Making Meaning of Narratives

· *in* **·**

The Narrative Study of Lives

Volume 6

The Narrative Study of Lives

The purpose of this Series is to publish studies of actual lives in progress, studies that use qualitative methods of investigation within a theoretical context drawn from psychology or other disciplines. The aim is to promote the study of lives and life history as a means of examining, illuminating, and spurring theoretical understanding. *The Narrative Study of Lives* will encourage longitudinal and retrospective in-depth studies of individual life narratives as well as theoretical consideration of innovative methodological approaches to this work.

Guidelines for authors:

The editors invite submissions of original manuscripts of up to 35 typed pages in the areas described above. As a publication of an interdisciplinary nature, we welcome authors from all disciplines concerned with narratives, psychobiography, and life-history. In matters of style, we encourage any creative format that best presents the work. Long quotations in the protagonists' voices are desirable as well as discussion of the author's place in the study.

References and footnotes should follow the guidelines of the *Publication Manual of the American Psychological Association* (4th ed.). A separate title page should include the chapter title and the author's name, affiliation, and address. Please type the entire manuscript, including footnotes and references, double-spaced, and submit three copies to:

Dan McAdams, Ph.D., Co-Editor
The Narrative Study of Lives
The Foley Center for the Study of Lives
Northwestern University
2116 Campus Drive
Evanston, IL 60208

THE NARRATIVE STUDY OF LIVES
Volume 6

THE NARRATIVE STUDY OF LIVES

Making Meaning of
Narratives
▪ in ▪
The Narrative Study
of Lives

Ruthellen Josselson
Amia Lieblich
editors

The Narrative Study of Lives ▪ Volume 6

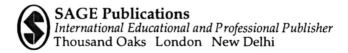

SAGE Publications
International Educational and Professional Publisher
Thousand Oaks London New Delhi

For information:

SAGE Publications, Inc.
2455 Teller Road
Thousand Oaks, California 91320
E-mail: order@sagepub.com

SAGE Publications Ltd.
6 Bonhill Street
London EC2A 4PU
United Kingdom

SAGE Publications India Pvt. Ltd.
M-32 Market
Greater Kailash I
New Delhi 110 048 India

Printed in the United States of America

Library of Congress Cataloging-in-Publication Data

Making meaning of narratives / edited by Ruthellen Josselson and
  Amia Lieblich.
    p. cm. — (The narrative study of lives; v. 6)
  Includes bibliographical references (p.) and index.
  ISBN 0-7619-0326-7 (cloth)
  ISBN 0-7619-0327-5 (pbk.)
    1. Narration (Rhetoric) 2. Autobiography. I. Josselson,
Ruthellen. II. Lieblich, Amia, 1939-   III. Series.
  PN212 .M35 1998
  808—dc21
                                                    98-40298
This book is printed on acid-free paper.

99 00 01 02 03 04 05 7 6 5 4 3 2 1

Acquiring Editor: C. Deborah Laughton
Editorial Assistant: Eileen Carr
Production Editor: Wendy Westgate
Production Assistant: Lynn Miyata
Typesetter: Christina M. Hill
Cover Designer: Candice Harman

Contents

Introduction

*I*s there—and should there be—a qualitative methodology? Or is the quest for such a thing itself an outgrowth of a positivistic paradigm that is fundamentally at odds with a hermeneutic approach? As narrative-based qualitative research attracts more practitioners, the wish to standardize and regulate grows. The wish is for modes of investigation parallel, say, to multiple regression designs or factor analysis. Or for clear criteria of "reliability." In general, the natural wish of students and beginning scholars is for a cookbook of some kind, a manual that will outline stages or steps in conducting a good narrative study—something that will guarantee success if you follow all the rules.

In quantitative research, all is regulated and rule-bound. Recently, a quantitative reviewer took me to task for asserting that two stories were "the same" without providing interrater reliabilities. That I presented the stories for all to see—and to verify for themselves the sameness—was overlooked. In the quantitative psychology world, evidently, there are clear and inviolable "rules."

How can we know what is good work in narrative research if there are no such methodological commandments? How can we measure such nonlinear concepts as persuasiveness, credibility, and insightfulness? And if we can't, then have we no "methodology"? I prefer to think of narrative research as a hermeneutic mode of inquiry, where the process of inquiry flows from the question—which is a question about a person's inner, subjective reality and, in particular, how a person makes meaning of some aspect of his or her experience. As we read submissions, we seldom criticize the method. Qualitative researchers are creative about method—this is a necessity. There is good (and bad) interviewing, there is well- (and poorly) grounded interpretation, there are (or are not) clear presentation, a compelling trail of evidence, and a logical link to conceptual understanding. As we review, we are most likely to find fault with the process of movement between interview data and conceptual framework (i.e., authors who want data to somehow "speak for themselves"). Researchers are often attracted to unusual people with unique life stories, but they do not manage to go beyond the presentation of a good story toward some kind of wider, theoretical meanings or implications. This is the most challenging aspect of narrative research.

We have become increasingly preoccupied with the problem of how to teach this work. As narrative researchers and as teachers of researchers who are preparing to use narrative approaches, we are concerned with transforming the ongoing discourse among us about our practices and our experience into communicable praxis in a written form. To this end, Amia and her students have recently completed a new book about narrative research, which documents their ways of analyzing and interpreting narrative material (Lieblich, Tuval-Mashiach, & Zilber, 1998). Frequently, we are asked to recommend texts in response to the question, What should I read (or have my students read) to learn about how to do qualitative research? As a result, we lead with the one invited paper in this volume, a critical review by June Price of a selection of the myriad books that have sprouted as guides to the doing of qualitative research. Dr. Price reported to us that answering what seemed like a simple question turned into "a nightmare." Her effort to take up this charge, however, led her to write a splendid review, which identifies and explores the salient issues in the field and offers a useful guide to what information is available where. We are grateful to her for pulling together such a cogent presentation, which we believe will serve many people in this field.

As work within this framework builds, it becomes ever more imperative for authors to stay in written discourse with one another. Our knowledge base grows not by accumulating statistics but by achieving like-mindedness among thoughtful scholars. Finding relevant literature, however, becomes more difficult, as search services are geared to key (content) words rather than key (interpretive) ideas. Even writing an abstract of the papers we publish violates the spirit of what we do: We traffic in subtle ideas that take lengthy expositions to explore. But this puts even greater demands on scholars to read widely and deeply, to cast a wide net before determining their idea of the "field." Sadly, we too often read submissions by authors who pose an interesting question, do the interviewing, and then write about their study as though no one else ever before thought about the things they are thinking about. We increasingly look with favor on authors who strive to place their work in some ongoing dialogue—as genuine conversation with other work.

Therefore, we are pleased to be publishing two related chapters in which scholars from two disciplines (literature and psychology) respond to an analysis of several autobiographies that had been published and analyzed by a third scholar. Both Paul John Eakin and Harriet Bjerrum Nielsen present their readings of the work of Marianne Gullestad, a Norwegian anthropologist whose work on autobiographies of ordinary people is little known in this country. Working with the same autobiographical material, Eakin and Nielsen demonstrate how placing life stories in a different conceptual context yields very different understandings, both of them, in our view, thought-provoking and useful. Taken together, their work embodies the way in which narrative research is a meaning-making endeavor with multiple truths.

Narrative research is a process of inquiry that embraces paradox and cannot therefore be defined in linear terms. Annie Rogers and her students engage one of the more elusive aspects of making meaning of narrative interviews by considering the problem of interpreting what is not said. In this pioneering effort, they attempt a poetics of the "language of the unsayable" and suggest an approach to reading that might identify pointers to experiences that a participant cannot articulate verbally. Their contribution offers us a structure that allows us, as narrative researchers, to venture into an uncharted sea that we have always known to be present but have struggled to bring into focus.

The remaining authors use a range of methods of inquiry, each deriving from the nature of the research question. Wendy Hollway and Tony Jefferson are also engaged in reading narratives beyond the words on the surface. Interested in the ways in which cultural meanings and values, particularly about gender, are transmitted across generations, they direct their analysis to the inherent interpretive grounds that exist, unnamed and often unseen, in families. Their intensive study of a working-class British family demonstrates how values are shaped by unconscious transmissions decipherable through careful reading of a narrative text.

Beverly Mizrachi also uses a single case study, but to different ends. Her aim is to explore how women are recruited into elite occupational positions, and she interviewed a large number of women. In her chapter, however, she explores one woman's life history, a woman who seems to represent the normative and dominant patterns of the larger group. At the same time, Mizrachi tries to discover the person who comprises the sociological and demographic factors identified by her own and others' research.

Two chapters are concerned with the function of narrative in the life course. Tineke Abma examines the political use of stories as they interweave in a mental hospital. In a fascinating presentation that leads us to question our own assumptions, she examines closely the use and nature of story and its relation to power in an action research project. Her chapter focuses on the transformational power of stories within societal organizations and the use of stories as an agent of change.

Barbara Crowther takes a careful, insightful look at girls' diaries and considers their developmental meanings. She argues for the ways in which the narratives contained in diaries are performances related to the growth and experience of the self in early adolescent girls. In her work, she engages in discussion with a chapter about diaries that we have previously published, and we are encouraged to see the *Annual* be a vehicle for ongoing scholarly conversation.

Working with related material, Dora Shu-fang Dien explores the question of how writing biographical fiction may relate to the author's own identity formation. Her subject is the well-known Chinese author, Ding Ling, and her thesis is that Ling's fictional character is a reflection of her own developmental process. This is the first psychobiographical article we have published, and we are pleased to present it; we find it of particular interest in that it considers these questions in a non-Western culture.

We continue to want to promote the integration of qualitative and quantitative findings. In her chapter, Elina Haavio-Mannila states, "A combination of detailed knowledge of the life of a relatively small number of individuals and quantifiable data on many people provides ideal possibilities for understanding and explaining the social world." Using detailed sexual autobiographies of Finnish men and women, as well as survey data, she seeks to understand what love means to people. Her investigation explores the effects of gender, age, and generation on the kinds of love stories that people construct and live.

In this volume, then, we believe we provide a sample of the range of work that can be undertaken under the broad umbrella of narrative research. The chapters in this volume come from five countries (England, Finland, Holland, Israel, and the United States) and five disciplines (criminology, literary studies, nursing, psychology, and sociology) In the end, teaching is best done through example, and we hope these examples will continue to spur and support others' quest for understanding through narrative—and to resist the reification of any "one way" to do this work.

—Ruthellen Josselson

Reference

Lieblich, A., Tuval-Mashiach, R., & Zilber, T. (1998). *Narrative research: Reading, analysis and interpretation.* Thousand Oaks, CA: Sage.

❦ 1 ❦

In Acknowledgment

A Review and Critique
of Qualitative Research Texts

June Price

*R*ecently, there has been a flood of general and discipline-specific textbooks about qualitative methodology, and the student or teacher may be bewildered about where to enter this conversation. In the following review, I acknowledge those writers who have provided me with insights, sensitivity, and technical knowledge about these methods; in doing so, I hope to provide a guide to those beginning to explore the possibilities in qualitative research. I was first introduced to these scholars during my years as a doctoral student, and now I use their works in teaching research methods myself. I chose the texts I review here for their readability, for their appeal to beginning researchers, and for their practical and transferable knowledge. The authors of these texts are regarded as both proficient and influential in the field.

Whose Science? Whose Knowledge?
(Harding, 1991)

Developing a qualitative study positions the author as artist, interpreter, and composer. Therefore, the initial step in the design of a study is an investigation and acknowledgment of one's own worldview about how we know what we know. The very act of posing a research question will influence and shape the answer. This personal stance may range from a rationalist, empiricist search for truth and underlying law to a postmodern, deconstructionist view of the world as complex, chaotic, and unknowable; from a highly structured process of inquiry to a more individualized perception and interpretation.

Works about qualitative methods illustrate this wide span, and each author is a firm believer at some point along this spectrum. For instance, Miles and Huberman's (1994) sourcebook clearly acknowledges the belief "that social phenomena exist not only in the mind but also in the objective world—and that some lawful and reasonably stable relationships are to be found among them" (p. 4). They provide interpretative forms most familiar to the quantitative approach: figures, graphs, tables, and conceptual frameworks of boxes and arrows.

Grounded theory (Glaser & Strauss, 1967; Strauss & Corbin, 1990) is further along the continuum; rather than testing hypotheses derived from theory, these researchers espouse generating theory based on the actual data through an inductive approach. Grounded theorists assume that science is a process of induction, deduction, then verification. Proof is not only possible; it is preferable.

Phenomenologists (Giorgi, 1985; Moustakas, 1994; van Manen, 1990) favor detailed descriptive documentation of experiences, relying on the interpretation of text in specific contexts for meaning making. Phenomenologists seek to discover what has been unknown or hidden rather than to verify and objectify an experience.

Deconstructionism, postmodernism, and feminism fall at the other end of the epistemological spectrum, philosophical stances that value the unique experience, multiple realities, and voices that are bound in the contexts of history and gender and that acknowledge the researcher as a participating influence of the product. Frequently, the goal is to challenge and re-view the received knowledge of the day.

At one time, the worldview/worthiness/scientific debate focused on qualitative versus quantitative methods. Today, pedagogical potshots are aimed at philosophical stances within the field. In choosing a text, it is wise to become familiar with the author's assumptions about how we know what we know, for this will direct and shape the entire process of developing and conducting the study.

Choosing a qualitative method is akin to choosing specific statistical analyses in quantitative research. The choice will frame the question and influence the answer; the method should be compatible with the researcher's philosophical assumptions regarding knowledge and the research question.

Research strategy is also determined by the experience and discipline of the researcher. In my own study of child-abusing mothers (Price, 1997), I chose a method that corresponded to the way I work as a clinician: intimately, intuitively, and with a frequent sense of puzzlement. In my clinical work with emotionally disturbed children and their families, I have come to view human behavior as frequently irrational: Any meaning attached to it is embedded in multiple contexts of an individual's history and culture. This stance led me to choose a feminist phenomenology, with its emphasis on description.

Method and Process

At first, methods appear so similar: gather data, examine data, make small interpretations by coding the text, make larger interpretations through the development of themes, write it up. The recent plethora of available texts and resource books can be overwhelming and confusing. But there is a significant difference in the underlying assumptions, the style, and the product among the main schools of thought.

Phenomenology

Phenomenologists describe their method as the study and description of lived experience. This human experience is viewed as contextual, subjectively interpreted, and complex in nature. Phenomenologists search for all possible interpretations and permutations emerging from the data through a hermeneutic process, a continuous review and reinterpretation of text. Initially, *meaning units* (Giorgi, 1985) are developed by coding very small units of the data. Insight and theme development evolve through personal interpretation. Intuitive leaps and the use of metaphors are encouraged, what Moustakas (1994) terms *imaginative variation* (p. 97). Other descriptions that may echo or interpret the phenomenon under study, such as those found in fiction, poetry, and visual media, may be incorporated to enrich understanding of the primary data source.

Masters of the phenomenological process include Spiegelberg (1975, 1976), Giorgi (1985), van Manen (1990), and Moustakas (1994). All of these authors provide a rich background in the philosophy of phenomenology, as well as the techniques of the method.

An example of the product is Oscar Lewis's (1966) *La Vida*. In his brief preface, Lewis describes the study of the lives of impoverished families in Puerto Rico and touches on his theory of the culture of poverty. Following the preface are the forceful and disturbing narratives in the participants' voices of the stories of their lives, without any commentary or interpretation by Lewis.

Grounded Theory

Based on the sociological concept of symbolic interaction (Blumer, 1969), the purpose of this method is to discover, describe, or develop a theoretical basis for social interaction. Interpretation of meaning is seen as a social contract, agreement among the players. Symbols, speech, dress, and gestures are all shared forms of communication. The interaction and interpretation of these symbols, the identification of shared meanings, and a description of the process of developing these meanings are the foci of inquiry.

Proponents feel that grounded theory is a reverse of the empirical approach. Rather than developing and testing hypotheses from theory, one relies on the data to develop theory, a bottom-up, inductive approach. Glaser and Strauss (1967), the fathers of grounded theory, assumed that one can detect universality of meaning and that generalizing is possible. Most frequently, grounded theorists stress constant comparative analyses, with the goal of developing relationships between concepts and a continual striving to verify these relationships or hypotheses. The emphasis is on conceptualization rather than on description.

Classic works of this genre include Glaser and Strauss (1967) and Strauss and Corbin's (1990) *Basis of Qualitative Research.* An excellent and brief overview is provided by Strauss and Corbin (1994). An exemplar of this school is Glaser and Strauss's (1968) *Time for Dying,* a study of terminally ill patients.

Ethnography

The study of a particular culture, whether foreign and exotic or homebound, was initially the bailiwick of anthropologists and sociologists. Ethnography relies on techniques of participant observation and was also influenced by the principles of symbolic interaction. The focus is on the investigation of shared meanings and on the interpretation of words and events in a particular society.

A general resource is Clifford and Marcus (1986) *Writing Culture: The Poetics and Politics of Ethnography.* An illustrative study of this school is *Tally's Corner* by Liebow (1967), a beautifully written account of the lives of black men on the urban streets. Van Maanen's (1988) *Tales of the Field* is an exceptional resource on how this methodology is presented as text and how social reality is created through the interpretation of the researcher. Three different formats are described in detail: the realist tale, which is a factual third-person presentation; the confessional tale, focusing on the researcher's experience as much as on the topic researched; and the impressionistic tale, a more free-wheeling and imaginative interpretation of fieldwork experience. Van Maanen (1988) provides detailed examples of each format, as well as an excellent reference list.

Historical Research

Tuchman (1994) provides an outstanding overview of this methodological format. Historical research relies on information (or the lack of information) recorded in the past or on oral history. Primary sources, or documented firsthand accounts, and secondary sources at least once removed provide the database. There are myriad approaches; some assume factual documentation, some acknowledge all sources to be an interpretation. There are also schools of the elitist approach versus the ordinary perspective; one may come to very different conclusions basing one's information on the memoirs of a general versus the diary of a foot soldier.

Historical researchers may focus on patterns, cause and effect relationships, or interpretations contextualized at a certain point in time. The product may be presented as factual, multivocal, or even idiosyncratic. Examples of these different approaches include Erikson's (1958) psychoanalytic interpretation of the Protestant revolution through the Great Man approach, *Young Man Luther,* and Carlos Ginzberg's (1966) work, *The Night Battles,* about witchcraft and cults from the perspective of peasants' belief systems.

Feminist Research

Philosophically, this research movement has relied on critical theory and postmodernism and has stemmed from the concern that science, at best, has neglected the influence of gender in the process of inquiry and in the interpretation of results. Adherents postulate that women's experiences and interpretations of meaning have been ignored. Simultaneously, feminists posit that Western, male-oriented science has been concerned with the control of events rather than the empowerment of the individual in a social context.

For postmodern feminist researchers, the research question vies in importance with the ethical purpose and product of the study. The goal is to enrich and empower the participants and to consciously avoid the exploitation of those individuals.

Within this framework, feminist research can range from experimental to action-oriented formats, as the researcher works "in the space between the personal and the political" (Olesen, 1994, p. 168). The works of Hekman (1990), Nielson (1990), Reinharz (1992), and Nicholson (1990), as well as Olesen's overview (1994), are among the most thoughtful representations of this school. A noteworthy study is Lather's (1995) study of women with HIV/AIDS. Her first full book publication is intended to be written by and for the participants. Lather refers to the product of her study as "a text that is as much trying to write me as the other way around" (p. 41).

Triangulation

Triangulation is the mixing of qualitative and quantitative methods within a study, and it remains a controversial approach. One camp views the process as enriching, whereas the opposition insists it represents muddied thinking, the apples and oranges of epistemology. Tripp-Reimer (1989) noted that the debate may be moot:

> As soon as you start looking for themes and categories in qualitative research, you have objectified the subjects, and that's no different than looking for statistical means. You take two similar experiences, and you "average" them, and that's your description or interpretation. (p. 12)

Triangulation is most often used to enrich presentations and to heighten the credibility of a study. Triangulation may also be accomplished through the use of multiple researchers, multiple disciplinary approaches, and multiple sites for data collection. Outstanding resources include Lincoln and Guba (1985), Miles and Huberman (1994), and Patton (1990).

General Resources

If you are choosing only one book for your personal library, I would recommend Denzin and Lincoln's (1994) *Handbook of Qualitative Research*. Although I was at first wary of any text entitled "handbook" (reminding me of a Cliff Notes approach), I have developed the highest regard for the scope and the consistent, outstanding quality of the work of the contributors. Denzin and Lincoln have gone to the masters in the field. Each contribution provides extensive coverage of a specific topic regarding paradigms, strategies, and methods, with excellent bibliographies. This sourcebook also has a highly usable, detailed, and logical index. It is the best overall resource available: sophisticated and scholarly, yet highly readable.

Ely's (1991) publication, *Doing Qualitative Research,* is unique in that it describes the process of doing qualitative research through the reflections and voices of researchers (including neophyte students). This work teaches by example, by inviting the reader to share in the struggles and emotions of the process, as well as in technique and procedure. Philosophical assumptions are up front. Chapter headings reflect the living nature of the process of inquiry: doing, feeling, interpreting, and reflecting.

Miles and Huberman's (1994) *Qualitative Data Analysis* lies near the positivist pole in its conceptual framework and is a clearly written, cogent, and invaluable sourcebook for its scope and richness in the analysis of findings of both within-case and between-case presentations. Chapter 10 on analysis and interpretation is useful and thought-provoking, regardless of the researcher's stance. Chapter 11 on ethical issues is a first-rate discussion on issues that are too frequently neglected by other authors.

Lincoln and Guba's (1985) *Naturalistic Inquiry* is a classic for what at the time was an emerging paradigm. The authors are a bit defensive of the qualitative process, defending against any claims that it is not scientifically verifiable. Chapters on design, logistics, and implementation of the study remain highly valuable. The authors also present a myriad of techniques to judge the quality of a study, what they term *trustworthiness,* including thick description, prolonged engagement in the field, triangulation of methods, checking results and interpretations with participants, and most important, the analysis of cases that do not fit the major interpretations of the study.

Discipline-specific general resources are also useful for both relevance to specific fields of knowledge and reference to outstanding models of the genre. In education, see Bogden and Biklen's (1992) *Qualitative Research for Education*; in sociology, Silverman's (1985) *Qualitative Methodology and Sociology*; and in nursing, Munhall and Boyd's (1993) *Nursing Research: A Qualitative Perspective.* The knowledge base is expanding dramatically, and discipline-specific and interdisciplinary journals are a rich source for updated and topical information. Journals now available include *Qualitative Sociology, Qualitative Studies in Education, Qualitative Health Research,* and the prominent interdisciplinary journals, *Qualitative Inquiry, Journal of Narrative and Life History,* and the annual *The Narrative Study of Lives.*

Maxwell's (1996) *Qualitative Research Design* is intended for students, uses the experience of students designing their dissertations, and provides exercises at the end of each chapter that allow the reader to work through each concept. Maxwell's stance is closest to Miles and Huberman's (1994) persuasion, unabashedly using terms such as *validity* and *generalizability,* with step-by-step design guidance to ensure both in the results. Maxwell's writing is very lucid, and he has the capacity for making a complicated issue clear and understandable. For example, regarding the debate about structure, he states,

> Structured approaches can help to ensure the comparability of data across sources and researchers and are thus particularly useful in answering variance questions, questions that deal with *differences* between things and their explanation. Unstructured approaches, in contrast, allow the researcher to focus on the *particular* phenomena studied; they trade generalizability and comparability for internal validity and contextual understanding. (p. 64)

Important issues in the design of a study are addressed, including gaining access to participants and planning the nature and the limits of the relationship the researcher will have with those participants.

The discussion of data analyses and the importance of analytical memos that begin with the conceptual design are valuable. Maxwell (1996) also devotes a chapter to writing a research proposal, which is exceptionally advantageous to students. This chapter outlines the inherent pitfalls and provides strategies for justifying one's research question, for writing a coherent outline, and for presenting a sound argument for design decisions.

A Foot in the Door

Little advice is available about gaining access to participants. My first field assignment in doing qualitative research was as an observer; neither conversation nor validation of my observations was allowed. I ended up spending hours in a Chinese laundry, but only after being rejected by the managers of a nail salon and a dry cleaner. Little did I know that the experience of being rebuffed, turned down, ignored, and dismissed would become an integral part of doing qualitative research.

Most informative on this topic is Ely's (1991) chapter on "Starting," as the author recognizes that "FIRST YOU HAVE TO GET INTO THE FIELD" (p. 17). Spradley (1979) also provides a multitude of tips on overcoming hurdles, identifying and negotiating with gate-keepers, and gaining entree to the world you wish to study.

Bogden and Biklen (1992) also discuss the courting ritual in gaining access (pp. 80-85) and tease out the different issues involved in dealing with the formal and the informal gatekeeping systems. Maxwell (1996) recognizes the ongoing nature of negotiating relationships during the study process, as well as the "philosophical, ethical, and political issues" (p. 67) that need to be considered from the beginning.

Collecting Data

The in-depth interview is the most frequent form of data collection, although participant observation, video (see Silverman, 1997), and documentation review are also used as techniques. Spradley's (1979) *The Ethnographic Interview* is the classic, useful for methods other than ethnography. Spradley provides options in the types of questions to ask and approaches for interviews that may span prolonged periods of time. Techniques include the concepts of a "grand tour" and a "mini tour"; the former designed to get a general overall description, and the latter to focus on particular events, people, or word usage by a participant.

Seidman (1991) addresses procedural issues such as the timing and frequency of interviews, how to choose informants, how many participants provide an adequate sample, and how to gain consent. Techniques of interviewing—listening, follow-up, and clarification are fully discussed. Seidman (1991) recognizes that, beyond technique, interviewing is also a "social relationship that must be nurtured, sustained, and then ended gracefully" (p. 72). Power issues of race, gender, class, and age are attended to as well.

Research Interviewing by Mishler (1986) provides a more theoretical discussion of gathering and analyzing interview data. Mishler (1986) speaks to the polemics of discourse and the politics of interpretation—of how the answer to a question evolves into a narrative format. Speech is viewed as a joint construction made by the speaker and the audience within the confines of a specific interview context. Interpretations must acknowledge the "textual, ideational, and interpersonal" components of language (p. 106).

Noteworthy recent books include *InterViews* by Kvale (1996a), which provides a postmodern perspective on the subject; and *Qualitative Interviewing* by Rubin and Rubin (1995), who address the cultural and personal contexts of the technique. Both texts encompass more than the process of interviewing and focus on design and evaluation as well as the techniques of interviewing.

Kvale (1996a), an educational psychologist, writes *InterViews* within a philosophical perspective. He describes interviewing as a "basic mode of constituting knowledge" (p. 37), more than simply a tool. Kvale (1996a) contrasts schools of thought by using the analogy of a miner seeking nuggets of buried knowledge, versus a traveler who "is on a journey that leads to a tale to be told upon returning home" (p. 4). Although this work is highly scholarly, Kvale (1996a) writes as if conversing with the reader. He is able to break down complicated ideas and make them comprehensible, as when he analyzes the interpretative, hermeneutic process or describes the technique of "deliberate naivete" as "curiosity, openness without preconceived assumptions seeing the participant as the expert in meaning making" (p. 31). Kvale provides a strong and cogent philosophical base for the methodology of interviewing.

Kvale (1996a) provides enough rich description of the interview process that one could follow his advice in lieu of a mentored experience. He covers the territory, including the qualities of the researcher, such as tone of voice and body language, and his or her influence on the process. Kvale's resources and references are excellent, and he provides a comprehensive bibliography. In contrast, Kvale's (1996a) chapter on ethics is a bit weak and mild-mannered, raising common issues such as confidentiality, while avoiding more controversial and loaded topics.

Irene Rubin, a public administrator, and Herb Rubin, an urbanologist, write a text (1995) that is more conversational in style while giving very practical and sound direction from the design of the study to the interpretation of the results. The authors are proponents of a feminist research model in the broad sense of collaboration, reflection on one's own emotional reactions, acknowledgment of findings as embedded in context versus fact, and an overriding ethical responsibility to the participants. They propose an emerging study design and a "self-correcting interview" (p. 164), with useful tips on how to judge your own results.

The authors rely on Spradley's (1979) work for structuring the interview process and provide detailed information on the types and purposes of questions. Criteria for the quality of an interview focus on design: "depth, detail, vividness, and nuance" (p. 76). The systematic discovery of themes is vividly described. The Rubins' (1995) chapter on ethics touches upon real world problems and copes with issues rarely discussed in other texts, such as hearing illegal or repugnant information, and cross-cultural/gender/class and race interview situations. Beyond data obtained directly from participants, other useful data stem from the researcher's observations, personal reactions, and descriptions of what is directly sensed and of what is intuited. Forms for this collection of data include fieldnotes, analytic memos, and personal journals, all reflecting the researcher as the instrument of the study.

Ely (1991), favoring hunches, and Maxwell (1996), favoring logic, both encourage the use of these documents to describe and reflect on nonverbal responses and the emotional reactions of the participant and the researcher. Analytical memos may be used throughout the study to reflect on ideas, insights, and hypotheses as they unfold and on their impact on the study. These memos provide a record of the data analyses as codes, themes, and meta-themes develop over time.

As an example of this, Reinharz (1997) analyzes 20 different personae that she identified in reviewing her fieldnotes of a study of kibbutz life, providing a wonderful illustration of the possibilities for analytic reflection based on sources other than interview data—her documented self: "The process transformed me into a data-based object of study. I found that I referred to myself in different ways throughout the year because different aspects of myself became salient over time and across contexts" (p. 5). Reinharz (1997) was influenced by her many roles, whether personal, such as being Jewish, or based on her task, such as being a person who will leave the field, or based on contexts during the actual study period, such as being a temporary resident on the kibbutz.

Recording and Transcribing

Rarely described are the mechanics of data collection and transcription to text from audiotapes. But for the novice, (and my hunch, the experienced as well), turning audiotapes into text is fraught with hazards. Transcribers have a knack for curious interpretation, turning taped interviews into the Mock Turtle's "uncommon nonsense" (Carroll, 1865/1965, p. 124). One transcriber I used was determined to clean up my participants' grammatical usage, thereby negating most of the color and the pacing of their speech. Another trick was "filling in the blanks"—if a passage was difficult to hear, the transcriber would kindly confabulate data. This necessitated my redoing hours of transcriptions. Poland's (1995) article is priceless in enumerating the faux pas and foibles inherent in the task and in providing suggestions for text notations that can identify nonverbal gestures, emphasis, inaudible words, and changes in voice as when a participant quotes another person. Poland (1995) also provides concrete advice on the mechanics involved in audiotaping and on how to avoid time-consuming mistakes and equipment malfunctions.

Kvale (1996a) speaks to the reliability and validity of transcriptions and encourages interrater reliability tests of tapes to transcripts. He provides a useful enumeration of the inherent problems, such as the subjectivity of translating emotional tones, repetitive sounds and phrases, and pauses. He notes that "transcripts are decontextualized conversations, they are abstractions, as topographical maps are abstractions from the original landscape" (p. 165). Kvale admits that the concept of validity is confounding in this context, that "there is no true objective transformation from the oral to the written mode" (p. 166).

In my study of child-abusing mothers (Price, 1997), the phrase "you know," which was spoken as frequently as "er" or "um," became surprisingly salient in my attempts at meaning making and in empathizing with the participants. I was later grateful for my attention, (although so tedious at the time), to such frequently "meaningless" figures of speech.

"The 1,000 Page Question"

Kvale (1996b) perceptively acknowledges the *big* question—what does one *do* with the information gathered in the study? He advises that this question be addressed in the design stage, rather than later.

Tesch (1990) provides step-by-step direction for descriptive, interpretative, and theory-building analyses, while recognizing the interpretative process of being in "constant interaction with the data" (p. 113). Tesch provides the means to see the forest and the trees. In her description of decontextualizing text, she speaks to the coding process that separates out meaningful items relevant to the study from the mass of information, while retaining the context. In recontextualization, the process becomes more abstract in the discovery of relationships. Tesch also discusses, in detail, how to physically handle the data, whether manually or electronically.

Silverman (1993) stands alone in his in-depth handling of data from texts and observations, as well as interview transcripts. Concepts are illustrated through detailed examples of previous research as process strategies toward interpretations. Specific student-oriented exercises in critical thinking are provided throughout the text in order to present situations for learning by doing. Silverman describes his point of view as antiromantic, values the concepts of validity and reliability, and is quite vocal in his stance against what he views as politically correct versus scientifically sound methods of analyses. A strong focus is on the search for data that do not support one's initial hunches or interpretations. Silverman sees generalizability as not only possible, but as necessary to the establishment of knowledge.

Once warned off Miles and Huberman's (1994) work because of its positivist approach, I found myself surreptitiously reading *Qualitative Data Analysis*. As the authors state, this book is specifically about "*doing analysis*" (p. 3). Miles and Huberman is a focused sourcebook on techniques, with detailed examples from research across disciplines; it is designed not only for students, but for the seasoned researcher, as well. The authors write so clearly that they can turn a maze of information into intelligible instructions. Issues addressed include how to focus and set boundaries on the data, code the data, identify patterns, use analytical memos, present data, and generate models of interpretation. The text is invaluable for those who wish to exhibit data findings in figures, graphs, and displays. The authors provide one of the best discussions on confirming findings, seeking and interpreting outlying cases, identifying the effects of researcher bias, obtaining feedback from participants, and handling disconfirming evidence that may negate one's interpretations. Their bibliography is a resource unto itself.

In *Transforming Qualitative Data*, Wolcott (1994) addresses the conceptual issues in presenting findings with solid and illustrative advice. Drowning in my own interview data, I was able to develop an outline and a story line right after reading his work. Wolcott describes three different emphases: description, or asking what is going on here; analysis, asking what is the essence of the data; and interpretation, asking what does it all mean. Through the use of exemplars, he identifies when each framework may be most appropriate. Decisions of emphasis, and the rationale for those decisions, are illustrated by Wolcott's own research. He moves from description, a close rendition of the actual voice of a participant; to analysis, grounded in the data and describing essential and common features of the narrative; to interpretation, broader and more conjectural abstractions that strive for explanatory power.

Kvale (1996a) also differentiates between analysis and interpretation. He outlines six steps of analysis: subjects describe, subjects discover relationships, researcher interprets during the interview, researcher interprets from the transcription, reinterviewing, and finally, action taken as a result of the experience (pp. 189-190). Similar to Tesch, he speaks of *meaning condensation* (decontextualization) and *meaning categorization* (recontextualization); from small coding units to larger relational themes (p. 192). Interpretation is seen as a higher level of abstraction, a perspective gained from a distance through reflection on what is less visible and less apparent, and in conjunction with theoretical and conceptual frameworks.

Electronic Analysis

There are a multitude of resources and software programs available for electronic analysis of data. For those not technologically challenged, the mechanics of analysis have gone far beyond cut and paste, photocopy, then file and hand shuffle thematic categories. Excellent sourcebooks and guides for choosing and using software tools are now available, including Weitzman and Miles's (1995) *Computer Programs for Qualitative Data Analysis* and Tesch's (1990) *Qualitative Research: Analysis Types and Software Tools.* Programs such as NUDIST, AQUAD, QUALPRO, and MECA are available for purposes such as text retrieval, coding, analysis, and theory development. Kvale (1996a) appeals to my fondest fantasies of avoiding drudgery as he describes the latest generation of computer programs, which make transcription of tapes an obsolete activity. Using KIT, tape recordings are actually converted to text and stored on compact discs (Kvale, 1996a, pp. 174-175).

Writing

Ely, Vinz, Downing, and Anzul's (1997) work, *On Writing Qualitative Research,* is highly recommended for its presentation of imaginative forms and literary devices. An exceptionally charismatic teacher, Ely captures the excitement of expressing voices unbound by traditional academic formats. Illustrations are derived from the work of both graduate students and accomplished scholars. Narrative formats are expanded into presentation of data as drama, poetry, and fables. Ely et al. write of the use of metaphors in theme development, and they value the power of presentation to provoke, disturb, and expand one's insight and awareness of another's experience.

Techniques are illustrated, such as using anecdotes and vignettes to make a pointed description of an event, posing a first-person narrative as an "I" story, or presenting multiple realities of perception as a layered story with many perspectives. In my own work (Price, 1997), I use what Ely terms *weaving and braiding* to make a quilt of perspectives and voices from participants, fictional characters, and poets. The text gained texture and weight and provided more than one path to understanding.

Harry Wolcott is another master in teaching the art of writing up qualitative research. His writing is intimate, clear, and succinct, and he is able to relate his own experience and mistakes. He is exceptionally cognizant of the dangers awaiting a student. Wolcott's (1990) earlier monograph, *Writing Up Qualitative Research,* should be read before beginning data collection and then again during the process of composition. Wolcott discusses the steps preparatory to writing, including decisions about what the story will be about, which voice will act as author, and who the audience will be. Concrete organizational problems such as developing an outline, handling revisions, editing, and getting feedback are discussed. Hints to overcome mundane problems such as a lack of working space, avoidance rituals, blocks, criticism, and the sense of being totally overwhelmed by the product are invaluable. Typical of Wolcott's advice is that the writer's task is not to gather as much data as possible but rather to get rid of as much as possible, to "winnow" the irrelevant from the essence.

Stories Lives Tell by Witherell and Noddings (1991) is a series of narratives that speak to the power of story telling as communication and interpretation of human behavior. The narrative form provides the descriptive example, grounds a concept in metaphorical rather than logical prose, and illuminates the meaning of our experiences. Storytelling is a "way of knowing" in Belenky, Clinchy, Goldberger, and Tarule's (1986) phrase. In "The Story That Saved Life" (Stafford, 1991), I learned a great deal about the process of writing another's story. The process of winnowing was made clear, as Stafford states that

"You have to forget 90% of what happens if you want to tell the story right" (p. 17). Stafford copes with the conflict of checking out an interpreted story with the participant when the participant disagrees with your interpretation: "'Yet none of that happened,' she says. What *did* happen, then, in my mind or to my mind? How did this story get made?" (p. 28). On interpretation, Stafford says, "[it] wasn't exactly true about that place . . . but it was true about my experience of the place" (p. 28); on composition: "It's making was invisible to me until it was essentially finished by springing whole to my mind" (p. 28). In *Imagining History*, Makler (1991) provides an example of a layered story, a biography of her grandmother, by juxtaposing three variations: her own childhood memories, a search for "facts" through the memories of other family members, and finally the effect on the story of the historical contexts of both the narrator and the subject.

In *Storied Lives*, Rosenwald and Ochberg (1992) compile a series of narrations and interpretations that are provocative and stimulating. Their framework poses essential questions such as what makes a good narrative? Is developing a coherent story an illusion? How do cultural values and mores affect the story and the storyteller? Contributions are from the fields of psychology, anthropology, sociology, education, and history.

Part I of *Storied Lives* (Rosenwald & Ochberg, 1992) focuses on identity formation, and the role of narration in that process. Part II illustrates how social and cultural limitations affect an individual's development, while Part III provides stories of escaping and overcoming those very restrictions. Issues such as the narrator's silences and omissions stemming from either intrapsychic phenomena or social, cultural, and historical constraints are discussed. The editors note that frequently, a story that is coherent lies within the boundaries of normal cultural standards, whereas those that do not conform are more disturbing and, possibly, more illuminating.

Values and Goodness

The notion of a "good" study in qualitative research has transformed itself from earlier concepts echoing the criteria of quantitative research, to more humanistic values, and then back again once more. Lincoln and Guba (1985) and Miles and Huberman (1994) speak of criteria reminiscent of the positivist point of view, such as credibility (internal validity), transferability (external validity), dependability (reliability), and confirmability (subjectivity). Lincoln and Guba's (1985) chapter on trustworthiness provides a multitude of techniques to ensure quality, including prolonged engagement in the field, thick description of data, peer review, member checking of interpretations, the identification and elimination of personal biases, provision for an audit trail, and a constant search for additional information or cases that do not fit the emerging overall conception.

Maxwell's (1996) chapter on "Validity: How Might You Be Wrong?" bases his criteria on the assumption that there is *a* real world to be discovered and described. He also speaks to what he terms commonsense errors, such as recording data inaccurately, having personal biases, and ignoring information that doesn't fit. Silverman's (1997) recent work also returns to the concepts of reliability and validity in judging the quality of results.

Yvonne Lincoln (1995) writes of criteria that are grounded in a different value system. She speaks of

> new commitments: first to new and emergent relations with respondents; second to a set of stances—professional, personal, and political—toward the uses of inquiry and towards its ability to foster action; and finally, to a vision of research that enables and promotes social justice. (p. 277)

In Lincoln's later vision, rather than avoiding researcher bias, the goal becomes incorporation of that bias while honestly acknowledging its existence. A more radical position on goodness holds that the product of inquiry should serve the community studied, rather than one's discipline, or the "knowledge producers and policy makers" (p. 280).

Relevant to this topic, *Doing Exemplary Research* by Frost and Stabein (1992) is an unusual series of research studies that focus on the process rather than the content and include vignettes of what really happens during the study process, including ethical conflicts and their resolution, solving erroneous design problems, and revising the study focus during the study period.

Hot Potatoes

Although there are notable exceptions, sex and politics are as verboten as topics in the literature as in my mother's world of conversation. Race, sexual orientation and gender, positions of power, the concept of using subjects for personal advancement, the Privileged studying the Marginalized, the tendency to emphasize "the exotic, the bizarre, the violent" (Fine & Weis, 1996, p. 260), covert research (see Mitchell, 1993), as well as endangering participants by exposure of their secrets and criminal behavior, avoiding the description and analysis of the "bad behavior" of minorities or oppressed social groups, or laundering results "to protect 'oppressed' respondents" (Warren, 1988, p. 64) are all topics not generally included in the texts of qualitative inquiry. There is a need for another reference book that honestly exposes the issues and struggles facing a researcher.

Thoughtful and provocative discussions of these loaded issues may be found in Michelle Fine's (1994) article, "Working the Hyphens," in Punch's (1994) article, "Politics and Ethics," in Josselson's (1996) article, "On Writing Other People's Lives," and in Lincoln's (1995) article, "Emerging Criteria for Quality in Qualitative and Interpretative Research." Lincoln illustrates this new genre in speaking of researchers who represent the new criteria, such as Brown (1992), who shares the royalties from her publication with her participant, a voodoo priestess.

Conclusion

In choosing a text, read the preface or introduction. Here the author(s) will identify their position along the continuum, their assumptions about knowledge, their style and audience, and a synopsis of the focus of each chapter. The texts chosen for this review have all been influential in developing my work, my interpretations, and my choice of a narrative voice in writing.

There is a profusion of books published on qualitative research today, and sources appear to expand exponentially each year. In writing this review, I decided to triangulate this narrative and discovered that I actually *own* 32 texts and resource books and subscribe to three journals on the subject. How do I interpret this evidence? It appears to be symptomatic of an addict, rather than a proponent of the field. Janesick (1994) warned against "methodolatry . . . a preoccupation with selecting and defending methods to the exclusion of the actual substance of the story being told" (p. 215). I think I'll go read a novel.

References

Belenky, M. F., Clinchy, B. M., Goldberger, N. R., & Tarule, J. M. (1986). *Women's ways of knowing*. New York: Basic Books.

Blumer, H. (1969). *Symbolic interactionism: Perspective and method*. Englewood Cliffs, NJ: Prentice Hall.

Bogden, R. C., & Biklen, S. K. (1992). *Qualitative research for education*. Boston: Allyn & Bacon.

Brown, K. M. (1992). *Mama Lola: A voudou priestess in Brooklyn*. Berkeley: University of California Press.

Carroll, L. (1965). *Alice's adventures in wonderland*. New York: Random House. (Original work published 1865)

Clifford, J., & Marcus, G. E. (Eds.). (1986). *Writing culture: The poetics and politics of ethnography*. Berkeley: University of California Press.

Denzin, N. K., & Lincoln, Y. S. (Eds.). (1994). *Handbook of qualitative research*. Thousand Oaks, CA: Sage.

Ely, M. (with Anzul, M., Friedman, T., Garner, D., & Steinmetz, A. M.). (1991). *Doing qualitative research: Circles within circles*. New York: Falmer.

Ely, M., Vinz, R., Downing, M., & Anzul, M. (1997). *On writing qualitative research*. New York: Falmer.

Erikson, E. (1958). *Young man Luther, a study in psychoanalysis and history*. New York: Norton.

Fine, M. (1994). Working the hyphens: Reinventing self and others in qualitative research. In N. K. Denzin & Y. S. Lincoln (Eds.), *Handbook of qualitative research* (pp. 70-82). Thousand Oaks, CA: Sage.

Fine, M., & Weis, L. (1996). Writing the "wrongs" of fieldwork: Confronting our own research/writing dilemmas in urban ethnographies. *Qualitative Inquiry, 2*(3), 251-274.

Frost, P., & Stabein, R. (Eds.). (1992). *Doing exemplary research.* Newbury Park, CA: Sage.

Ginzberg, C. (1966). *The night battles: Witchcraft and agrarian cults in the sixteenth and seventeenth centuries.* Baltimore, MD: Johns Hopkins University Press.

Giorgi, A. (Ed.). (1985). *Phenomenology and psychological research.* Pittsburgh, PA: Duquesne University Press.

Glaser, B., & Strauss, A. (1967). *The discovery of grounded theory.* New York: Aldine de Gruyter.

Glaser, B., & Strauss, A. (1968). *Time for dying.* Chicago: Aldine de Gruyter.

Harding, S. (1991). *Whose science? whose knowledge?* Ithaca, NY: Cornell University Press.

Hekman, S. (1990). *Gender and knowledge: Elements of a postmodern feminism.* Boston: Northeastern University.

Janesick, V. J. (1994). The dance of qualitative research design: Metaphor, methodolatry, and meaning. In N. K. Denzin & Y. S. Lincoln (Eds.), *Handbook of qualitative research* (pp. 209-219). Thousand Oaks, CA: Sage.

Josselson, R. (1996). On writing other peoples lives: Self-analytic reflections of a narrative researcher. In R. Josselson (Ed.), *Ethics and process in the narrative study of lives* (Vol. 4, pp. 60-71). Thousand Oaks, CA: Sage.

Kvale, S. (1996a). *InterViews: An introduction to qualitative research interviewing.* Thousand Oaks, CA: Sage.

Kvale, S. (1996b). The 1,000-page question. *Qualitative Inquiry, 2*(3), 275-284.

Lather, P. (1995). The validity of angels: Interpretative and textual strategies in researching the lives of women with HIV/AIDS. *Qualitative Inquiry, 1,* 41-68.

Lewis, O. (1966). *La vida.* New York: Vintage.

Liebow, E. (1967). *Tally's corner.* Boston: Little, Brown.

Lincoln, Y. S. (1995). Emerging criteria for quality in qualitative and interpretative research. *Qualitative Inquiry, 1*(3), 275-289.

Lincoln, Y. S., & Guba, E. G. (1985). *Naturalistic inquiry.* Beverly Hills, CA: Sage.

Makler, A. (1991). Imagining history: "A good story and a well-formed argument." In C. Witherell & N. Noddings (Eds.), *Stories lives tell: Narrative and dialogue in education* (pp. 29-47). New York: Teachers College Press.

Maxwell, J. A. (1996). *Qualitative research design.* Thousand Oaks, CA: Sage.

Miles, M. B., & Huberman, A. M. (1994). *Qualitative data analyses.* Thousand Oaks, CA: Sage.

Mishler, E. G. (1986). *Research interviewing: Context and narrative.* Cambridge, MA: Harvard University Press.

Mitchell, R. G. (1993). *Secrecy and fieldwork.* Newbury Park, CA: Sage.

Moustakas, C. (1994). *Phenomenological research methods.* Thousand Oaks, CA: Sage.

Munhall, P. L., & Boyd, C. O. (Eds.). (1993). *Nursing research: A qualitative perspective.* New York: National League for Nursing.

Nicholson, J. M. (Ed.). (1990). *Feminism/postmodernism.* New York: Routledge, Chapman & Hall.

Nielson, J. M. (Ed.). (1990). *Feminist research methods.* Boulder, CO: Westview.

Olesen, V. (1994). Feminism and models of qualitative research. In N. K. Denzin & Y. S. Lincoln (Eds.), *Handbook of qualitative research* (pp. 158-174). Thousand Oaks, CA: Sage.

Patton, M. Q. (1990). *Qualitative evaluation and research methods.* Newbury Park, CA: Sage.

Poland, B. D. (1995). Transcription quality as an aspect of rigor in qualitative research. *Qualitative Inquiry, 1*(3), 290-310.

Price, J. (1997). *"Suffer the little children . . . ": The relational history of women reported for child abuse.* Unpublished doctoral dissertation, New York University, New York.

Punch, M. (1994). Politics and ethics in qualitative research. In N. K. Denzin & Y. S. Lincoln (Eds.), *Handbook of qualitative research* (pp. 83-97). Thousand Oaks, CA: Sage.

Reinharz, S. (1992). *Feminist methods in social research.* New York: Oxford University Press.

Reinharz, S. (1997). Who am I? In R. Hertz (Ed.), *Reflexivity and voice* (pp. 3-20). Thousand Oaks, CA: Sage.

Rosenwald, G. C., & Ochberg, R. L. (Eds.). (1992). *Storied lives: The cultural politics of self-understandings.* New Haven, CT: Yale University Press.

Rubin, H. J., & Rubin, I. S. (1995). *Qualitative interviewing: The art of hearing data.* Thousand Oaks, CA: Sage.

Seidman, I. E. (1991). *Interviewing as qualitative research.* New York: Teachers College Press.

Silverman, D. (1985). *Qualitative methodology and sociology.* Brookefield, VT: Gower.

Silverman, D. (1993). *Interpreting qualitative data: Methods for analyzing talk, text, and interaction.* London: Sage.

Silverman, D. (Ed.). (1997). *Qualitative research: Theory, method, and practice.* London: Sage.

Spiegelberg, H. (1975). *Doing phenomenology.* The Hague, Netherlands: Martinus Nijhoff.

Spiegelberg, H. (1976). *The phenomenological movement: Vols. I and II* (2nd ed.). The Hague, Netherlands: Martinus Nijhoff.

Spradley, J. (1979). *The ethnographic interview.* New York: Holt, Rinehart & Winston.

Stafford, K. R. (1991). The story that saved life. In C. Witherell & N. Noddings (Eds.), *Stories lives tell: Narrative and dialogue in education* (pp. 15-28). New York: Teachers College Press.

Strauss, A., & Corbin, J. (1990). *Basis of qualitative research: Grounded theory, procedures, and techniques.* Newbury Park, CA: Sage.

Strauss, A., & Corbin, J. (1994). Grounded theory methodology: An overview. In N. K. Denzin & Y. S. Lincoln (Eds.), *Handbook of qualitative research* (pp. 273-285). Thousand Oaks, CA: Sage.

Tesch, R. (1990). *Qualitative research: Analysis types and software tools.* London: Falmer.

Tripp-Reimer, T. (1989). Dialogue: On bracketing. In J. M. Morse (Ed.), *Qualitative nursing research* (pp. 11-13). Rockville, MD: Aspen.

Tuchman, G. (1994). Historical social science: Methodologies, methods, and meanings. In N. K. Denzin & Y. S. Lincoln (Eds.), *Handbook of qualitative research* (pp. 306-323). Thousand Oaks, CA: Sage.

Van Maanen, J. (1988). *Tales of the field.* Chicago: University of Chicago Press.

van Manen, M. (1990). *Researching lived experience.* London, Ontario: State University of New York Press.

Warren, C. A. B. (1988). *Gender issues in field research*. Newbury Park, CA: Sage.

Weitzman, E. B., & Miles, M. B. (1995). *Computer programs for qualitative data analysis*. Thousand Oaks, CA: Sage.

Witherell, C., & Noddings, N. (Eds.). (1991). *Stories lives tell: Narrative and dialogue in education*. New York: Teachers College Press.

Wolcott, H. F. (1990). *Writing up qualitative research*. Newbury Park, CA: Sage.

Wolcott, H.F. (1994). *Transforming qualitative data*. Thousand Oaks, CA: Sage.

❦ 2 ❦

Autobiography and the Value Structures of Ordinary Experience

Marianne Gullestad's Everyday Life Philosophers

Paul John Eakin

Constructed Selves, an Autobiography Contest, and the Social Sciences

In her recent book, *Everyday Life Philosophers: Modernity, Morality, and Autobiography in Norway,* anthropologist Marianne Gullestad (1996) investigates the transmission of moral values in 20th-century Norwegian society, opening up a fresh perspective on the social construction of selfhood. She seeks "to grasp and understand certain aspects of the structures within which people live their lives and from which they draw in making sense of their lives" (p. 31). Refusing a deterministic view of the individual as passively disciplined or inter-pellated by social institutions, Gullestad sees individuals instead as engaged in a dynamic process of self-invention in which "they crea-

AUTHOR'S NOTE: I want to thank Marianne Gullestad not only for inviting me to the University of Trondheim, where an earlier version of this paper was given in March, 1996, but also for making invaluable subsequent comments and suggestions.

tively refashion and adapt the knowledge, values, and ideas they receive" (p. 31).[1]

Gullestad (1996) bases her findings on four autobiographies drawn from an archive of some 630 narratives that she and sociologist Reidar Almås gathered through a nationwide autobiography competition, "Write Your Life," held in Norway in 1988-1989.[2] Although the use of an autobiography contest as an instrument of social and cultural analysis is not new—Gullestad points to those in Poland and Finland (p. 5)[3]—what is new is Gullestad's interest in the textuality of the artifacts she and Almås collected in the "Write Your Life" project. In *Everyday Life Philosophers,* she approaches the narratives they elicited *as narratives* and not merely as quarries from which to extract quantifiable information. As historiographer Hayden White (1987) memorably argues, form itself *is* a content and ought, accordingly, to be the object of historical inquiry.

Gullestad believes, however, that the social scientist, embracing an empiricist disciplinary paradigm, is conditioned to regard the constructed, literary nature of autobiographical texts with suspicion; the very imaginative qualities that she prizes in life writing are precisely those that might seem to interfere with the social-scientific scrutiny of objective fact. Rejecting this notion that the constructedness of a life story vitiates its value for cultural analysis, Gullestad (1996) reformulates constructedness as *"reflexivity,* a central quality which needs to be studied" (p. 7). This constructedness of autobiographies, of the selves we say we are and the lives we say we have lived, is the focus of her research in this project: rightly seen, and *Everyday Life Philosophers* helps us to see this, constructedness is itself an objective fact, a fact reflecting the structure of subjectivity.

Although a certain narrow strain of empiricism may indeed refuse the factuality of facts of this kind, cultural anthropologists and especially ethnopsychologists have made such facts the primary target of their research. Clifford Geertz (1976), for example, identifies the ethnographer's concern as a study of "the symbolic forms . . . in terms of which, in each place, people actually represented themselves to themselves and to one another" (p. 225). Viewed in this perspective, autobiographies in particular, and self-narration in general, document what Jerome Bruner (1991) terms our sense-making cultural "toolkits" (p. 2), giving us Geertzian evidence of what individuals in a particular culture "perceive 'with'—or 'by means of,' or 'through' " (Geertz, 1976, p. 225).[4] What, we might ask, do the four autobiographies in Gullestad's (1996) study tell us about their writers' knowledge of the symbolic forms available to them? We could, of course, develop a typology of the forms they draw on, reconstructing a kind of repertoire of cultural scripts.[5] Gullestad's research, however, points in a different direction, suggesting that form is transmitted not only through story as such but also through value.

As I have argued in *Fictions in Autobiography* (Eakin, 1985) and *Touching the World* (Eakin, 1992), autobiographies offer a precious record of the process of identity formation, of the ways in which individuals employ cultural models of identity and life story—subsets of Geertz's *symbolic forms*—to make sense of their experience. But where exactly do such models come from and what is the manner of their dissemination? (Eakin, 1992, pp. 89-90). Predictably, literary scholars have given literary answers to these questions. Embracing a theory of intertextuality, Avrom Fleishman (1983), for example, traces the history of autobiographical "figures," the "verbal formulas, iconographic images, and intellectual commonplaces" that cumulatively, over the centuries, constitute "the lingua franca of literary discourse" (p. 49). Briefly, books beget books.

Such theories of intertextuality, however, omit any account of the transmission of texts as a primary cultural process. How, we should ask, do texts come to be as they are? For an answer, social scientists, especially cultural anthropologists and developmental psychologists, direct our attention to the ways in which institutions—notably family, school, and church—contribute to the formation of the individual's subjectivity.

Complementing this familiar picture of the cultural sources of self and life story—literary texts, social institutions—is Gullestad's (1996) stress on values. "Constructions of self and identity," she observes, "are . . . dependent upon moral notions" (p. 20). Taking Gullestad's key insight that value is a repository of form, I want to extend her analyses by exploring the narrative structures that emerge in the value dilemmas faced by three of her everyday philosophers—Einar, Kari, and Øivind.[6] Latent in the discourses used to express values, I will argue, are metaphors for self and life story, rudiments of plot and character that individuals draw on as they live their lives and—sometimes—write them.

Einar and the Narrative of Disaffiliation

"I . . . remained 'nobody' "; "you go to and fro and there is nothing much to write about."

Einar titles his autobiography *My Childhood and Youth in a Periphery of the Periphery,* whereas Gullestad (1996) titles her analysis of it *Einar: From Fisherman to Bureaucrat.* The disjunction between the two titles—the opposing narrative destinations—is immediately apparent and instructive. On the face of it, Einar's move from a peripheral, marginalized Sami fishing community to a clerical job, marriage, and family life in the city has all the markings of the conventional success story, and Gullestad likens it to the trajectory of traditional *Bildungsromanen* (p. 115). Interestingly, however, in a statement of life purpose remarkable for its negatives, Einar himself insists that he rejected the success story: "I left fishing in order to get something to do, not in order to make a career. I never made a career and, this is also not what I set out to do" (Gullestad, 1996, p. 120).[7] Nor does he write that story of career: "After you marry and have a family of your own, you go to and fro and there is nothing much to write about" (p. 117).

In place of the unwritten *Bildungsroman,* Einar writes what Gullestad (1996, p. 106) characterizes as a narrative of apology to justify why he had to abandon the traditional Sami way of life he had known as a child. Reconstructing his situation at the decisive moment of vocation, Einar presents himself as a kind of liminal, transitional individual caught between two models of identity, two ways of life, affiliating with neither, yet accepting to his own discomfort the terms of the alternative model of *Bildung,* which he nonetheless did not choose to embrace.[8] He writes of his peers that "they went to school in order to 'become somebody,' " while he "was still at home and remained 'nobody' " (p. 104). Further evidence of his conflicted stance comes in his view that the school should have inculcated the very model he could not embrace.

The long and short of it, however, is that Einar *did do something* but it wasn't "a career" and it wasn't fishing, which he wasn't interested in and which made him sick. As I see it, Einar's story is finally neither a *Bildungsroman* nor an apology, although it contains elements of both; it is really something else, something, moreover, that perhaps the autobiography contest itself assisted him to work through and construct, what I would term a *narrative of disaffiliation.* I see him as between stories—Gullestad (1996) suggests this to me when she speaks of him as "commuting" (p. 121) between two ways of life.[9] Einar does not enter *narratively* into either one. Thus, he may have enacted the *Bildung* trajectory in his living, but it is largely unrepresented in his telling, whereas he focuses his counternarrative of his childhood world precisely on the moment of his decision to abandon it.[10] I want to look briefly at this unusually rich passage, which Gullestad identifies as a pivotal "moment of interpretation" (p. 110) leading to a kind of Sartrean choice of life project.

As he stands looking out to sea, reflecting on his life, Einar seems to identify with the freedom of birds making their way in a hostile environment: "the fulmar bird flying in the storm" and "the black-backed gull which . . . had started to search for a travel space and probably told me with some juicy expressions in black-backed gull language that he was first" (Gullestad, 1996, p. 110). The black-backed gull models for Einar a solitary alter ego who possesses a positive identity ("first") and the will to enact its capacities ("search for a travel space"), an identity endowed with the possibility of action and the discourse in which to express it in story. What I am suggesting is that Einar may have found a therapeutic opening in the "Write Your Life" contest, a travel space in which to express self and life, not in the language of the *Bildungsroman* or the apology but in a "black-backed gull language" of resistance: He makes a model of the lack of model from which he suffered as a young man, telling his story and in so doing making himself not "somebody" in the "career" sense but *someone with a story to tell.* Gullestad's analysis and publication of this non-story story, moreover, validates it as a life narrative, giving it status and standing. I suspect, in fact, that the contest and subsequent scholarly commentary have answered to the contestants' deeply felt need for validation and recognition. God's eye, we are told, is on the sparrow, and in the context of contemporary Norway's "transformed modernity" (Gullestad, 1996, pp. 10-14), its increasingly secularized culture, doubtless it was deeply satisfying for the contestants to know that someone was paying attention to them, not only reading them but talking and writing about them: They were worthy subjects of institutional discourse.

Kari and Value as Character

"She had several 'not so good characteristics' "

The mismatch between the cultural resources for identity formation and the individual's circumstances, which I believe Einar experienced as a kind of double displacement, an existence on the "periphery of the periphery," is experienced by Kari, in the second of Gullestad's (1996) autobiographies, as a psychological breakdown requiring hospitalization. Her therapist apparently concluded that Kari was too dependent, that she had failed to achieve a suitably adult measure of autonomy. Kari herself believes that she had become ill "because she had several 'not so good characteristics' " (p. 173)—in Kari's own understanding of her situation, character and value have become inextricably intertwined.

Values provide the simple structure of Kari's story: a focal episode in youth in which she accepts a guiding life principle, followed in midlife by a psychological crisis in which this principle is disconfirmed. Kari herself makes the link between the two episodes. Although she finds herself at 13 suddenly adrift and on her own when her grandmother dies, she is sustained by a piece of the grandmother's advice that "came to determine most of the years of my life: 'if I should pass away, and you are in doubt about what to do, then try to think of what I would have told you.' " The role of the other in this self-defining moment is central, yet interestingly, the grandmother's advice, despite its apparent demand of deference, functions simultaneously as a rationale for independence and autonomy. Kari makes this point clearly when, recalling the day of her grandmother's burial, she observes, "I felt a kind of self-confidence." Characteristically, this recognition of autonomy dawns as a kind of authoritative instruction from the other: "Now childhood is over and you have to start taking care of yourself" (Gullestad, 1996, p. 134). Although Kari's therapist failed to grasp it, the grandmother herself was apparently a quite complex figure who, despite her associations with hearth and home, encouraged Kari to "reach out for something better" (p. 152)—better, for example, than working in a factory. Kari clearly got her grandmother's *Bildung*-like message: "I fought my way upwards and forwards, the way Grandmother recommended" (p. 156).

The pattern of independent action formulated as obedience to advice is repeated when Kari recalls her decision to adopt a more refined style of speech despite family criticism. Relationally conditioned, she fights family with family in a decisive moment of introspection before her mirror, in which, again, we hear Kari in "thought-correspondence with Grandmother" (Gullestad, 1996, p. 174): "You are going to manage on your own, Kari, and you are going to behave in such a way that nobody will have any reason to blame you" (p. 153). Kari will achieve autonomy in obedience to the other, and it is precisely the anticipated approval of the other that authorizes her budding individualism. Kari instinctively recognizes the paradox of her grandmother's life-defining advice: She had been given permission to be herself.

Which brings me to the therapist who treated her during her midlife breakdown—a flat-footed figure who comes off rather badly in Gullestad's (1996) account. This patronizing fellow, the voice of the institution at its prescriptive worst, tells her that she "had never made an independent decision all [her] life," and Kari, ever obedient to the voice of authority, seems to accept the therapist's view that her grandmother "had decided [her] life," although she immediately qualifies this admission by saying, "It was probably not her intention." The therapist proceeds to enact precisely the authoritarian posture he had criticized in the grandmother as damaging to Kari's self-esteem: "Now let us put Grandmother away here, and let her rest in peace." Notwithstanding the smug condescension of the therapist's "now let us," Kari reports that his request "sounded like an order, and believe it or not, she disappeared from me" (Gullestad, 1996, p. 174).

Gullestad's (1996) delicate and discriminating analysis of the role of the grandmother in Kari's life and decision making underlines the simplistic nature of the therapist's interpretation: what he had seen as dependence was rather a way of "grounding moral decisions in popular forms of knowledge transmitted orally in important social relations" (p. 174). There is an important difference, she argues, between obedience and responsibility, defining the responsible individual as "somebody who acts in terms of deeply held and actively chosen moral values and convictions" (p. 176). In this case, Grandmother really did know best, best for Kari at any rate, and Kari eventually confided to Gullestad that she had resumed her "thought-correspondence" with her grandmother: "I have brought her forth again, and that's fine" (p. 175). Kari intuitively grasped, as the therapist did not, the latent individualism of the grandmother's advice. Perhaps, in the relational world of Kari's childhood, individualism could reach her only in the form of the advice the grandmother gave her, the grandmother who bridged two worlds, who was both worker and homemaker, who "reached out for something better" for Kari. The lesson of Kari's story is that autonomous and relational modes of identity are not mutually exclusive alternatives. We should rather think of them as poles at either end of a spectrum of identity patterning along which any individual, regardless of gender, will be located.

Gullestad (1996) discerns two "ideal structures" (p. 181) in Kari's autobiography, a chronological life-course plot from childhood to advanced age and an "attempt to achieve completeness" through the performance of the autobiographical act itself. Gullestad's analysis makes me see a third structuring element in value itself and in its transmission, for the transmission of value is thematized in so many of the episodes she analyzes, especially those that feature Kari's thought-correspondence with her grandmother. It is especially note-worthy that in the grandmother's admonition, Kari is enjoined to imagine "what I would have told you"; she was invited to imagine the grandmother giving her advice without the advice being specified. And Kari is herself notably preoccupied with the transmission of value, not merely in thought-correspondence with her grandmother but also, in her turn, in her views on childrearing and on the writing of her autobiography, for she desires to transmit her story to her descendants. What is important to Kari is to locate a value-appropriate discourse, a course of conduct that will be "blameless." Her search for a language of self-expression, as Gullestad makes clear, is made more difficult by the therapist's delegitimation of the grandmother's discourse.

Nevertheless, although the therapist's diagnosis seems simplistic, it is also true that Kari *was* sick, and Gullestad (1996) hypothesizes that her ailments—and perhaps those especially of women—represent a "somatisation" of social and cultural experience that affords Kari a "vocabulary" to articulate her suffering (p. 149). If I were to speculate about the reasons for Gullestad's selection of these four autobiographies for analysis out of the hundreds in the contest archive, I would suggest that she is especially drawn to individuals who find themselves at odds with their culture's received patterns of value: Kari's illness functions for her as the "black-backed gull language" did for Einar, expressing experience that the familiar discourses of the culture and its institutions contrive to silence.[11] Despite the reductive nature of Kari's view that her breakdown was caused by "several 'not so good characteristics,' " it points nonetheless to a fundamental perception that emerges from this autobiography: that value may be the source of identity and life-story action.

Øivind and Value as Plot

"Don't go too far."

Scrutiny of the "Write Your Life" autobiographies reminds us that we should never underestimate the creativity of the ordinary individual. As we might expect, these narratives display the imprint of the culture and its institutions on the individual's sense of identity. At the same time, however, each narrative reworks shared cultural material in unique and distinctive ways. Einar locates a life story between stories in a narrative of disaffiliation, whereas Kari struggles to claim her story as her own in the face of the therapist's charge that her grandmother "had decided [her] life." By contrast, Øivind, the third and in many ways most interesting of Gullestad's (1996) "everyday life philosophers," emerges as a man who never mustered the courage to embrace the story that would have realized his youthful ambitions: In the memorable final image of his narrative, Øivind exposes the "black holes" lurking beneath his treasured childhood "memories" (p. 219); autobiography and the identity it confers open onto the void.

Gullestad (1996) discerns in Øivind's narrative a "three-layered model of society," a model, she contends, that many Norwegians subscribe to today: in the middle are "people like us," who "stick together," determined not to "sink down" to the level of the poor, while the few, the rich, "stand out" on top. In addition, and complementing this three-layered vertical model, she detects a binary set of value oppositions between inside and outside, between home and the world beyond, and so forth (pp. 198-199). Implicit in the metaphoric structure of this value system is a series of life-course plots, those risings and sinkings of economic and social status that are the stuff of Ibsen's plays. Recalling the questions I posed at the outset concerning the relation between the individual and the models for self and life story supplied by a culture, I want to ask once more: How, exactly, are such models communicated to a child? To the young Øivind, for example?

Øivind is 13 when he accepts a permanent job to assist his mother in supporting a family in straitened circumstances—"we were three to provide for six"; this step foreclosed his chance for an education and his vague dreams of the future. When the aging autobiographer reconstructs this turning point in the life of his younger self, he draws precisely on the metaphoric potential for action latent in the three-tier model of society: "The bold ones can break out, rise towards the surface and become their own decision makers. But not me. The family in No. 25 became my destiny. I was part of it" (Gullestad, 1996, p. 206). Self and life story, act and character, become interchangeable in this moment of choice that isn't choice, which follows the logic of the boy's passive model of selfhood: He is someone to whom things happen, someone who does not really choose (p. 214). It is scarcely surprising, then, that Øivind's narrative terminates with the end of his childhood, and Gullestad notes that his story, unlike Kari's and Einar's, lacks a "specific interpretive moment in which the young man takes charge of his life and formulates an explicit life project of his own" (p. 208).

There are, however, what I would term two "anti-interpretive" moments, episodes in which the youth does *not* take charge of his life but accepts instead the role he believes his family has assigned him, an acceptance that lays the groundwork for his embracing at age 13 his sense of their project for him as his own. In these two passages, we see the boy trust in what he has been given, in what has been "chosen" for him. Probing Øivind's story, Gullestad (1996) concludes that "*something* [italics added] in him was preventing him from making the choice that would give him an education, and thereby a chance to 'rise to the surface'" (p. 208). What was that "something"? The two anti-interpretive, self and story-determining moments point to an answer.

The first of these moments concerns the child—now able to open the heavy gate—as he begins to cross the boundary between home and the world: "*Don't go too far*. Be careful," he was warned, and Øivind himself treats this admonition metaphorically, interpreting it as fore-shadowing the destiny of the older self who "took no risks." Gullestad (1996) emphasizes the moral values of restraint, control, and care in the mother's warning; not going "too far" becomes for her "a meta-level description" of Øivind's reticence about his most intimate concerns in the autobiography as a whole (pp. 200-201). Gullestad's stress on the "symbolic tensions between inside and outside" (p. 201) opens up additional registers of meaning: don't succeed, don't "stand out," stick with us, and you will be rewarded with love and security (this last is Øivind's own point). That is to say that these daily admonitions functioned as a dress rehearsal for the turning point at age 13, a turning point in name only, for, figuratively and psychologically speaking, Øivind was the boy who didn't turn out into the world but remained at home, behind the gate.

"Don't go too far"—all this may seem like a heavy freight of interpretation for the simple language of the parent's warning to bear, and it is fair to ask whether the boy could possibly have attached to it the import claimed by Gullestad (1996) and the aging autobiographer. The question is unanswerable, or rather, Øivind himself supplies the only available answer, and it is revealing: what he allows us to say for sure is that the parent's admonition lent itself to the metaphoric elaboration that he (and Gullestad later on) relate, testifying that even the simplest expression of value may carry the seeds of self and story that structure our self-narrations. Øivind focuses our attention on his going in and out through the gate accompanied by his mother's voice, and he proceeds to set in motion the whole set of metaphoric inter-pretations I have just rehearsed. Going in and out through the gate may seem rather trivial, but I suspect that it is precisely through the medium of frequently performed, habitual actions that values are most likely to be transmitted. The very nature of the action, its daily-ness, its simplicity, suggests that the metaphoric charge it gradually acquired for Øivind developed in the most natural way. Observing Gullestad observe Øivind, I conclude that this is what the transmission of value looks like from the vantage point of experience.

If we seek to identify the sources of the principal large-scale metaphors of autobiography, the self and its life story, we need to pay attention to the *narrativity* of the values Gullestad examines in these life stories—"reaching out for something better," "sinking down," "standing out," "going far," and so forth. We need to read the figures backward to their grounding in experience. In *Metaphors We Live By,* George Lakoff and Mark Johnson (1980) argue that metaphors are not merely distinctive features of the language we use to express thought; instead, they argue, "human *thought processes*" themselves are "largely metaphorical" (p. 6). Believing that metaphors "structure how we perceive, how we think, and what we do" (p. 4), they proceed to create a typology of the metaphors that organize our lives. In every case, they locate the origins of metaphor in cultural and especially in physical, bodily experience. Metaphors of value are no exception, and Gullestad (1996) gets at this, I think, when, speaking of Kari's asser-tion that she never thought she "was something," Gullestad com-ments, "values imply hierarchy" (p. 156). If we live by metaphors, we also write our lives by them, and these autobiographies afford a privileged glimpse into the workings of this process of self-construction.

I want now to look at the second of the two anti-interpretive moments, Øivind's painful recollection of a childhood disappointment. Gullestad (1996) interprets this particular Christmas memory as an authentic expression of the child's point of view. In general, she acknowledges that memories will necessarily be colored by the perspective of the remembering adult, but she singles out this one as allowing a glimpse of the boy Øivind had been, both because of its unusual emotional intensity ("the story's strongest") and because it "does not quite fit into the general theme" of Øivind's narrative (p. 213).[12] Sitting around the Christmas tree on Christmas Eve, the child recalls his excitement before opening his present from his father, for he tells us that "we expected most from the presents from father." The present proves to be "a big, stylish, marzipan figure," and Øivind bites off the head, only to discover that it was made out of soap. The bitter disappointment and humiliation are simply and sharply declared as a series of blows: "Father laughed! Everybody laughed. At me!" (pp. 211-212). I agree with Gullestad that the experience touched a nerve in the child that continues to ache a lifetime later, but I would stress the dialogic interplay between the child Øivind and the aging autobiographer. As she points out, it is the adult with his literary strategies who invests this memory with special significance (the repetitions, etc.), and we should ask why. What is behind his pouring so much literary energy into representing the child's disappointment?

The rest of Øivind's narrative makes me suspect that *he* suspects that his 13-year-old self had been betrayed by his family when he made a life-defining decision to give up his education and start working to help support them: He had chosen a marzipan figure that proved to be made out of soap. It is as though the youth had been tricked by the adults, conned into accepting their values, which they didn't themselves believe in, just as, earlier, the child had been betrayed by the father. In this reading, then, the Christmas memory is also a replay—as is the entire narrative—of the choice that wasn't a choice, the choice to stick with and support the family.[13] If my hunch is correct, then Øivind's story is a peculiarly painful one, in which the autobiographer confronts his doubts about the moral grounding of the life he has lived and the self he has become. If I am right, then the entire narrative functions as the "interpretive moment" Gullestad finds missing in

Øivind's tale. Gullestad (1996) believes that Øivind's primary motive for writing his narrative of childhood was that "out of his experiences during these years he was able to create a pattern describing his self that seemed to hold for the next six decades" (p. 221). Perhaps, but the marzipan deception—at least *as Øivind now recalls it*—seems to disconfirm the pattern, and I think it is telling that the final sentences of the narrative should repeat in capsule form the expectation/ disappointment, marzipan/soap tension that structures the Christmas memory: speaking of the house in which he had spent his childhood, he writes: "And it is filled with memories. And black holes." (p. 219).[14]

Discourses of Value, Discourses of Self and Life Story

Ethnopsychologists attempt to identify the tools we use to organize and understand our experience. "How," they ask, "do culturally contrasting peoples conceptualize their human nature and their personal-social processes?" (Smith, 1985, p. 62). Prominent among these tools are certain primary sense-making categories, including concepts of time and of the person. Drawing on these categories, autobiographers (re)construct their lives, and the cultural anthropologist who proposes to use such material as a source for social analysis must ask—and here I return to my opening questions—where does the individual's sense of self and life story come from? One answer has been from books, whereas another would point to the institutions that authorize, inculcate, and disseminate particular narratives and identity scripts.[15] Complementing these sources, Gullestad (1996) focuses our attention on discourses of value. In reviewing her analyses of the stories of Einar, Kari, and Øivind, I have emphasized how models of self and story are derived from values, for I think that Gullestad's work on the transmission of value can expand our understanding of identity formation.

We have long recognized that self and language are mutually implicated in an interdependent system of symbolic behavior. We know that the acquisition of language marks a milestone in the child's emerging sense of self, although Daniel Stern (1985) traces the sense of self back to the very dawn of infancy. Moreover, the research of Jerome Bruner (1991) and the so-called "narrative psychologists" has helped us to recognize the narrative dimension of identity formation. As Oliver Sacks (1987) observes, "Each of us constructs and lives a 'narrative,' and . . . this narrative *is* us, our identities" (p. 110). But what exactly is the content of this narrative discourse that produces the sense of self, of life story? Gullestad's (1996) studies of her "everyday life philosophers" reveal the models of identity that are coded in the discourse of values, models that precipitate out in the autobiographies produced by the "Write Your Life" contest. Working over her autobiographers' texts with patience and tact, she teases key value words back to their origins in everyday discourse, discourses spoken in schools and churches but especially in families, and—yes— across kitchen tables. In particular, Gullestad makes me see the self-and-narrative potential of what we *say* we believe—"Don't go too far," "reach out for something better," and so forth. Her study of the transmission of such values as these shows how social institutions are *experientially* linked to the individual: "Values," she urges, "do not only exist as explicit notions, but may also be reproduced in subtle ways through embodied practices in everyday life" (p. 265). Sensitizing us to recognize these "embodied practices" that make up the texture of the quotidian, Gullestad puts us in a good position to recognize how identity formation functions as cultural process.

In making so much of Øivind's going back and forth through the gate, however, his movement toward autonomy disciplined by the cautionary parental injunction not to go "too far," I don't want to embrace some impossible quest for origins. We can never expect to witness the emergent sense of self, of life story, as an observable event, for it is an ongoing process. The datable moments—Einar standing by the sea, Kari standing in front of her mirror, Øivind biting into the marzipan figure—are explicit or implicit moments of recognition that the sense of self and its story has *already* taken a decisive turn; we never catch ourselves in the act of *becoming selves*. We are always out of sync with our selves, always lagging behind, always trying to catch up retrospectively, for the self we seek turns out to be a self *in process.* Thus, the autobiographies Gullestad (1996) studies are themselves attempts to recapture the decisive moments in which the autobiographers believe they became what they think they are. But the self, of course, which we take to be experiential fact, is also finally a fiction, an elusive creature that we construct even as we seek to encounter it. In this sense, writing autobiography is like weaving Penelope's web, a making that is also an unmaking. Ironically, even when we train an ethnographic gaze upon ourselves, even when we are our own subjects, our own informants, there is always a gap or rupture that divides us from the knowledge that we seek. Nevertheless, I think that in *Everyday Life Philosophers,* Gullestad goes very far indeed toward giving us what Clifford Geertz (1973) has proposed as "a scientific phenomenology of culture, . . . a developed method of describing and analyzing the meaningful structure of experience (here, the experience of persons) as it is apprehended by representative members of a particular society at a particular point in time" (p. 364).

Notes

1. Similarly, in *Touching the World: Reference in Autobiography* (Eakin, 1992), I draw on psychologist Andrew Lock's notion of a *positive-feedback* loop to conceptualize my own sense of identity formation as an organic, experiential, constantly evolving *interaction* between the individual and cultural forms and forces (pp. 99-100).

2. For information about the contest and the methodology that informed it, see Gullestad and Almås, "Write Your Life."

3. The whole subject of autobiography contests is fascinating, and in addition to the commentaries Gullestad cites by Bertaux and Kohli (1984) and Roos (1985) on this phenomenon, see also Lejeune (1985, pp. 70-73) for a 19th-century French example, and Lejeune (1989a) for a 20th-century Italian one.

4. In a parallel fashion, Gullestad (1992) writes,

> I am interested in the implicit cultural knowledge embodied in social practices. Culture is not a thing that human beings have, but an analytic aspect of their practices. I am, in other words, not only interested in what people think and do, but also in what they think and act with, [that is], the ideas, values, concepts, and beliefs that they routinely use as tools for thinking and acting" (p. 21).

5. Lejeune has pioneered the typology of autobiographical forms: see, for example, "Autobiography and Social History" (1989b) and "En famille" (1986, pp. 199-200).

6. I should caution that my knowledge of the "Write Your Life" contest materials that I comment on is derived exclusively from Gullestad's presentation of them. I am, as it were, reading over her shoulder, at one remove from the primary sources.

7. It may be merely an effect of translation, but the statement "I never made a career and, this is also not what I set out to do" (Gullestad, 1996, p. 120) has an interesting and perhaps revealing ambiguity about it: (1) I never made a career, and I never intended to; (2) I never made a career *but* this is not what I intended. In any case, the conflicted discourse strikes me as characteristic of Einar and his liminal identity situation.

8. This accepting of the terms of the model he doesn't embrace is echoed in the title as well in which he speaks of the "periphery of the periphery."

9. Gullestad (1996) interprets Einar's situation rather differently, contending that he maintains a double affiliation with both the old life he left behind and the new life he made for himself in the city. He develops, she suggests, a "commuting, hybrid self" (personal communication to the author). For further insight into this notion of cultural commuting, see Gullestad (1992). Gullestad's notion of Einar commuting between two cultural affiliations parallels her view of Øivind "oscillating" between two different assessments of his identity and life choices (see Note 14). Individuals today, she argues, may belong to several "partcultures" simultaneously (Gullestad, 1992, pp. 18-20). Both instances reflect Gullestad's effort to articulate a concept of culture that is sufficiently supple to address the complexities of contemporary life: "What we need . . . is not to abandon completely the concept of culture, but rather to reconfigure it as a set of permeable, less bounded, and less tightly integrated structures and practices" (Gullestad, 1992, p. 14).

10. Einar's narrative of disaffiliation is thus a disaffiliation from what historian Carolyn Kay Steedman (1986/1987) has described as the "central interpretative devices of the culture" (p. 5). Steedman makes a case for "lives lived out on the borderlands," lives that don't square with the culture's received scripts for life history.

11. I have discussed this issue with Gullestad, and she comments: "I think I am drawn not to individuals at odds, but to their *texts*. In fieldwork, too, I found that the best informants were often people who were a little marginal in the group: They were able to make explicit the general rules for inclusion and exclusion, for example, in ways that more centrally located individuals were not. I think that there is a general point here—that cultural values and ideas are best studied at the margins and in interstices between institutions and groups" (personal communication to the author).

12. Gullestad (1996) prefaces her analysis of this episode by distinguishing between "historical accuracy" on the one hand and "authentic expressions of the sentiments of a child" on the other (pp. 210-211). Although she discerns the adult's retrospective presence in the literary language and strategies used to reconstruct the episode, she believes nonetheless that "we are closer to Øivind the child in this passage than anywhere else in the story," that the child's emotion "has not grown old but has kept its raw vitality and force" (p. 213).

13. Interestingly, Gullestad (1996) links this memory to another moment in which Øivind portrays himself as a child who suspects "that somebody *little* does not understand everything the big ones understand" (p. 213). If she is correct in making this

connection, the passage would seem to support the interpretive weight that Øivind, Gullestad, and I have given to the marzipan episode: The autobiographer portrays the child as intuiting the existence of a latent kernel of meaning that he lacks the power to articulate.

14. Gullestad (1996) argues that Øivind "oscillated" between two views of himself, such that the marzipan deception does not so much disconfirm his "pattern" or model of identity but is rather a part of it. I come back to what strikes me as a highly charged image: Øivind's linking of memory with "black holes." I note an interesting gap between what Øivind wrote and the impression he seems to have made on Gullestad in his subsequent conversations with her about his life and narrative. The follow-up interviews with the informants obviously enrich and complement the written narratives in interesting ways, but I suspect that they also raise problems for ethnographic interpretation that are not easily solved. In this case, for example, I would suggest that Øivind may have been prepared to own in writing a starker interpretation of his life than he was prepared to own to Gullestad in person.

15. For additional discussion of these issues, see Eakin (1992), Chapter 3, "Self and Culture: Models of Identity and the Limits of Language."

References

Bertaux, D., & Kohli, M. (1984). The life story approach: A continental view. *Annual Review of Sociology, 10*, 215-237.

Bruner, J. (1991). The narrative construction of reality. *Critical Inquiry, 18*, 1-21.

Eakin, P. J. (1985). *Fictions in autobiography: Studies in the art of self-invention.* Princeton, NJ: Princeton University Press.

Eakin, P. J. (1992). *Touching the world: Reference in autobiography.* Princeton, NJ: Princeton University Press.

Fleishman, A. (1983). *Figures of autobiography: The language of self-writing in Victorian and modern England.* Berkeley: University of California Press.

Geertz, C. (1973). *The interpretation of cultures.* New York: Basic Books.

Geertz, C. (1976). From the native's point of view: On the nature of anthropological understanding. In K. H. Basso & H. A. Selby (Eds.), *Meaning in anthropology* (pp. 221-237). Albuquerque: University of New Mexico Press.

Gullestad, M. (1992). *The art of social relations: Essays on culture, social action, and everyday life in modern Norway.* Oslo: Scandinavian University Press.

Gullestad, M. (1996). *Everyday life philosophers: Modernity, morality, and autobiography in Norway.* Oslo: Scandinavian University Press.

Gullestad, M., & Almås, R. (1992). Write your life: A Norwegian life story contest. *Oral History, 20*, 61-65.

Lakoff, G., & Johnson, M. (1980). *Metaphors we live by.* Chicago: University of Chicago Press.

Lejeune, P. (1985, janvier). Les instituteurs du XIXe siècle racontent leur vie. *Histoire de l'éducation, 25*, 53-104.

Lejeune, P. (1986). En famille. In *Moi aussi* (pp. 181-202). Paris: Seuil.

Lejeune, P. (1989a, mars-avril). Archives autobiographiques. *Le débat, 54*, 68-76.

Lejeune, P. (1989b). Autobiography and social history in the nineteenth century (K. Leary, Trans.). In P. J. Eakin (Ed.), *On autobiography* (pp. 163-184). Minneapolis: University of Minnesota Press.

Roos, J. P. (1985). Life stories of social changes: Four generations in Finland. *International Journal of Oral History, 6,* 179-190.

Sacks, O. (1987). *The man who mistook his wife for a hat and other clinical tales.* New York: Harper.

Smith, M. B. (1985). The metaphorical basis of selfhood. In A. J. Marsella, G. DeVos, & F. L. K. Hsu (Eds.), *Culture and self: Asian and Western perspectives* (pp. 56-88). New York: Tavistock.

Steedman, C. K. (1987). *Landscape for a good woman: A story of two lives.* New Brunswick, NJ: Rutgers University Press. (Original work published 1986)

Stern, D. N. (1985). *The interpersonal world of the infant: A view from psychoanalysis and developmental psychology.* New York: Basic Books.

White, H. (1987). *The content of the form: Narrative discourse and historical representation.* Baltimore: Johns Hopkins University Press.

❦ 3 ❦

"Black Holes" as Sites for Self-Constructions

Harriet Bjerrum Nielsen

Agency and Agents

Today, the notion of agency is one of the most highly valued terms in the social sciences. In the aftermath of structuralism, much effort has been put into revitalizing the subject and conceptualizing it as an active contributor to the formation and change of social structures and cultural forms. Thus, ethnographic studies of everyday life, in-depth interviews, life stories, and autobiographies of ordinary people (as opposed to the great and famous) have gained significance as empirical sources in the social sciences.

Agency, however, is also a very disputed and ambiguous term. In the postmodern version of agency, for instance, the idea either becomes rather voluntaristic (as in *identity politics*) or seems to vanish into linguistic systems that are believed to make up the agent. In more mainstream interpretative research in sociology, anthropology, and even social psychology, agents often seem to merge into the cultural meanings they are claimed to be making (Bjerrum Nielsen, 1996; Chodorow, 1995; Moore, 1994).

The question I shall address in this article is whether a notion of agency can do without a theory of the agent—that is, a theory of how humans, in conscious and unconscious ways, process their experiences of life and act on them. With respect to textual constructions by the agent (life stories, etc.), to what degree are interpretations that tend to leave out the psychological/emotional level of textual organization limited in their understanding of the contributions of the individuals to the process of cultural change? In a commentary on Clifford Geertz's image of man as a spider amid the web of meanings he himself has created, the Indian/North American anthropologist Gananat Obeyesekere (1990) reminds us that Geertz shows us the web, but not the spider. What is missing are the *life-forms in the making*: "It seems to me that to ignore deep motivation in the formation and transformation of culture is to miss an important dimension in our species condition" (p. 287). The point Obeyesekere makes is that psychoanalytical readings should not just be understood as supplementary interpretations for those especially interested in the psychology of the individual, but as essential to anyone who wants to understand the *work of culture*:

> With respect to unconscious materials the anthropologist is in a peculiar dilemma. He must either deny that they exist; or he must adopt a comfortable sociologism that says that while they exist they do not manifest themselves in cultural form or social life; or he might ignore them and invoke his lack of training to handle them; or he must adopt a theory that helps him to understand them—whatever that theory might be. All but the last position would leave a large area of symbolic form and social life uninvestigated by the anthropologist and unexplained by his informant (. . .) resulting in badly slanted descriptions of cultural life. (pp. 223-224)

In my opinion, this should certainly not amount to saying that interpretations that remain on the level of cultural configurations are worthless. On the contrary, such readings can give us important insights into how people actually use cultural concepts to organize their social world and to make sense of what is going on around them. These readings can also give us important information about which cultural discourses are available and who uses them at any given time. In this way, we can "see history from below." The question I will raise, however, is whether one can grasp the other side of the dialectic between the individual and the social without a psychological perspective: not only how people make use of cultural concepts to construct themselves and their social world, but also how such personal constructions may give rise to cultural and social change. This entails not only writing history from below, but also grasping how all these small histories continuously and in multiple ways change the big historical picture.

Everyday Life Philosophers

I will approach my topic via a re-reading of an autobiography presented in an intriguing new book, *Everyday Life Philosophers*, by the Norwegian social-anthropologist Marianne Gullestad (1996). The aim of the book is to grasp the rhetorically central value concepts by which people organize their understanding of their own lives, and thus to describe the societal changes in moral understandings in contemporary Norway through the lens of life narratives. How are the self and society constructed in these autobiographical accounts, and what kind of moral dilemmas emerge in different stories? What can these models and dilemmas tell us about social and cultural change? Marianne Gullestad depicts, through her interpretations, the cultural resources that the writers draw on, and how they use these resources. In her introductory chapter, she writes,

> I hope to show that "ordinary people" relate in creative and complex ways to structural conditions and to social categories, labels, and concepts associated with such conditions. There is a dynamic relationship between hegemonic values— transmitted through institutions such as schools, churches, and mass media—and individual efforts at making sense of what goes on around them (. . .) The overall problem of this book can be put as a question of what human beings receive from other people, and how they creatively refashion and adapt knowledges, values, and ideas, they receive (. . .) Traditions are not just inherited; individuals choose among

elements and make them theirs in processes of active construction and reconstruction. People live their lives and tell
their stories within socially structured conditions, but their
actions and stories also have a potentially transformative impact on "society." (pp. 3, 31-32)

The process of moral transformation is seen from the perspective of
modernity, according to which the self becomes a reflexive project
under the responsibility of the individual. When "grand" narratives
lose power, says Gullestad (1996), little narratives, such as autobiography, gain credibility. The art of moral living in our time, according
to Gullestad, is to be able to live with tensions, contradictions,
dilemmas, paradoxes, and ambiguities—and to find solutions not in
terms of either/or, but in terms of integration (p. 21). In a bold move,
Gullestad presents an instructive, moving, and well-written monograph about contemporary Norwegian society by analyzing only four
life stories, written by Einar, a middle-aged civil servant and (in his
own words) a "closet Sami" from northern Norway; Kari, a working-
class housewife in her sixties from Oslo; Øivind, a businessman in his
seventies from Norway's third-largest city; and Cecilia, a sixteen-year-
old girl from a small coastal city. Gullestad traces an interesting change
of emphasis in popular ideologies from *being of use* to *being (and
finding) one self,* and she sketches some of the considerable sociocultural implications and consequences of this change. In her concluding chapter, "Anchorage Points for the Self," she discusses how egalitarian values are simultaneously reinforced and transformed as many
Norwegians engage in creating more plural images of self through new
combinations of roles and identities.

In her interpretation of the autobiographies, Marianne Gullestad
(1996) draws on an impressively wide array of theoretical and substantial knowledge from historical, sociological, anthropological, and
literary studies, but she explicitly chooses to exclude psychoanalytic
interpretation and theory, which, in her view, "reduces the imaginative
and reflexive qualities of the autobiographical account to 'distortions'
of a deeper and more authentic meaning, and, thus, works with 'tight
causal relations in one direction' " (p. 7). While I agree with Gullestad
that a life story is shaped by material facts of social existence, deeply

embedded notions and expectations about what constitutes a culturally normal life, and conscious and unconscious rules about what constitutes a good story (p. 7), I would add that stories are also influenced by the emotional life and unconscious motivations of the writer, not in terms of authentic meanings to which everything else can be reduced, but as sources no less important than those included by Gullestad.

By reinterpreting one of the autobiographies in *Everyday Life Philosophers* (Gullestad, 1996), I wish to highlight what a reading from a psychological perspective can add to a cultural analysis, particularly insofar as the question of agency is concerned. My discussion of this point should not overshadow the fact that I am in other respects very impressed by Gullestad's refined analyses of her material. I have no objections to her shrewd account of the Norwegian process of modernization and its general impact on self-construction and identity. The very openness and richness of her analysis[1] is what allowed for my re-reading, and thus my endeavor is quite in the spirit of Gullestad's book:

> The many quotations from their text provide the reader with ample material for making different interpretations than the ones I have made. The life stories, as well as the social realities that shaped them, are open to future interpretations from new perspectives, and, therefore, open to challenge. (p. 42)

Nonetheless, I do believe that a more psychologically informed understanding of identity and of the art of self-construction might have shed some light on her own research questions.

Activity and Passion

Paul Ricoeur (1991) says that life can be seen as "an activity and a passion in search of a narrative" (p. 29). When we construct a narrative of our life, we produce a textual structure that "underscore(s) the mixture of acting and suffering which constitutes the very fabric of life. It is this mixture which the narrative attempts to imitate in a creative way" (p. 28). When analyzing a narrative, says Ricoeur, we should thus look for the points of support that the narrative can find in the living experience, as well as that which, in this experience, demands the assistance of a narrative and expresses the need for it. Thus, the passion inherent in the creating of a text is not only to make sense of what goes on around the narrator but also to make sense of unconscious passions and sufferings within the narrator. When we tell stories about our lives, the point is to make our lives not only more intelligible, but also more bearable. We can make ourselves heroes of our own story—we cannot, however, actually become the authors of our own lives. Thus, even though narrative strives toward homogeneity, it will always be a synthesis of the heterogeneous—a structure of "discordant concordance" (p. 31).

The German psychoanalyst Alfred Lorenzer (1986) and his colleagues, working in the field of cultural studies in the tradition of the late Frankfurter school, have developed a method of *deep-hermeneutic cultural interpretation,* according to which a text can simultaneously convey a conscious and an unconscious structure of meaning. Notwithstanding Gullestad's (1996) ostensible conception of psychoanalytic interpretation of cultural forms, Lorenzer's aim is not to reduce the manifest meaning of a text to a latent meaning. In his view, the unconscious structure is not something that lies behind the text, but rather another structure of meaning in the text. Whereas the latent meaning of a dream will often require additional information from the dreamer, the latent meaning of a written text has to be in the text; otherwise, it makes little sense. Thus, the connection between the conscious and the unconscious is to be found in the symbolic accounts themselves.

These coexisting structures of meanings are related to each other in multiple ways: The unconscious structure softens the contradictions of the conscious structure, and the conscious structure softens the forbidden nature of the unconscious. In this way, a text can be a means of presenting a forbidden passion (and the conflicts and compromises that go with it) in a public room. In this way, the text also presents what Lorenzer (1986) calls alternative "life-sketches" to its readers. Obeyesekere (1990) makes much the same point in his discussion of *personal symbols:* By engaging in cultural practices, a person can enact an inner personal conflict, but by doing so he mediates this conflict to the realm of culture. His action is perfectly intelligible to others, even if they don't know his unconscious motivations for engaging in it. In this way, personal symbols act as a mediating language between the privatized language of symptoms and the communicative language of everyday life, and this mediation may change both. Drawing on Freud and Ricoeur, both Obeyesekere and Lorenzer suggest that symbolization can control loss and help one to bear, relieve, or transform suffering. Whether transformation actually takes place, depends on the degree of *symbolic remove*—whether the energy of the unconscious motivations takes a regressive or a progressive direction. In the first case, cultural symbols are used to express and control personal conflicts; in the second case, personal conflicts are used to create new cultural forms: "A symbol and a symptom contain both motive and meaning, but whereas a symptom is under the domination of motive, a symbol is under the rule of meaning" (Obeyesekere, 1990, p. 12).

To find the unconscious structure in a text, according to Lorenzer (1986), we have to be as open to the text as an analyst is open to the communications of the patient. We look at the spots where it "irritates" (Prokop, 1996)—where something "does not fit" or seems to be missing, where the text becomes contradictory or maybe too coherent, where the rhetoric is experienced as ambiguous, touching, or untrustworthy. These instances may be related to content but are more often issues of form—selection, ordering, rhetorical figures, textual images. It is by virtue of our capacities as humans and our knowledge of a particular culture that we are able to sense these irritations.

Whether the conflictual themes in the text are general or specific to a certain culture or family, they are marked by repression and by a manifestation in the text as irritations. To interpret these irritations, knowledge of the values and norms in the culture of the narrator, as well as knowledge of psychoanalytic metatheory, is indispensable. Yet, as both Lorenzer (1986) and Obeyesekere (1990) point out, interpretation begins with empathic response to the text itself, and only afterward are results systematized in relation to cultural and psychoanalytic theory. Direct relation of text to theory will at best yield a dry classification or illustration of what is already known. It is essential to combine a "thick description" of the object of study with a generalized and conceptual framework related to objective as well as subjective structures of the narrator and his or her culture. A poststructuralist would, of course, object that such generalized conceptual frameworks are nothing but *master-narratives*, assaulting the text and the self-identity of the writer, but in my opinion—and here I believe Gullestad (1996) concurs with me—generalized concepts and theory are always involved in interpretation. The fact that a psychoanalytic reading provides a frame of interpretation does not disqualify it, any more than any other reading that provides an interpretative frame. The main point in all cases is to establish an empathic and reflexive space between the object of interpretation and the theoretical framing of the interpretation.

In the following, I will try to demonstrate how a simultaneous reading of the conscious and the unconscious structure of an autobi-ography can help us to see how a specific narrator not only makes creative use of cultural categories to construct a self-identity, but also how this specific self-construction endorses his forbidden desires and thus gives them a form in which they can have an impact on social change.

Øivind's Story

The life story I am going to reinterpret was written by an old man, then in his early seventies. His name is Øivind, and he insisted that his real name be used by the researchers in their presentation of his story.[2] Born in 1917, he has lived through the history of social democracy and the welfare state in Norway. Marianne Gullestad (1994) gives a short discussion of Øivind's autobiography in *Cultural Studies,* where the following summary of the story introduces her analysis:

> Øivind's story is 33 typed pages and treats his childhood from approx. 4 years to approx. 14 years. The story is well written, with obvious literary qualities.[3] The story is called "No. 25. (The frame of a childhood)" and a description of No. 25 as it was then and how it is now frames the story.

No. 25 is a house in Queen's street in the city of Trondheim (Norway's third largest). Øivind was 4 years old when the family moved in. He was the youngest child in the family (three elder sisters and one elder brother). His father, a businessman, had recently bought the whole building and the family took possession of a large apartment in it. Øivind describes vividly no. 25 as a "castle" and its back yard as the yard of the castle. Not long after, the building lost its fairytale qualities. Øivind's father died, and the family was forced to let most of their own apartment, leaving mother and five children only two rooms and a back door. There is a development in the story from the naivete of the child to the 13-year-old boy who has made the choice of his life—to work and thereby contribute to supporting his mother and siblings rather than getting the education he wanted.

Sticking Together or Standing Out?

The central frame of interpretation that both Øivind himself and Gullestad (1996) apply to Øivind's life is his choice at age 13 and the tension between duty and loyalty toward one's family and the ability to take one's life into one's own hands; the moral imperative of duty versus the moral imperative of self-realization. Gullestad discusses Øivind's oscillation in his text between images of himself as a person who is loyal and dutiful and a person who is unable to break out and take charge of his own life. She identifies two complexly interrelated models of society in his life story (one consisting of three layers with himself and most others in the middle, and one consisting of an opposition between home and the outside world) and discusses the relation between choice and constraint in present-day modernity. She concludes by pointing out parallels between Øivind's dilemmas about how to understand himself and his life as an aging man, on the one hand, and current dilemmas of the social democratic welfare states, on the other. The stress on solidarity is being overrun by the growing emphasis of a transformed modernity on individual freedom and choice. This dilemma can also be seen as a tension within the social democratic project itself: Solidarity is a central value, but it is also a necessary means of defense for those who have been denied access to societal power for self-realization.

Øivind is rather vague when it comes to his choice of duty/loyalty over individualization. The decision to go to work when he was 13 was, as Gullestad (1996) depicts it, both a choice and a nonchoice, his own move and yet an act that was forced on him:

> The bold ones can break out, rise towards the surface and become their own decision makers. But not me. The family in No. 25 became my destiny. I was part of it (. . .) We were three to provide for six . . . I was an ordinary case. (p. 206)

Øivind appeals to our pity and at the same time seems to be proud of his choice and quite content with his life. Something in the text irritates here.

The tension in Øivind's story between his solidarity with his family and his desire to go out on his own is depicted by Gullestad (1996) in two opposing sets of values throughout the narrative. By extracting the values from Gullestad's fluent prose, it is possible to compose the following two lists. And as Gullestad puts it, Øivind sympathizes with and feels obligated to the values I have put in the left column, whereas he desires the position of those few who "stand out":

Duty/Solidarity	Self-Realization
Sticking together	Standing out
Group	Individual
Safety	Freedom
Inside	Outside
Home	Places far away
Everyday life	The exotic
Family	Society at large

The opposing sets of values are constructed as a dichotomy in Øivind's narrative, which corresponds to other familiar dichotomous constructions. One, which Gullestad stresses, is the dichotomy between then and now, between the then of experienced past and the now of the writing. Another, which is not explicitly mentioned either by

Gullestad or by Øivind, is that of gender. No one with a knowledge of modern Western culture would have trouble deciding which column connotes femininity and which connotes masculinity. This coincidence is not surprising—femininity is often portrayed as a premodern relic in modernity. Evaluations of this half of the dichotomy range from a view that it is anachronistic with respect to the demands on a modern individual to the belief that it may be regarded as representative of superior values: essential human traits of care, emotions, and connections among people, which are protected by women from the coldness, destructiveness, and irresponsibility of modern society. After "the death of God," it is women who represent morality in society, a point also made by Gullestad in another chapter in her book. The English sociologist Barbara Marshall (1994) puts it this way: "The purpose of the family, and woman within it, becomes, depending on the theorist, a moral regulator of, a reproducer of, or a haven for, the male individual" (p. 9). In other words, women and the intimate sphere of the family represent, on the one hand, a sort of paradise to which a modern man can sentimentally long to return, and on the other hand, a threat to the praised modern project that precisely demands that he free himself from stagnation and dependency.

In the case of Øivind, this suggests a different story than the one he tells explicitly: Did he, by choosing duty and solidarity, also choose to stay in a female world even though he desired the male? Øivind himself does not expressly make the connection to gender, even though, as we shall see in a moment, he lets us know indirectly, that he is aware of the implicit gendered meaning in the two sets of values.

A Male and a Female World

Øivind discusses family and kinship in quite an ungendered manner, and he seldom talks about brothers and sisters, mostly just about siblings. Degenderization of this type may not be remarkable in and of itself, given that many families consist of both men and women, mothers and fathers, grandmothers and grandfathers, aunts and uncles, and both brothers and sisters. What is interesting, however, is that this norm does not apply to Øivind, in whose family there are mostly women: a mother, innumerable aunts, several sisters, and women who come to work for the family. This fact makes the degenderization in the language chosen by Øivind remarkable and worthy of note.

After the death of Øivind's father, when Øivind is 6 years old, this ungendered, indeed prominently female kin group takes over, an event that is described very vividly in his story:

> Into the one and only living room came the family, the kin group, the relatives, with their support. The living room was not very big, but our family was. Mother was one of sixteen siblings, most of them married and living in town. The times were bad for all of them. Some were better off than us, some worse. We all stuck together . . .
>
> We understood that the visits of the aunts were a great support for mother. She regained her spirits. And we grew happier too. Laughter came back to No. 25. I can still hear them laugh over the cups of coffee, Aunt Ann, Aunt Dagmar, mother who was "Aunt Laura," and all the others. (Gullestad, 1996, p. 193)[4]

Although Øivind does not explicitly connect the two sets of values with gender, he does do it implicitly, by describing the women and the few men of his childhood in terms that are aligned with the two sets of values: Mother is definitely and explicitly tied to the pole of care, safety, and family: When Øivind is tempted, as a small child, to go outside, mother calls him back: "I turned around and went inside again. Into security, into no. 25. Here was mother" (p. 200). The female world is associated with food (often mentioned as part of the social life: coffee, pancakes, a bite to eat at the homes of his relatives, the daily meals). It is also a realm of cultural ambitions and interests that match the language and the curriculum of school (books/education), and it is a world connected with music and poetic/aesthetic qualities.

Apart from his epileptic elder brother, the very few men that are mentioned are just as clearly connected to the other set of values. The father is a salesman, often traveling away from home, and therefore distant in the family. "The person I knew the least was Father" says Øivind. With his money, however, Father could buy the "castle" at no. 25. And Father could let the family have maids who hugged Øivind. When Father died, the castle shrank and lost its fairytale qualities. Instead of the maids came washing-Anna and sewing-Anna, with no time or inclination for hugging. So Father's death also meant a social descent and the loss of the sweet maids. Father is remembered for his strong arms, which lifted little Øivind high into the air, so close to the ceiling that he could reach toward the bunches of fruits and flowers on the ceiling's wallpaper, and Father is remembered for his postcards to Øivind from the world outside. In one of these, Father prompts Øivind to get away from the chimney corner and out into the fresh air.

There is also a grandfather in the story, but he dies long before Øivind's birth, and is only mentioned because he couldn't stand being at home with his wife and 16 children (these 16 children are later referred to as the aunts—we don't know if there were any boys). During his holiday week, after only two days, Grandfather went back to work, leaving his wife baking pancakes for the 16 children.

Øivind has a 10-year-older brother who is mentioned only briefly in the story. He is physically disabled—an epileptic who cannot work. His maleness comes up in the context of his sexuality: He sleeps by himself and goes to the men's changing room at the public bath, while little Øivind can sleep in his mother's bed and shower with his sisters. The brother is a pianist, and his friends turn up to practice, which Øivind enjoys. He is also taught to play the piano by his brother.

In addition to these three either distant, working, and dead or disabled, nonworking males, we meet, also very briefly, four other men:

- A rich factory owner who lives across the street, owns a Buick convertible, and has an unattainable fairy princess of a daughter. He is described in his capacity of being rich and as a person who "stands out" from the rest. He is in sharp contrast to two poor women in the narrative—washing-Anna and sewing-Anna.
- The employer at the office where Øivind gets his first job at 13. He is a patriarchal figure who assesses Øivind thoroughly before taking him on. He also owns a car, and his wealth is in contrast

to the state of three old, poor, and bad smelling women who come to his office every Saturday for charity.
- The headmaster of the school, who twice intervenes in Øivind's life, once by rescuing his hard-earned pocket money from his mother's plans to use it for winter boots, and once by offering the then 13-year-old Øivind a summer job. It is this job that puts Øivind in the situation where he makes the pivotal decision of his life, going out to work instead of continuing in school.
- A farmer whom Øivind gets to know during the summer of his fateful decision. Øivind admires this farmer for his work skills. He is described in terms that oppose the laughing and talking aunts of no. 25 in the city: silent and dressed in black homespun clothes, "not used to urban talk." He smells of horses, while the farm itself is described in terms of exciting smells.

Some generalized groups of men are also mentioned: the strict teachers at school, the playmates from the street who provide Øivind with sex education, and first and foremost the seamen in the harbor who come in from their exotic journeys to foreign countries. They are dirty, smoke cigarettes, and have survived the dangers of the sea. They too are connected with the exciting smells of the harbor: oil, coal, tar, hemp, dried fish. Øivind writes: "I admired them and dreamed about these men of excitement, standing there, little me, with my experiences limited to the frame around no. 25" (Gullestad, 1996, p. 203).

So even if Øivind does not explicitly connect the tension in his life to his experience of gender, his own narrative shows that he knows perfectly well that this is a gender split. And thus, from his specific life experiences come additional qualities connected to the two poles, making the parallel to the dilemma of the welfare state only partial. We can add to the male/freedom column:

- "Rising up" (the rich man, the boss, father)
- Work for money
- Access (through money) to pleasures (cars, castle, hugging maids, the rich man's daughter, sweets)
- Exciting smells and tastes/sweets/fruits/cigarettes/dirt
- Country life/the wild sea/fresh air

And to the female/duty column:

- "Sinking down" (social descent, a latent danger in the family, which is kept at bay only through sticking together, talking, and laughing; the two Annas; the three old women)
- Education/talk
- Poetic/aesthetic qualities
- Food
- Urban life/chimney corner

Books and music seem to be the only gender-ambiguous areas. As we have seen, music is tied to the home but still played and introduced by a (disabled) male. Books are combined with the educational atmosphere of the home and family evenings of reading aloud, but they are also borrowed from the public library and described as luring Øivind toward the wider world. Looking at the backs of books on the shelves in the library, Øivind hints at the seductions they present:

> Backs that do not reveal the secrets they confine. Come, take me! they say. Lay me open! We have waited for you. Here you will find your dreams in writing and signs. And our fantasy world reaches so far, and farther than that. We are going to shape your life. And we have power. Use us in the right way, and you will become rich! And I carry the richness with me home. The journey has started.

But apart from these mediating areas, to which I will return later, the gender split is very clear and still so indirectly conveyed. Why? Why is it both explicitly there and still concealed by terms such as family, kinship, children, kids, adults, grown-ups, relatives, and siblings? To answer this question, I think we have to move to the emotional meanings of these things. We have to trace the black holes in his narrative in order to understand what use the moral discourse of duty/freedom has for this specific individual in his processing of the emotional tensions of his life.

Black Holes and Childhood Memories

Øivind begins and ends his story with a reference to the "black holes" in his memory. An atmosphere of sorrow permeates the subject of these black holes. In the very last words of his story, he depicts himself as an old man, sitting at a modern cafe opposite no. 25, looking at what was his childhood castle:

> But the scene is empty, the actors are gone. Another kind of life takes place behind the windows now—no children's voices, no comforting mother. Only the frame is still there. And it is filled with memories. And black holes. (Gullestad, 1996, p. 219)

At the same time the black holes also impart a distance to the narrative structure he presents, and this is subtly implied before he even begins the story. In a short preface, he admits that other stories could have been told:

> Everything is accidental (. . .) Time unhooks the images, reshuffles, loses most of them, and lets the remaining ones rise in memory like glimpses of light among black holes. In this accidental way history[5] is made. This is my story. A part of it. Framed by Number 25. (p. 192)

Almost deliberately, Øivind tells us that he knows something that he does not know—and that these black holes between his treasured childhood memories may confer on the memories a significance other than the one he "accidentally" has given them. Can we spot some of these black holes in the text?

According to Alfred Lorenzer (1986), unconscious forms of inter-action have a scenic character. More than single verbal symbols, they are complexes of different sensations and thus can only be conveyed in the text through scenic representations. He refers here to the capacity of poets to transform human suffering to images with multi-ple layers of meanings. Obeyesekere (1990) has much the same to say about how personal symbols are tied to life in a way that makes them primarily nonverbal, even though their collective representations will give them more verbal embodiment. According to this line of thought, the black holes do not exist alongside the reported memories but are likely to be found in them, hidden, but still containing a lot of energy—as black holes do—and thus, they are important sites for the self-construction in the narrative. Such black holes are what makes us sing. Julia Kristeva (1994) says that whereas imagination is driven by loss and melancholy, the act of writing is driven by desire to get something instead of this loss.

As Gullestad (1996) notes, there is one scene in Øivind's story that stands out from the rest of the narrative for its marked literary form and emotional strength, as well as for the marked disappointment that contrasts so strikingly with the otherwise rather idyllic descriptions of family life. It is interesting that Øivind somehow senses the dynamic of black holes and scenic representation:

> As a grown up, it is easy to analyse. As a child, it is not. And all these emotions without name in the mind of the child are probably the reason why one of the strongest memories I have about my father stems from a Christmas Eve: the presents were about to be distributed. They were lying in a pile under the Christmas tree. Candle lights flickered on the branches, and the glitter-star shone at the top, close to the ceiling. We, the children, were sitting around the Christmas tree, as if mirroring the lights of the candles of expectation before the high point of all Christmas Eves: receiving the presents. To find the secret hidden inside crackly paper, behind all things, and let the excitement turn into joy. We expected most from the presents from father. They were the most secret ones. Time passes slowly sometimes! The minutes feel like hours. But at last I hear: "To Øivind from Father." I see nothing but the parcel, I tear off the ribbons and the wrappings, and inside the tissue paper, a big, stylish marzipan figure! Does anybody believe I was disappointed? Far from it. The expectations then were not on the high level of today. I was ever so grateful, I hugged Father and thanked him nicely, sat down, bit off the head of the figure in order to save the rest for later.

Then it happened. Then it happened. What I tasted was
not sweet lovely marzipan, but soap foaming in the mouth.
It was a soap figure! What a disappointment! What an
abrupt escalation from the delights of expectation to the
depths of bitterness. And then something more happened: Father laughed! Everybody laughed. At me! No comforting
words. No comforting hand. They screamed with laughter
because of this ridiculous character, sunk in disappointment
and foam. I will never forget it. I will never forget it.
(pp. 211-212)

This is Øivind's strongest memory of his father, who died shortly
afterward. Øivind himself openly connects the memory to the experience of rivalry between himself and his father. He remembers how
he wanted to marry mother when he grew up and the ambivalent
feelings of joy and jealousy when his father came home from business
travels and mother decorated both herself and the home in advance.
"Mother had to be won," he writes, and then continues with
the recollection of the Christmas Eve: "As a grown up, it is easy to
analyse . . . "

As we all know—and obviously Øivind also knew—this part of the
story is also a beautifully scenic rendition of what Freud coined the
Oedipal conflict: Through a symbolic castration by the father of the
boy, the boy gives up mother, identifies with father and acquires a
motive for becoming like him. He learns to understand himself inside
the symbolic order, as a boy and thus as a potential man. The message
to the boy in the Oedipal defeat is that he is a boy, not a man. He is
given a gender identity, but is located at the bottom of a male hierarchy.
With the help of the father, however, he can grow up to be a man and
attain access to sexuality. His success in this endeavor has much to do
with the father's ability to fill the position as an admirable object in
the boy's eyes and thus to contain the narcissistic wound of the boy,
which follows the symbolic castration (Shalin, 1983).

Many details of Øivind's recollection of the Christmas Eve actually
do gain significance when read as a memory of the symbolic castration:
The tense atmosphere of enormous expectations of getting to know

father's secrets, the most secret ones of all, Øivind tells us. The joy of getting the sweet and desired thing (what vision of shape and materiality does Øivind bring about in the mind of his readers, by describing this wonderful gift as a "big, stylish marzipan figure"?). Then it happens. Then comes the cut, the abrupt escalation—Øivind bites of the head—zack!—the sweet things have disappeared, they are not for little Øivind, and he is left with soap bubbles in his greedy little mouth. The association between soap and purity is also notable, while the contrast between luxurious marzipan and everyday soap connects the scene to the opposition between freedom and duty. Everybody is roaring with laughter. Øivind's littleness and powerlessness are brutally demonstrated in front of the social group to which he belongs, including mother, of course, and arranged by father, who keeps the sweet secrets for himself. Father's power is boundless—maybe even anticipated by Øivind's description of the Christmas tree: a hierarchical structure where the waiting children resemble flickering candles well below the glitter-star at the top.

Øivind really sings here—but where are the black holes that deliver the emotional energy to his description? Why is the humiliation remembered so vividly? Could this be a screen memory for him, carrying a charge from other memories that are less clearly or directly displayed?[6] According to the French psychoanalyst Micheline Enriques (1990), emotionally distressful moments sometimes can seem to be totally wiped out of the memory, but they are always accompanied by the more or less open expression of their hidden faces. She mentions three possible expressions of this hidden face:

- *a frantic refusal to forget,* playing on hate, resentment, and guilt
- *an extreme vigilance* for anything that could turn out to be a cause of psychic suffering and the disappearance of identificatory reference points that have been so costly to acquire
- *a hypercathexis,* sometimes successful but always restrictive, of a narcissistic object that can never fail, over which the exercise of power and mastery is set up as though it knew no bounds. (p. 100)

Enriques (1990) calls these distressful moments "memories that can neither be remembered or forgotten." Øivind's memory reflects at least the first and third of her expressions of the hidden face of the memory: the frantic refusal to forget and a hypercathexis to a narcissistic object whose power and mastery know no bounds. The second may also be seen in the fact that Øivind generally ignores themes of gender, body, and sexuality in his narrative.

One of the most important discoveries by Freud—a discovery that was decisive in lifting psychoanalysis out of the realm of instinct theory and into the realm of hermeneutics, language, and construction—was the concept of 'nachträglichkeit' (in English the translation is *deferred action,* in French, *après-coup*). By this insight, Freud discovers that infantile experience and the meaning of that experience are not related in a simple one-to-one relationship. Incidents can be experienced as unremarkable or even satisfying while they occur—but can later be reinterpreted—or maybe interpreted for the first time—and become suddenly traumatic. The fact that Øivind's father died shortly after this episode may have effected such a 'nachträglich' reinterpretation of the humiliation felt this Christmas Eve—or at some other time. First of all, Øivind loses a father with whom to identify in his striving to overcome symbolic castration and become a man—and it seems that no other grown men were available to fill this function for him. Second, this situation brings Øivind into the very ambiguous situation of Oedipal triumph. The boy actually wins over father—not as a man, but as a mother's baby, which threatens his gender identity and his existence as a separate being. Unconsciously, this death is also a fulfillment of his murderous impulses toward his father, whom he simultaneously admires and loves. The effect of all this will therefore often be an intense feeling of guilt and efforts at self-castration—denying himself the right to the pleasures of sexuality. This corresponds to Gullestad's (1996) observation that control of emotions seems to be of supreme importance for Øivind and that this trait is reflected in his narrative: he never "goes too far" (p. 214). Could it be, that the black holes of Øivind's story have to do with conflicts connected to gender identity and that he is left to strive against Oedipal desires all on his own? Did he become a man—and at what price?

Mother Fooled Him When
She Told Him He Was a Boy

When remembering the tasks he performed as a child, Øivind offers us this little recollection: "And grinding the coffee and polishing the knives were tasks that mother fooled me to do, by saying that this was work for somebody with muscles. And I had muscles. I was a boy" (Gullestad, 1996, p. 215). What is Øivind actually telling us here? The text is ambiguous. Did mother fool him by making him believe that coffee grinding and polishing knives require muscles and thus are a man's work or by leading him to believe that he was such a creature? This is one of the very few places where Øivind even mentions his gender, and it seems that he is not quite convinced by the fact of his masculinity.

When his father dies, Øivind reports an emotional state of guilt and confusion rather than one of grief and sorrow. "Be good to mother," father says on his death bed, and Øivind bows politely and doesn't understand. He remembers vividly how the women of the family let him know that he was little:

> I am so little, I learn. As an excuse. As a hidden reproach.
> And as a little child I start suspecting that somebody little
> does not understand everything the big ones understand, and
> that this is wrong. But when the fall comes, I start school,
> and then, then I will learn. (Gullestad, 1996, p. 213)

As we can see, Øivind experiences the humiliation of not being good enough as a man, both as an excuse and as a hidden reproach from the women. No wonder that he looks forward to starting school—in this way, he may both hope to grow to be respected as a man and escape from suffocation in a totally female world. But the teachers at school are too harsh and frightening. As a small, powerless boy without a father, Øivind develops what he himself calls "a contaminating fear" of the outside world.

Another difficulty in escaping the female world is that in many ways, it is quite satisfying: both mother and the family are portrayed

as warm and giving, but as Gullestad (1996) notices, in very generalized terms. There are not many persons, just generalized aunts and
siblings. There is no individuality in this engulfing world of femininity.
It is described as a narcissistic haven: "It was so good to be back in no.
25. To let the house close in on me, be home. Be surrounded by dear,
near things protecting me against all the strangeness of the outside"
(p. 201). No. 25 at Queen's street—in the beginning of the story is
even metaphorically described as a bride (while the next-door house
is described as the groom). It is tempting to sink down in the comforting world of mother, even though it is also extremely threatening to
his identity as a separate being. Is Øivind actually a boy or just a part
of the satisfying maternal body? Does this enclosing maternal body
nourish him or eat him? Is mother fooling him by comforting him? In
the recollection where Øivind returns to the safety of mother instead
of going outside, he attaches to himself the label: "the baby child."
When he writes about the bold ones who break out, he uses the
expression "rising towards the surface." These individuals, he later
explains in a conversation with Gullestad, are the few who contrast
with the "grey mass" of nonindividuality.

The sense of not being taken seriously as a man is also seen other
places in the narrative: "How sweet," the aunts say and return to the
chatter of the living room after little Øivind has said his evening
prayers in the conjugal bed of his mother—with his hands kept over
the blanket. And this feeling may also explain why the words of the
attendant at the public bath hit so hard: "Aren't you getting a little too
old to go to the ladies' room?" The problem is both one of establishing
a male identity, and, on a deeper level, about Oedipal desires: as long
as he is not considered a man, he will never be able to "marry mother,"
however dead his father is.

Both his Oedipal guilt and the restricted development of his
identity as a boy can be connected to Øivind's marked separation of
sexuality from the female world of the family. When later, for other
reasons, he is told to keep his hands over the blanket, he moves out
of mother's bed and to a separate couch in his brother's room. Mother
is portrayed through poetic and aesthetic memories with a definite
feminine flair ("white curtains, the pedestal, the flowery wallpaper";

p. 214), but with no traces of sexuality whatsoever. As we saw before, the exciting sensuous pleasures are placed in the men's world—and connected to having money from work to buy them. Money seems to be a prime symbol of masculinity and access to sexuality for Øivind. It is associated to work, the real world, pleasures, and sinfulness. This is also evident in Øivind's almost obsessive memories of sweets and what they cost.

The Choice of Becoming a Man

From this perspective, Øivind's memories of his headmaster's intervention in his life get saturated with meaning. Here—for the first time in his life—a male figure with positive fatherly authority comes to the boy's assistance. What he does is precisely to rescue Øivind's small amount of money, a saving that has been his own hard achievement, from mother's plans. The headmaster is abundantly portrayed as a Santa Claus with a long beard. The memory, indeed, seems to mark a turning point in Øivind's development, when the old, powerful, and mean Santa Claus begins to give way to a sympathetic Santa with practical advice for the boy and the competence to work things out. No wonder then, that when this Santa comes back with more money-gaining devices, in the guise of a job, Øivind makes a choice that is so self-evident it is actually not experienced as choice. In contrast to the other autobiographies, where Gullestad (1996) detects a clear "interpretative moment"—a moment where the writers understand their life and take it in their own hands—the choice of the job in Øivind's case seems to have been much more a choice of the unconscious. "Something inside him" (Gullestad, 1996, p. 208) prevented him from choosing the education he also wanted. Øivind says in a conversation with Gullestad, "I have always felt that life was something outside me that would seize me and lead me where I wanted to go" (p. 190). The expression is remarkable, for on the one hand, he was seized by something, but on the other, he was led in a direction where he—a part of him at least—actually wanted to go. The somewhat sorrowful tone in his narrative, connected to later reflections on his choice, doesn't match the thrill he also conveys as he remembers the first day of his new job, being on his own, and not least, earning money, the proof of manhood:

> I felt that I lived my own life—outside the family. A paid life, outside No. 25. And I could do it! The roots started to loosen. I thought. Until they came back from the countryside and I once more became one of six around a common table, one of the family, with the same problems, but with different solutions and experiences. I remember ever so well the experience of bringing home my first salary—putting five ten-kroner notes on the table in front of mother, saying, "these are for you!" I got five kroner back for myself. It was my payment for the month. (p. 206)

Although Øivind tries to appeal to our pity, he simultaneously conveys what a triumph it was to hand over 50 kr. to mother—and even to get 5 kr. back for his own sensuous pleasures. In the recollections of his ongoing work life, he stresses that he saw the money and learned to handle it, he learned to know the offices and the streets. He says that he came to live in the world of adults without being an adult himself—or should we replace adult by men? By making his choice and going to the men's world, Øivind gradually and belatedly constructed a gender identity as a male. In my view, he actually belonged to the "few bold ones" because he was one of the few who managed to earn a wage during the economic depression.

But in his own narrative, things are framed the opposite way. He withdrew from education and the possibility to stand out, out of duty to his family. What he tells us indirectly, however, is that the sphere of education connotes too much femaleness for him on a unconscious level. Even though the books promise escape, it is also stressed that they lead to a fantasy world, rather than the real thing. And given the symbolic position of the books, as mediators between home and the outside world, pursuing their allure could very easily assume incestuous meanings. So what would standing out through education actually have meant—becoming Mother's phallus?

Øivind chooses work, whereby he separates himself from his family in a psychological and sexual sense but keeps his family in a social sense as a male breadwinner. Symbolically, work can also be seen as a perfect compromise between the two worlds. He becomes a man through his work, choosing exactly the same occupation his father had, yet at the same time, he combines going outside with retaining the love and recognition of the inside. The work and the money connect with food and everyday life. With a safeguarded masculine identity, he can also approach the temptation of books in a less frightened way and use them to develop himself, not only to dream, even though the sensuous pleasures they give access to are channeled in a less carnal direction. This can be seen as a way to mitigate guilt feelings for sexual desires or as a capacity for sublimation.

Self-Construction

Is Øivind's narrative a story of wrecked masculinity or of a successful effort to make a man of himself when his father couldn't do it for him? Is it a story of defeat or of mastery? As is true of most stories, it seems to be both. There are wounds that did not heal properly, as the traumatic Christmas Eve memory reminds us, and as is suggested by Øivind's striking failure to recognize his own implicit gender dichotomies, his fear of the brutal world of men, his sense of a lack of energy and enterprise, and his everlasting unrest: did he make the right choice? Did he become a man in this way? Was his a bold action—or another self-castration?

On the other hand, there is also another voice in Øivind's narrative: a pride in having made it, of having made the choices that he did, a satisfaction with his own life. There is a certain air of subtlety in this old man. In spite of the sense of an irretrievable loss, Øivind seems to have been not only an everyday philosopher, but also an everyday artist of living. In addition to having earned his money as a respectable businessman who actually made it as a manager, a profession he talks of with pride, he portrays a rich life full of books, writing, art, music (as a skilled amateur jazz pianist), membership in several cultural and political organizations, and a large circle of intellectual friends. When

Gullestad (1996) asks him what he thinks of the Jante Law,[7] he subtly informs her that he also knows about a "reversed version" of the Jante Law, which tells you that you shall believe that you are somebody.

In many ways, we can see how the explicit structure of the narrative, duty versus freedom and self-realization, intertwines with the implicit conflict of gender identity and conflictual Oedipal desires. The timeline of the story goes from the Oedipal conflict to its resolution in puberty, and the two central scenes—the symbolic castration and the choice of becoming a man—frame the story. Something is clearly released in Øivind after making this choice:

> Now the period of youth could begin. I had money which many others did not have. And next year I was going to get myself a bike. On Saturday evenings I could go to the "Nordre" and watch the girls. But only watch.

For Øivind, choosing to become a man, actually also means becoming a man to his mother: With the help of his wage, the family is able to move to an apartment even bigger than the one father gave them in no. 25. At the same time, this symbolic fulfillment of an Oedipal wish is legitimized by the concept of duty, of not doing what he really wanted. It also softens some of the contradictions in the explicit structure: the free choice of whether to take the job versus the experience of the compulsory nature of the choice, the thrill over the job versus his regret for not having chosen otherwise, the appeal to our pity versus the pride of having made it, the disappointment of the Christmas Eve episode and the otherwise loving family. And as already noted, it also explains why the choice of taking the job must have been experienced as this strange mixture of a nonchoice and a choice. The cultural discourse of duty versus freedom is thus an important device that actually helps Øivind to fulfil some of his desires—mediating them to a form that is compatible with the societal norms, and with the demands of a family in straitened circumstances in the midst of the economic depression—they were in fact only three who could provide for the six of them.

The reciprocal scaffolding of the conscious and the unconscious structure of meaning in the narrative does not, of course, dissolve the conflicts within them and between them. Several areas in Øivind's life seem to have had the function of trying to bridge such unsolvable conflicts. Music and books have been mentioned. The writing also combines the two spheres. It is connected to the intellectual, cultural, and aesthetic values of the feminine world, and at the same time, it is an activity that causes Øivind to stand out, makes him into an individual (cf. his insistence on his real name being used)—and he even expects to earn money by it. At the same time, the writing can be seen—as Gullestad does—as a medium of self-construction, a way of working through and mastering tensions in his life, both the tensions in his contemporary culture and society and those that are specific to his life story. And it seems that it is the "black holes" of his memory that deliver the energy for working on both kind of tensions.

Contributing to a New Masculinity?

Highlighting the unconscious structure of Øivind's story may give us more insight into this specific individual, but is this exercise of any interest to the study of culture? According to both Obeyesekere (1990) and Lorenzer (1986), the purpose of drawing attention to the unconscious structures in symbolic forms (for instance, fiction or rituals) is not to understand the specific biography of the narrator, as it would be in therapy, but to understand how unconscious desires and cultural activity are intertwined. Whereas the psychoanalytic interpretation in therapy aims at changing the analysand, deep hermeneutic cultural interpretation, by drawing attention to hidden "life sketches," aims at changing the analyst (or her/his readers). Lorenzer (p. 68) calls this the distinction between analyzing the production and analyzing the effects of the text. Through an autobiographical text, we may gain insight in how a narrator can contribute to the change of culture through the impact his symbolic behaviors—be they stories he tells or embodied practices he engages in—have on his fellow men and women. The ways ordinary people influence other people, and thus make their contribution to the change of culture, are only rarely through written stories. I believe, however, that what Øivind does in his narrative can be seen as an image of what he also does in his life, as embodied practice. The choices he has made, the way he has related to other people, can be seen as a lived narrative—directed by both conscious and unconscious structures of meanings.

Øivind tells Marianne Gullestad (1996) that he wrote his autobiography first and foremost for himself. At the same time, she notices his wish that his son will read the story—and his disappointment when the son does not do so at first. Is the story also written to his son? In that case, Øivind is giving his son a message about a father who is successful enough, but without the endless power and superhuman qualities that Øivind saw in his own father. He is a man of the real world (not the star close to heaven)—and uses his real name. Does some of the subtleness of this old man lie in the fact that he managed to transform the father images of his own life (the image of both his father and his grandfather) to a much more human father image and an actually present father for his own son? This would also accord with the fact that at a certain point, Øivind chose to get a new job that allowed him to spend more time with his wife and son than his own father and grandfather had spent with their families. If this is the case, his work on his own psychological tensions can also be seen as a contribution to the transformation of culture and society.

By his work of identity, Øivind seems to have changed the traditional male role somewhat, combining life as a businessman with artistic expression and with a socialist political stand. In this way, he has exposed his son to a different model of masculinity—which again may have given his son the inner psychological readiness to take part in the transformation of gender roles that later took place. We don't know if this was what actually happened, but that is not the point here.[8] The theoretical point is to see how Øivind's black holes become part of the process of cultural change through their influence over the ways he builds his own life and his interactions with others.

By taking his black holes into account, we can understand that the processing between the inner tension (am I really a man?) and outer tension (the conflicting demands made on the successful individual) can speak to each other. Øivind connects money to masculinity. His father dies just before the period of economic depression, and this coincidence of disappearing money in the inner psychological arena and in the societal arena makes a special impact on Øivind's experience of the economic depression, as well of the actual financial situation of the family. One could say that he has an *inner psychological readiness* to be affected in a special way by this societal problem and the moral obligations connected to it, an inner readiness to live out and thus work on the dilemma of the welfare state. The rising societal possibilities for higher education for young urban males, on the other hand, were rejected by Øivind, both because books might have gained an ambiguous symbolic meaning in his inner world and because of the material needs of the family. The choice when he was 13 can be seen as an active solution both to an outer and an inner tension.

Psychology and Culture

In many minds, the object of psychology is to study the invariant and universal traits of the human being, or the nonsocial dimension, if such a thing exists. Although some branches of psychology actually do this, this is not my conception of either psychology as such or of psychoanalysis. One should not deduce from psychoanalytic theory that every boy who loses his father will have problems attaining a masculine gender identity. One cannot even deduce that a boy has to attain a strong gender identity at all. That depends on the specific life situation and life course of that boy, as well as on the cultural categories and the social practices of the given historical time in which the boy comes to know himself. But this variability should not prevent us from attaching importance to cases in which the loss of a father actually makes a boy suffer a crisis of gender identity—as is true of Øivind. His sufferings and tensions are present in his own text and we have to take them seriously, which is not the same as universalizing them. Monica Rudberg and I, for instance, have argued that the effect of father absence will vary with the social and the psychological significance of a father in the development of specific historical forms of gender subjectivity. A father can be important for quite different psychological reasons (Bjerrum Nielsen & Rudberg, 1994).

Psychoanalytic theory should be understood as a hermeneutic and constructive endeavor. We construct our lives in accordance with our time—but we do so with emotions, desires, dreams, and fantasies. It is difficult to analyze human beings and actions without some presuppositions of psychology, and paradoxically, one often finds the most implicitly ahistorical accounts precisely where psychology is not reflected on explicitly. For instance, when some constructionists argue that only conceptions of the self, and not the self itself, change historically, they implicitly convey a picture of a human creature who is invariably the same, but whose expressions of this sameness will vary according to available discourses. By maintaining this, one does not grasp that subjectivity itself is historically changeable. What is historically constructed is thus not only the discourses, but also subjectivity. In my opinion, it is the processing between these two kinds of historical structures (the structure of discourses and the structure of subjectivity) that is the key to understanding agency and thus the relations between psychology and cultural change

Notes

1. My article was originally presented in March 1996—in a somewhat different form—at a seminar in connection with the launching of Gullestad's book. At that time, I relied only on Gullestad's interpretation of the autobiography. The richness of her analysis allowed me to see other structures in the text. Afterward, Gullestad was so kind as to lend me an unabridged version of this particular text, the only one in her book that is not anonymous, and is thus open to a full reading. Much information, however, is still drawn from Gullestad's book, as she also did several interviews with the writer.

2. This autobiography is one of 630 life stories, elicited by a nationwide autobiography contest, "Write Your Life," in Norway from 1988 to 1989, organized by Marianne Gullestad and the sociologist Reidar Almås. The method is presented in Gullestad's book.

3. It is telling that both Paul John Eakin, who also gave a lecture about Marianne Gullestad's book at the launching seminar (Eakin, 1996), and I were drawn most to Øivind's story. The same applies for Marianne Gullestad, who chose this story as the first among the 630 to analyze. I believe this has to do with the richness and the ambiguity of this particular text. I am grateful to Marianne Gullestad, Paul John Eakin, and Henrietta Moore for their valuable comments on my analysis of Øivind's story.

4. The page reference is to Gullestad (1996), where the cited text is translated by her. If there is no page-reference after citations of Øivind's text, this part of the text does not appear in Gullestad, and in these cases, the translation is by me.

5. The Norwegian word for history—historie—has a double meaning of history and story.

6. I am grateful to Paul John Eakin for having suggested to me the possibility of the Christmas Eve collection being a screen memory.

7. The Jante Law is a well-known concept in Scandinavian culture. It stems from the novel *En flyktning krysser sitt spor* (A refugee crosses his track) by the Norwegian-Danish author Axel Sandemose and expresses the reverse side of egalitarianism: putting down anybody who tries to stand out above the rest. The first paragraph of the Jante Law is "You shall not believe that you *are* somebody" (Gullestad, 1996, appendix C).

8. What we do know, however, is that Øivind's son did a university degree in literature. The access to higher education expanded dramatically between these two generations as an effect of the social democratic policy in the Norwegian society, but his choice of literature may tell us that this field for him was no longer connected to femaleness as it might have been, on an unconscious level, for his father when he was a young man. Again, we catch a glimpse of the interaction between cultural change and psychological change.

References

Bjerrum Nielsen, H. (1996). The magic writing-pad: On gender and identity work. *Young Nordic Journal of Youth Research, 4*(3), 2-18.

Bjerrum Nielsen, H., & Rudberg, M. (1994). *Psychological gender and modernity.* Oslo: Scandinavian University Press.

Chodorow, N. (1995). Gender as a personal and cultural construction. *Signs, 20*(3), 516-544.

Enriquez, M. (1990). The memory envelope and its holes. In D. Anzieu (Ed.), *Psychic envelopes.* London: Karnac Books.

Gullestad, M. (1994). Sticking together or standing out? A Scandinavian life story. *Cultural Studies, 8*(2), 253-268.

Gullestad, M. (1996). *Everyday life philosophers.* Oslo: Scandinavian University Press. (Norwegian edition: *Hverdagsfilosofer: Verdier, selvforstöelse og samfunnssyn i det moderne Norge.* Oslo: Universitetesforlaget)

Kristeva, J. (1994). *Svart sol—depresjon og melankoli* [Black sun—depression and melancholia]. Oslo: Pax forlag.

Lorenzer, A. (1986). Tiefenhermeneutische Kulturanalyse. In H-D. K'nig et al., *Kulturanalysen.* Franfurt an Main: Fischer Verlag.

Marshall, B. (1994). *Engendering modernity.* Oxford, UK: Polity Press.

Moore, H. (1994). *A passion for difference.* Cambridge, UK: Polity Press.

Obeyesekere, G. (1990). *The work of culture.* Chicago: The University of Chicago Press.

Prokop, U. (1996). Cultural pattern of the feminine—On the construction of the ideal woman in Rousseau. In U. Prokop, *Kvinnelighetens symbolikk—kvinnelige livsutkast i det moderne* (Arbeidsnotat 7). Oslo: Centre of Women's Studies, University of Oslo.

Ricoeur, P. (1991). Life in quest of a narrative. In D. Wood (Ed.), *On Paul Ricoeur: Narrative and interpretation.* London: Routledge.

Shalin, L. J. (1983). Phallic integration and male identity development. *Scandinavian Psychoanalytic Review, 6*, 21-42.

4

An Interpretive Poetics of Languages of the Unsayable

Annie G. Rogers   James Holland
Mary E. Casey   Victoria Nakkula
Jennifer Ekert   Nurit Sheinberg

Conceptions of the Said and Not-Said

The Snow Man

> One must have a mind of winter
> To regard the frost and the boughs
> Of the pine-trees crusted with snow;
> And have been cold a long time
> To behold the junipers shagged with ice,
> The spruces rough in the distant glitter
> Of the January sun; and not to think
> Of any misery in the sound of the wind,
> In the sound of a few leaves,
> Which is the sound of the land
> Full of the same wind
> That is blowing in the same bare place
> For the listener, who listens in the snow,
> And, nothing himself, beholds
> Nothing that is not there and the nothing that is.

In "The Snow Man," Wallace Stevens (1954) imagines a cold and virtually empty landscape in which we can see:

> the frost and the boughs
> Of the pine-trees crusted with snow;

and

> the junipers shagged with ice,
> The spruces rough in the distant glitter
> Of the January sun

We place ourselves in this landscape not only as perceivers, but also as interpreters and researchers. What we must perceive and interpret, however, includes more than what may be directly present. Stevens recognizes two potential errors of judgment in the transition from perception to interpretation. In presenting his minimalist landscape, Stevens first recognizes our temptation to ascribe meaning to the emptiness, to project our own feelings into the landscape. He acknowledges how difficult it is to apprehend this landscape and "not to think/Of any misery in the sound of the wind." Stevens's adjectives are vivid and precise in their descriptiveness (crusted, shagged, rough) but devoid of emotional coloring. His verbs convey an apparently passive receptivity (regard, behold) without interpretation, perceiving without thinking "of" anything.

Thus far, Stevens has portrayed a conventional, careful observer who wishes to record "Nothing that is not there." Yet careful observation of what "is there" will not suffice. In the final cryptic and startling line, Stevens expresses the goal of the observer/interpreter: to behold "Nothing that is not there *and the nothing that is* [italics added]." This complex image expresses a paradoxical threat to our ability to take in and comprehend the world around us, whether the natural or the human world. As both observers and researchers, we sharpen our perception to avoid ascribing meaning or overwriting our data (nothing that is not there); at the same time, however, we risk overlooking or ignoring the meaning of what is absent (the nothing that is). Stevens depicts the dilemma of the researcher who knows what, by conventional methods, can be said to be "there," yet who knows as well that such criteria may not exhaust the possibilities of understanding. "There are more things in heaven and earth than are dreamt of in your philosophy," as Hamlet reminds Horatio. In this chapter, we suggest an approach—an interpretive poetics of "languages of the unsayable"—that acknowledges the presence and importance of what is unsaid, and perhaps unsayable, in research interviews.

We have adopted the phrase "languages of the unsayable" from *Languages of the Unsayable: The Play of Negativity in Literature and Literary Theory* (Budick & Iser, 1987). These essays examine "the negative gestures that seem to be implicit in virtually all poetic, philosophical, and even historiographical language" (p. xi) and explore a variety of ways that "negativity" in speech and writing can "allow the unsayable to speak" (p. xii). In applying the concept of languages of the unsayable to research interviews, we explore the psychological significance of such expression and also affirm the central role played by figurative thought in everyday speech. Perhaps most important, as we will explain below, we have chosen languages of the unsayable because this method allows us to distinguish between what is merely unsaid, and what may be, in some crucial sense, unsayable.

We have struggled to find effective language to speak about what is unsaid without falling into the trap of objectification and reification. Unlike Stevens, we must do more than to speak simply of "the nothing that is." What is unsaid cannot be pinned down, reified, or segmented into discrete categories. Evidence of what is unsaid can be found, however, in data that we have designated languages of the unsayable. Paradoxically, in our interpretations, we still cannot speak what is unsaid; we can, however, illustrate the doublings of meaning that mark the dynamic interplay between the said and not-said in moments of negation, evasion, revision, denial, hesitation, and silence. Throughout this chapter we use the terms *what is unsaid, the unsaid,* and *the not-said* interchangeably to refer to what is not named, either by the participant or in our interpretation. Further specifying these ideas, we select data from the interview texts that we designate *language of negation, language of revision, language of smokescreen,* and *language of silence.* This discussion points to a crisis of knowledge for researchers. If we assume, as we do, that the unsaid can contribute something valuable to our understanding of how an individual understands the world, then what language can we use to present what is unsaid? Furthermore, how can we interpret its meaning in a systematic way while remaining sensitive to issues of authority and validity? At the heart of these questions lies our interest in the psychological processes by which children make sense of and communicate, in spoken and unspoken ways, disturbing experiences and/or knowledge. From a psychological point of view, we distinguish a range of significance in various constructions of the unsaid, from something merely omitted, to something that cannot be expressed in the context of a particular interview, to something difficult to say in any context, and finally, to something too dangerous to speak or even to know.

The concept of negative space in the visual arts provides a parallel for us. Empty space defined by shape and substance forms an integral part of what we "see." The significance of the shapes and substance that are present depends on what is absent. In the same way, what is said depends on what is not said for its full significance. An analysis that considers only the spoken, no matter how complex, risks overlooking an essential aspect of expression and meaning.

In interpreting interview texts, we begin with the obvious: what is said. We are aware, however, that spoken words tell only part of a person's story; even a verbatim account does not capture the part of the story communicated in or through gesture, facial expression, shifts in emotion, or silence. These forms of expression constitute what is literally unsaid; silence, as a form of communication, poses a particular challenge for any listener or interpreter. To preserve the integrity of the interview as a whole, we must be willing to hear silence as a presence rather than an absence and to attend to silence as systematically in our analysis as we attend to the words that have been said. What is said helps us define the landscape of the interview and supplies an interpretive ground for considering what may be missing or unsaid.

Another challenge in exploring interpretive dimensions of the unsaid is the unavoidable and inevitable imbalance of power between interviewer and interviewee. This imbalance is even more pervasive and potentially threatening when a child is being interviewed by an adult. In our work with children, we were particularly sensitive to the dynamics of the relationship and issues of authority. Because the interview relationship is central to analysis, crucial questions of authority arise in all interpretations. For example, by what authority does any researcher resound another person's story or life? The imbalance of power in the relationship between a child and an adult in an interview, as well as the use of conventional rhetorical expressions, make interpreting the unsaid a challenging task. In interpretations that include the significance of the not-said, the researcher assumes the additional responsibility of naming, in some way, what is unspoken, and perhaps unspeakable, from the participant's point of view. The participant may be unwilling to confirm, or even unable to know, what the researcher concludes. Implications related to the power and responsibility inherent in such research require our careful consideration.

Reading for and apprehending what is unsaid in relation to what is said means listening to simultaneous presence of both the said and the not-said and the interplay between them. In our interpretive poetics of languages of the unsayable, what is unspoken becomes an opening and a resource for exploring the layers of another person's experiences and understandings. In the following sections, we outline and illustrate our way of reading for languages of the unsayable.

Background:
An Interpretive Poetics

The method presented in this chapter for identifying and interpreting languages of the unsayable is one of four dimensions of a theoretical approach outlined in "An Interpretive Poetics: The Artistry of Figurative Thought in Qualitative Inquiry" (Rogers et al., 1997).[1] In its initial formulation, a *poetics of research* was defined as "a sensitivity and responsiveness to emergent images and the associative logic of poetry" (Rogers, 1993, p. 268). Over the past several years, our research has led us to recognize and appreciate more deeply the value and potential of an approach that seeks to preserve the complexity of figurative thought and language. As a result, we have elaborated a theoretical and methodological basis of an interpretive poetics. Two hallmarks of this poetics are variation and multiplicity as they inform this method of qualitative inquiry and analysis.

Susanne Langer (1942) asserts, "Artistic form is congruent with the dynamic forms of our direct sensuous life; works of art are projections of 'felt life,' as Henry James called it. They are images of feeling that formulate it for our conception" (p. 159). In this chapter, we formulate the landscape of our research using an interpretive poetics that reflects the complexity of experience by drawing on the qualities of "artistic form" that Langer outlines. This process acknowledges variational thought and figurative associations as irreducible aspects of human experience and understanding.

Incorporating variational thought and figurative associations explicitly into our approach encourages us to reconceptualize our research design and analysis. In his book, *The Poetics of Space,* the philosopher Gaston Bachelard (1962/1994) espouses an approach to knowledge that does not rely exclusively on convergence of observation and interpretation. "The poetic image is essentially variational, and not, as is the case of the concept, constitutive" (p. xix). For Bachelard, variation in the meaning of images leads to the richness of their texture, and not to the confusion of avoidable ambiguity. Poetic images cannot be assigned to single categories without losing their multiple connotations and their capacity to evoke new and fresh responses each time they are encountered. Bachelard's emphasis on the variational nature of poetic images has provided us with a useful model for approaching data in research. Therefore, we acknowledge the presence of complex and irreducible images, as well as concepts, in data.

In addition to the variational quality of images, our approach draws upon the human capacity to hold multiple interpretations simultaneously. As we read texts, we create ways to heighten our experience and awareness of multiplicity in perception, memory, and consciousness. A poetic approach that values such multiplicity remains open to emergent associations throughout the interpretive process. Being attentive to the images that a child's words evoke in us, we are able to read and respond associatively to interview text. This way of working creates complex interpretations of language data that are rich in detail and imbued with what James called "felt life." Following this approach in qualitative inquiry, what we call an interpretive poetics, we have discovered that variational and multiple interpretations offer new possibilities for conducting and writing research. Working interpretively in a poetic framework allows us to understand our data in a way that remains vital and fresh, seeking congruence and continuity among all aspects of the research process: observing, interpreting, and writing.

Our individual associations, when joined together, begin to build toward a logic of interpretation that provides a trail of evidence (Brown et al., 1988) from multiple sources and perspectives. Critical to this process of data analysis is an interpretive community (Taylor, Gilligan, & Sullivan, 1995) in which any individual's associations and interpretations may be challenged, abandoned, or expanded. At this level of analysis, it is only by working collaboratively that we are able to explore creatively the landscape of figurative thought and imagery in children's experiences while remaining grounded in our data.

A Poetic Interpretation of
Languages of the Unsayable

A poetic interpretation of languages of the unsayable is crucial, for the not-said is itself layered and multilingual. In other words, there is no single language through which "the sayings of things can be undone" (Budick & Iser, 1987, p. xvii). The articulation and interpretations of associated themes (variational thinking with sound, sight, and sense impressions upon repetitions of what is actually said) can be juxtaposed against an analysis of languages of the unsayable to understand the liminality of human knowledge: those borders and boundaries we inhabit at the edge of conscious knowing. Between the said and the not-said, we can hear and trace languages of the unsayable. They lie in the realm of the timeless dream, which works by an associative logic and is often coded in metaphoric or figurative language.

Tracing this associative logic through a trail of evidence, it is possible to apprehend another's world indirectly, without distorting that world. To do so, one must interpret by making another's words reverberate, allowing spoken and unspoken themes to come to life through the cadences and metaphors of a poetic language, the musical speech of the unconscious. This construction of variational thinking, joined with building interpretations to clarify new constructs and theories (making, shattering, and remaking conceptual patterns), is central to our interpretive poetics, as we seek to understand, in Stevens's words, "the nothing that is."

This approach reframes certain questions about validity by expanding the concept of text. In qualitative research, a fundamental criterion of validity requires that interpretations and conclusions follow a trail of evidence that originates in the text. Both interpretive and theoretical validity rest on the foundation of descriptive validity, the accuracy with which data are recorded and preserved (Maxwell, 1996). With regard to interview texts, descriptive validity traditionally requires only the verbatim transcription of what was said. To consider the unsaid as well as the said, however, we must determine criteria for establishing the descriptive validity of what is unsaid. We face the daunting task of capturing, in words, what was not, and perhaps could not be, spoken. Because this enterprise ventures into uncharted territory, we recognize the importance of developing strategies to address the significance of the unsaid that are open to critical scrutiny, and we invite responses to this preliminary sketch of our approach.

The Relational Nature of Languages of the Unsayable

In " 'To Take Them at Their Word': Language Data in the Study of Teachers' Knowledge," Donald Freeman (1996) questions research that is based on the assumption that "teacher's words are . . . isomorphic to their mental worlds" (p. 734). He includes three principles of structural linguistics in his analysis of language data from interviews, emphasizing that language is "systematic, that it is collective before it is individual, and that it gains meaning by presence or lack of contrast" (p. 747). Freeman observes that these principles "all center on the notion of relationship" (p. 747). Focusing on what is said without any awareness of how it is said reduces an interview to the mere exchange of information. Such an orientation does not consider that, in speaking, a person's "aim is to be recognized, not simply to communicate" (p. 749). Using the concept of language communities, Freeman traces the ways that being recognized plays a role in the negotiation of meaning and understanding within particular interview relationships.

Building on Freeman's (1996) argument, we can explore the psychological significance of the contrasts that form an essential part of each response in an interview. These contrasts include, among other things, the implicit presence of the not-said. If contrasts are integral to the meaning of positive statements, they become even more crucial, and elusive, in statements that are explicitly or implicitly negative. For example, if a child says, "Meet me on the playground after lunch," she has excluded all other times and places from the request; after lunch contrasts with before lunch and after school and every other time—what is "not-said." Such simple contrasts are not likely to have psychological significance. Yet, to understand the psychological meaning of what is not-said, and is in some cases unsayable and even unspeakable, we need to have a strategy for identifying and exploring the variety of ways that the not-said can give shape to the said, just as negative space can give shape to what is seen.

Expressing the Not-Said

Our interest in reading for expressions of the "not-said" is historically grounded in Annie Rogers's (1992) understanding of this aspect of language elaborated in her chapter, "Marguerite Sechehaye and Renee: A feminist reading of two accounts of a treatment." Rogers examines two discrepant texts of a psychoanalytic relationship, a firsthand account by a young French woman, Renee, and another version by Sechehaye, Renee's therapist. Drawing on the idea of "locating the feminine not-said" introduced by feminist literary critic Elaine Showalter (1985), Rogers introduces a method of reading for the not-said through contrastive subject and object clauses within and across different accounts of the treatment relationship. What cannot be said overtly in subject clauses gets revealed more covertly and implicitly in object clauses following the verb constructions of the sentences. This strategy provides a revealing way to read written texts, but it is more limiting when applied to interview transcripts where there is a wide range of ways of expressing the not-said.

In our efforts to understand variations in expressions of the not-said, we turned to Budick and Iser (1987), who write about this dimension of language in their book, *Languages of the Unsayable: The Play of Negativity in Literature and Literary Theory*. They argue that what is not-said can be expressed in different dialects or languages, specifically in languages of the unsayable (Budick & Iser, 1987). Listening to children speak about difficult and disturbing relationships in their lives in our research, we elaborated the idea of languages of the unsayable to include what is unsaid as well as what is potentially unspeakable. We considered these languages as dynamic, one moving into the next, taking various forms along a continuum of knowledge and consciousness. For instance, what is unsaid may include missing information or negations that shred the borders of what is asserted, even what is stated with emphasis and certainty, so that knowledge is eroded. The unsayable is pervasive and encompasses in its reach reverberations of the unsaid and the unspeakable, yet it is neither of these. The unsayable is that which is read or understood in what is both said and not-said; the unsayable stumbles along and tries to find words for its own inarticulate understanding, and it also tries to undo or erase understanding that is dangerous. For example, a child trying to articulate a memory that is unsayable revises the story in the telling, longing for words to express a memory that is not known fully. She or he may also revise or erase what is recalled because some aspects might be too dangerous, or simply too hard, to know. What is unsayable lies just under the surface of conscious knowing, whereas what is unspeakable exists as a deep and haunting sense of something present that begs for words but is also absolutely forbidden to be spoken.[2] For example, survivors of terror "long to forget" and are sometimes also forbidden to remember, much less to reveal their stories, and at the same time, "the unspeakable must be spoken and heard" (Herman, 1997).

The tension between what is known and what lies beneath the surface of conscious knowing, or what is spoken and what is known but not spoken, produces a phenomenon of double meaning that is common in our lives. We experience this doubling in a variety of ways, including living with contradictions, "being of two minds" about something, and the internal dialogues that accompany ambivalence. These dialogues may be less conscious but are nevertheless evident in children's thinking. According to Budick and Iser (1987), "practically all formulations (written or spoken) contain a tacit dimension, so that each manifest text has a kind of latent double" (p. xii). Furthermore, the play, or movement, between what is said and not-said through languages of the unsayable makes this analysis necessarily dynamic and contextual.

Identifying and Interpreting Languages of the Unsayable

In our research, we distinguish four ways that the not-said can play a role in interview data. Our provisional ways of identifying and interpreting languages of the unsayable include (a) a language of negation, (b) a language of revision, (c) a language of smokescreen and evasion, and (d) a language of silence. In our interpretive analysis, we order our readings for the four languages according to the explicitness of the evidence, from the most explicit evidence to the least explicit: negation, revision, smokescreen, silence. In providing examples of each, our intention is to point toward ways of identifying and interpreting instances without offering the kind of detailed interpretations that depend on much more extensive consideration of context and content from an entire set of interview transcripts. We interpret the languages in sequence to illustrate how the less explicit and, plausibly, less conscious languages are informed by the more explicit ones. After a preliminary outline of these four languages, we will provide illustrations from our research data. This layered process allows researchers to interpret a text through multiple readings; it is modeled on a voice-centered method of interpretation (see Brown et al., 1988; Brown & Gilligan, 1992; Gilligan, Brown, & Rogers, 1990; Rogers, 1994; Rogers, Brown, & Tappan, 1993). Our examples focus on participant responses in the context of the dramatic interplay of question and response in the presence of an interviewer.

Language of negation expresses an idea or feeling through the explicit negation of its opposite. Instances of such negation can be identified by the use of either *not* or negative prefixes such as *un-* and *in-*. For example, a child may say, in describing a teacher, "She doesn't yell" or "He is impatient." In any case where a statement is expressed through negation, the simultaneous presence of the positive and negative (yelling and speaking softly, patience and impatience) introduces multiplicity into both the expression and the interpretation.

Language of revision, or undoing knowledge, encompasses a range of instances, from the self-correction of details to explicit contradiction or denial, such as "I was in third grade—no, I was in fourth grade" on one hand, or "I didn't really want my mother to be there after all" on the other. Like instances of explicit negation, these expressions create multiplicity in the narration of a story. They also provide evidence of the process of remembering, constructing, and reconstructing narratives, the process of imagining, identifying, selecting, and revising details and impressions.

Language of smokescreens and evasions is more difficult to identify. Unlike language of negation or revision, language of smokescreens does not contain explicit contradiction or multiplicity. Evasions are more easily identified than smokescreens: hesitation, vagueness, and brevity can all indicate evasion, in which what is evaded remains unsaid. Nonverbal indications of discomfort or withdrawal ("shutting down") can also mark such moments in an interview. These moments are usually recognizable, even though their meaning may not be immediately apparent. Successful smokescreens, on the other hand, whether conscious or unconscious, direct the attention of the interviewer and the interpreter to what is said, the positive spoken, rather than what is not-said, the implied unspoken. What is said, the "screen," becomes the figure, while the unsaid serves as the ground. For that reason, these moments of smokescreen are harder to recognize, even though potentially more crucial in interpretation.

Language of silence is the most elusive language of the unsayable. The mere absence of some information from an interview does not necessarily indicate a silence. Information is always absent from an interview, simply because some questions are not asked. Information about topics that were not addressed (even ones within the scope of the research) must be regarded simply as omissions, rather than as silences. Other information, however, which might have been offered but was not, may be more appropriately regarded as a silence. Similarly, a silence that follows upon hints at forbidden or taboo knowledge and a fear of speaking may be interpreted as a silence that arises in response to something unspeakable.

Whereas all these readings assume the importance of what is not-said, smokescreens and evasions, as well as silence, raise the question of whether what is not-said may also be, in some sense, unsayable and even unspeakable. Drawing such distinctions requires proceeding not only with caution to avoid projecting meaning into silence, but also with care to "hear" silence when it occurs. In maintaining a focus on the interview relationship, we seek to affirm Freeman's (1996) emphasis on recognition along with communication as a goal of speaking.

Reading for Languages of the Unsayable in Interview Transcripts

Overview

Our approach to the analysis of interview data consists of three processes: (a) identifying languages of the unsayable in interview transcripts, (b) building interpretations from quotations for each of the four languages, and (c) writing narrative summaries that integrate these analyses in relation to particular interpretive questions. Each step in this process builds on the previous steps; thus, as inferences become more theoretical and integrated, they remain grounded in the data.

The identification of languages of the unsayable requires a reader to understand what is not said in relation to what is said and to trace moments of recognition and evasions or missed opportunities for acknowledgment in the interviewing relationship. We quote both the interviewer and the interviewee to preserve the crucial elements of a relational context in this analysis.

Building interpretations is a systematic and careful process. Our approach invites the reader to make inferences from excerpts of interview data for each of the four languages by first interpreting each excerpt separately and then creating a narrative summary (Miller, 1988) of the relation of the various excerpts to one another for each of the four languages. Approaching data in this way leaves a "trail of evidence" (Brown et al., 1988) for each interpretation that other readers may challenge or confirm in further analyses. The narrative summaries invite the reader to bring various interpreted excerpts from a text together into a coherent understanding of the whole. These summaries provide a way to contextualize the process of interpretation, which can be experienced as fragmentary at this level of analysis (Maxwell & Miller, 1996).

Method

We identify examples of each language through a series of sequential readings, marking each language distinctively, yet recognizing that the languages are not mutually exclusive, so that individual passages may incorporate more than one language. Marginal notes for each example form the basis of integrative analytic summaries. Initially, we read the text of the interview for language of negations—for places where the speaker recognized something through its negation, for repetitious denials, and for negative constructions, such as "I could not avoid being seen." We mark these places for later reference as examples of negation and comment briefly on what is being negated or expressed through negation.

We then return to the start of the interview and read carefully for language of revising or undoing knowledge—for any revisions, erasures, retractions, or statements that would unravel an acknowledgment or recognition made earlier. After marking these places, we note the kind of knowledge that is being undone, erased, or revised.

Reading the transcript a third time, we listen for language of evasions and smokescreens—for hesitations, stumbling, avoidance of questions, consistently short responses to particular questions, diversions, and aversions, such as changing the topic abruptly. We mark these passages, noting both what we think is being averted or avoided and how the interviewer responds.

Finally, we read the text for language of silences—for missing information, unresolved puzzles, contradictions that leave us confused, and gaps in our knowledge or understanding. We pay particular attention to the boundaries around what is spoken (and what may be conscious for the speaker) by listening for the limits of her or his voice and imagination. We also listen for hints at dangerous knowing or fear in telling, followed by silences, which may indicate topics that are taboo or unspeakable. Again, we note both the child's and the interviewer's language, with provisional interpretations of what these silences imply.

Once the four languages have been identified in the transcripts, we begin the process of building our interpretations. Examples of each language are extracted from the text and joined with all the other examples of that language. Through collaborative discussion, we focus on examples that express the range and depth of the child's use of each kind of language. Guided by our marginal notes, we write an interpretive summary based on these examples, one summary for each language. To conclude this part of the analysis, we join all analyses of the individual languages into a single narrative summary.

Having reached an understanding of how each of the four languages is expressed, first by itself and then in relation to the others, we bring two overarching interpretive questions to our analysis. Posing new interpretive questions about the languages of the unsayable at this point allows us to begin to link the interpretations made thus far to a wider theoretical and developmental perspective. The first interpretive question we pose is: What is unsaid, unsayable, and potentially unspeakable in this relationship? Answering this question requires that we consider the four languages along a continuum—from those that are most explicit and easily identified to those that are more difficult to identify and to interpret. In making these distinctions, we recognize a range of unspoken expressions: from the unsaid (what is simply not said or missing), to the unsayable (what is difficult to say, but may be implied through negation, revision, evasion, or silence), to the unspeakable (what points to a knowledge that is dangerous or taboo). In these interpretations, the roles of figure and ground are reversed, so that what is unsaid, unsayable, and unspeakable emerge as figures to the ground formed by what is spoken, or the actual words of the transcript.

The second interpretive question—What are the limits of what can be known or recognized in this relationship?—reintroduces the relational aspects of the previous analyses that may have been submerged in the narrative summaries. In this part of the analysis, we are interested in the ways that the interviewer participates in the creation, maintenance, or disruption of the four languages of the unsayable in the interview. To answer this question, we focus on how the interviewer follows the child's responses and silences, opening up or closing down particular avenues of inquiry, exploration, or feeling. We also attend to the ways the child might not hear or acknowledge the interviewer's questions or responses. Our interpretive summary of this analysis outlines the limits of what can be known or recognized by the interviewer, as well as what can be known by the interviewer and child together.

Examples of
Languages of the Unsayable

To illustrate how analyzing languages of the unsayable can inform psychological inquiry, we draw on interviews and case studies developed through a longitudinal study of children's accounts of relationships at an urban K-8 public school. The project, called "Telling All One's Heart," takes its name from an early definition of the word *courage* (Rogers, 1993). All of the examples that follow are taken from interviews with four students: Mark, David, Andrea, and Sonia. Mark and David are of European ancestry; Andrea is Asian American, and Sonia is Puerto Rican. The interviewers, Margaret, Jenny, Elisabeth, and Eliane, are graduate students trained and supervised by members of the "Telling All One's Heart" research team. Mark, at 13, tells Margaret stories of his impulsive lying and being scapegoated, yet speaks about his "many" friends. In his interviews with Jenny, 9-year-old David speaks of his experiences of physical punishment. Ten-year-old Andrea tells Elisabeth stories of conflict and hurt in family relationships, although she expresses surprisingly little affect. At 10, Sonia speaks to Eliane about going to church, and although they are both Latina and speak Spanish, together they struggle to communicate across differences in religious backgrounds.

Language of Negation

The following illustration shows how analyzing language of the unsayable that focuses on negation can provide a lens into a child's world of relationships. In his conversations with Margaret, Mark uses a language of negation as he returns repeatedly to two themes in his interviews: not being scapegoated and not lying. However, it is impossible to appreciate Mark's use of negations without also considering what he reveals and conceals about himself, his relationships with peers, and his family.

At 13, Mark is large for his age, overweight, and known within his school as a loner. At one point in his interview, Mark describes being teased and leaving school early to avoid further teasing, "just annoying, little pestering stuff. I try to get along with my school work and then go home." On the heels of this comment, he says, "Then I have many, many, many, many, many friends. I go to the park. I go to Foster (a former school), and Foster is, it wasn't so bad. . . . There was hardly any scapegoating. I mean, if there was, I wasn't in it." Here, it seems that Mark exaggerates the number of his friends away from school ("many" is mentioned five times). He also insinuates through his negations ("it wasn't so bad. . . . There was hardly any scapegoating. I mean, if there was, I wasn't in it") that scapegoating was not a problem for him at his former school. Although Mark makes every attempt to appear tough and to portray himself as a boy with many friends, he also tells Margaret that he has been scapegoated by other children "since kindergarten." At one point, he muses, "I don't understand why I keep setting myself up." Indeed, we, too, wonder how Mark may set himself up for such treatment and what is at stake for Mark in his relationships at school and home.

One of the most interesting and self-revelatory statements Mark makes is utterly spontaneous. As he is putting the final touches on a family drawing, he suddenly turns to Margaret and comments, "I've adopted a new policy. In my life." Margaret wonders what this new policy is. "Uh, um, I believe the world would be a better p—much, much, much, much, much better place, if people were just a lot more honest." Here Mark laughs, and when Margaret comments on his attempt to downplay what he is saying through his laughter, he continues,

> Um, I lie a lot. Um, I like can acknowledge that as one of my problems. I, I lie, a lot, sometimes? Um, not at school as much, actually in school I really can lie a lot, but like at camp, or different places, it's just sort of an impulse in me to lie. I've been trying to cut down on this, and it's interesting. You know, I haven't lied for an entire month. And it hasn't affected my life in any possible, way.

We notice and follow the contrasts in Mark's language. What is first overstated ("I've adopted a new policy . . . the world would be a much [5X] better place if people were honest") is then negated through laughter and qualified ("sometimes?," "not at school"). Mark then reverses what he's just said ("in school I really can lie a lot; it's just an impulse in me to lie"), and immediately reclaims his original assertion about not lying ("You know, I haven't lied for an entire month"). These words are once again negated in their importance to Mark ("And it hasn't affected my life in any, possible, way"). In this poignant passage, Mark seems to be earnestly seeking truths about himself even as he speaks so haltingly about lying and his attempts to stop.

Language of negation conveys implicit unspoken contrasts. "I haven't lied" implies, but is not the same thing as, "I have been truthful." In fact, as Mark continues to talk to Margaret, he clarifies this point. In a story about Julia, a friend from summer camp, he tells Margaret that he feels bad that he was not truthful in his comments to her about other kids in their camp and now he wants to "come clean" with her:

I'm trying to find Julia's number, because I lost it a while ago? Um, I just want to come clean about everything, you know. I didn't, I never lied to her, I just didn't tell the full truth about everything to her.

While Mark indicates that he feels bad for not being honest with Julia, he does not reveal what would have been the "full truth." It is still unclear what his commitment to the truth means to him, and, therefore, it is difficult to know if what Mark is saying about wanting to live according to a new life policy of being honest is a statement about not lying anymore or about being able to tell the truth.

Our understanding of languages of the unsayable leads us to see the complexity of what Mark is able to know, if not to say clearly. Through his negations, Mark shows us the multiple truths and potentially slippery identifications he makes as he struggles to know what to say, how to speak. After Mark talks about his wish to stop lying, he brags that one of the lies he told at camp was that he was a year older than he actually was last summer—nearly, but not quite, getting away with this one. Margaret questions, "But you felt bad about it?" Mark retreats, "No, not really [short laugh], I still don't feel bad about it." Margaret allies herself again with the impulse in Mark to stop lying and says, "I want to know more about this lying because you said that you want to change it about yourself." And Mark retreats further,

Oh it's not a real problem, you know, just I like, I like to um, see people's reactions to different things. I think it's interesting, so I'll like make up, not a fantastic story, just something that wouldn't affect them in any way and see their reaction to it?

Mark slips away from Margaret again through his negation ("Oh it's not a real problem"), while at the same time conveying multiple truths: what is denied is vividly evoked. Despite his denial, lying seems to be "a real problem" for Mark. He appears to us to be a young adolescent boy who needs desperately to see others' responses to his lies—so he makes up lies that are "not a fantastic story" and "something that wouldn't affect them in any way," as if he wishes not only to "see their reaction" but also to be found out.

This see-sawing between "wanting to come clean," "never lying," and not telling "the full truth" or telling lies just to "see their reaction" reverberates throughout the interview as Mark paints a picture of himself to Margaret that is at once confident and insecure, strong and vulnerable. Embedded in these stories is a more worrisome image of a boy whose life is ordered by multiple and shifting truths and who, by enacting these truths (and struggling against his own enactment), reveals himself to others as an impulsive liar and a scapegoat among his peers.

Language of Revision

When present in an interview text, a language of revision introduces another layer of multiplicity in understanding a child's world of relationships. Because the original story and the revised account coexist in the child's narrative, an interpretive method that includes both versions offers an opportunity for understanding the complexity of how a child perceives, remembers, and expresses experiences. As David talks with Jenny, he uses a language of revision in two ways: to correct accounts of past events ("My uncle had to walk [my] dog[s], no, he had to feed them") and to undo previously expressed knowledge ("My dad and mom stopped [hitting me] like last year . . . [but] just, you see, my mom still hits me"). Tracing a language of revisions through these interviews helps us to understand David's process of remembering and reconstructing events, selecting details and impressions. This analysis provides us with hints about knowledge that may be difficult, or perhaps impossible, for David to hold.

David explains to Jenny that it's "normal" for him and his three siblings to pick on one another, including "hitting" and "smacking." When his mother observes this behavior, David says that "We're all in trouble, we all get sent to our rooms." Jenny wonders aloud whether David's mother gets angry in these situations:

David: Mm Hm.
Jenny: How does she show her anger?

David: Well, it's a law that you can't hit kids, so they don't, my, my dad and my mom stopped like last year and now it's a law that you can't hit kids and now, she just yells at us and tells us to get in our room.

Jenny: Did they used to hit the kids?

David: (nods)

Jenny: Did they hit you?

David: (nods)

Jenny: What did they do? How did they hit you?

David: Just, you see, my mom still hits me.

Jenny: Oh, she does?

David: I just pretend that I'm hurt and as soon as she leaves, I'm not hurt.

Jenny: How does she hit you?

David: She doesn't hit me hard, she just goes like (slaps his hand on the table) that.

Jenny: Where does her hand fall?

David: Sometimes on my back or, usually on my back. And I just pretend that I'm hurt.

Jenny: How do you do that?

David: I usually, like, hold my back or something like that. /MMM/ And then she leaves the room, and them I'm, and then, but I'm not hurt.

In response to Jenny's question about how his mother expresses anger toward her children, David reveals that she used to hit them but quickly adds that she stopped a year ago. Later, however, David admits that "you see, my mom still hits me." Through this apparent contradiction, David may be testing Jenny to see whether to trust her with a story that is painful for him. Jenny's reaction, "Oh, she does?," invites David to speak honestly, and David begins to share and to elaborate on experiences that he denied moments before. For Jenny, this revision, combined with what she described as his subdued affect, signals David's feelings of vulnerability related to being hit.

Jenny learns that David has watched his mother hit his brother and sisters, including the youngest, who is a baby, and that David is afraid of his father, especially when he is in a bad mood ("I ain't afraid of my mother, I'm afraid of my dad"). This section of the interview stands out because David responds to many of Jenny's questions about being hurt or feeling afraid of his parents only by shaking his head or nodding. In the end, David signals to Jenny that he has gone far enough and tells her, "I want to stop those questions." At the end of this second and final interview, Jenny shares with David that hearing about him getting hit concerns her. David then introduces another layer of contradiction by assuring her, once again, that "they don't really hit me anymore . . . so I'm not worried about it anymore." Jenny tells David that his story makes her "really sad," and he replies, "Ah, it doesn't hurt. . . . I can't let it bother me."

Following these shifts in David's story helps us to understand how David and Jenny respond to one another around a story that is difficult for David. Even more, David's shifts and contradictions show us how he manages both to stay connected to and to move away from knowledge about hurt and fear in his relationships with his parents. When the reality of being hit and scared by them becomes too much for David to bear, he moves toward a language of revision that erodes knowledge, as if he is trying to convince himself that his parents really have stopped hitting and hurting him. David's initial articulation and subsequent revision of his story of being hit by his mother leads us to question whether or not this knowledge and experience are too hard for David to hold, pushing the bounds of what is speakable for him.

Language of Smokescreen

Some interview questions elicit feelings and memories that make the respondent uncomfortable, in a variety of ways and for a variety of reasons. The extent and nature of this discomfort can be discerned in responses that both conceal and reveal in language that we characterize through the image of a smokescreen.

In her first interview with Elisabeth, Andrea relates stories of being physically hurt by members of her family, most explicitly by her grandmother. Later, however, she shifts the attention away from her being hurt by others toward getting hurt by herself. Although Andrea is reticent during most parts of the interview, she offers an impressive level of detail around experiences of being physically hurt. For example, in response to Elisabeth's question about an early memory, Andrea describes a time when "I cracked my head":

> My big sister pushed me against the heater, and I ran down-
> stairs to my mother crying, and my mother whacked my sis-
> ter, and my mother, my dad told me to lay down on the
> couch, and then when I got up from the couch, my sister saw
> some blood, and then my dad looked in my head and saw a
> crack, and my mother whacked my sister again, and my dad
> called my aunt, and my aunt went to Osco Drug and bought
> some sprays, and my dad took a little can of blue spray and
> sprayed it on my head, and he put a band-aid on my head,
> and I had to stay home for two days.

Andrea later explains that she knew her head was "broken" because
her finger could go inside. Andrea indicates that she was not taken to
a doctor after that incident. In another instance, asked about someone
in her family who she does not remember, Andrea again responds with
a story of getting hurt:

> When we went to California to go to someone's, I think,
> wedding, and we were going to drop, umm, people off to
> go to a movie, and my sister said, "Arachnaphobia," and I
> wanted to get a drink because I wanted to open the Coke in
> the coolers and then my grandmother said, "No, no, no,
> wait 'til we get to a stop." And I said, "I'm thirsty, I'm
> thirsty, I'm thirsty," and, umm, my grandmother, hit me on
> the nose and my nose started bleeding.

As Andrea initially tells these stories, it is clear that getting hurt
was the result of other people's actions—her sister's pushing and her
grandmother's hitting. Yet, later in the interview, Andrea introduces
an additional factor, her own clumsiness: "When I cracked my head
. . . [my sister] pushed me, and I fell and I tripped, I think, against the
heater." By adding a detail that could attribute partial responsibility
to herself ("I tripped"), Andrea diverts attention from those whose
behavior originally led to her injuries. In the third interview, Elisabeth
returns to the incident of Andrea's nose being hit, and Andrea says
that she does not remember telling Elisabeth about such an incident.
When Elisabeth then asks about other times when Andrea has been

hit, Andrea describes being struck on the hand by her mother as a punishment. After Andrea replies that she feels "nothing" when she is hit, Elisabeth asks,

> Elisabeth: Do you get angry when it happens? [Andrea shakes her head] No?
>
> Andrea: Because I always get hurt.
>
> Elisabeth: What do you mean?
>
> Andrea: Mm . . . I play soccer, and sometimes the ball hits my face. Sometimes, someone kicks me in the leg, and sometimes they step on my toe. And, I always trip over some chairs and fall, and then sometimes I just fall off the stairs and go tumbling down, when I was young, and sometimes I trip over the stairs and bang my head, and sometimes, I don't know, I get hurt by going down the stairs into the basement and then stepping on some wood and then I get a splinter in my foot.
>
> Elisabeth: Oh.
>
> Andrea: And sometimes I just kick something and it hurts.

In a context where Elisabeth's question refers directly to punishment by Andrea's mother, Andrea replies with examples of being hurt in other situations, shifting responsibility away from others and toward herself without even mentioning her mother. The frequency and consistency with which Andrea assigns responsibility to or blames herself suggest the possibility of an unspoken and, perhaps for her, unspeakable account of these events.

In her reflections on the final interview, Elisabeth expresses her surprise that Andrea would not acknowledge incidents that she had recounted in previous interviews. Elisabeth describes her struggle to maintain her connection with Andrea, to understand what Andrea is trying to communicate through what she is saying and not saying:

> I had not anticipated that she would change her story because she had seemed so careful in answering all previous questions accurately. I asked her directly if she had ever been hit. When she said yes, on the hand by her mother, I felt somewhat relieved. But then she spoke rather spontaneously about always hurting herself. And it was at this point, she

> held my gaze. I felt the room (the sight and sound of it) melt
> away, and all that mattered and all that existed was her and
> me. It seemed to me that she was trying to communicate
> something more than she hurting herself, but that she could
> not use ordinary language.

Elisabeth feels her attention directed away from Andrea's being hit
and instead toward Andrea always hurting herself. In this moment,
Andrea appears to have reached a limit to her ability to speak, while
still conveying a desire to be recognized.

Language of Silence

The final layer of analysis includes the language of silence which,
by virtue of being the least explicit, is the most difficult to identify.
Silences in conversations have different meaning and play different
roles. In her interview, Sonia uses silence to communicate her sense of
frustration when she is unsuccessful in her attempts to describe an
experience to Eliane. An important question to consider in this
example is how much of the silence is a reaction to Eliane's lack of
understanding and/or Sonia's own inability to describe the experience
clearly.

Sonia is a friendly and somewhat feisty girl who is ordinarily quite
outgoing in school. Because Sonia's first language is Spanish, Eliane
spoke to her in both Spanish and English throughout the interviews.
Sonia, however, chose to answer most of Eliane's questions in English.
The following interchange between Sonia and Eliane is one example
of the way in which silence can be read as a language in the context
of an interview. In response to Eliane's questions regarding things she
does with her family, Sonia begins to share something about her
experience of going to church: "I go to church and ummm . . . like
you know . . . the umm . . . the guard . . . the person who's like . . .
there's a . . . ."

In this instance, Sonia speaks haltingly, as if she is uncertain of the
correct terms to use to describe her experience or the people associated with the church she attends. In her frustration to find the words,

she looks to Eliane for help, perhaps hoping that Eliane will know what she is trying to say. "Do you go to church?" Sonia asks, to which Eliane responds, "No." Eliane goes on to suggest that perhaps that is the reason that she cannot understand what Sonia is trying to say. So, Sonia asks another question: "But do you know what a sacerdote is?" Eliane ventures a guess: "Well, he is like a God . . . is he?" With each question Sonia seems to grow more frustrated. She tries to explain to Eliane who the sacerdote is, but mid-sentence, her voice begins to trail off and then she simply stops speaking. Eliane pursues the story and tries in vain to get Sonia to tell her why she stopped speaking:

> Sonia: No, the sacerdote is not like a god he's like a priest but above the priest. I meant like . . . a . . . [Sonia leans back on the chair. She seems to be puzzled, a little shy, a little confused and maybe even more frustrated.]
>
> Eliane: What? So the sacerdote came to your church? So did he come to your church?
>
> Sonia: [Sonia puts both hands over her eyes and smiles very shyly.]
>
> Eliane: Qué te pasó? (What happened?) Why did you get all shy? Did you want to tell me about something you do with your family in church?
>
> Sonia: No. [She is still leaning back with her hands over her eyes smiling shyly.]
>
> Eliane: Do you want to skip the whole thing?
>
> Sonia: [Sonia shakes her head, meaning "no."]
>
> Eliane: Do you go to church every Sunday? With your whole family?
>
> Sonia: [Sonia nods but is still leaning back, with her hands covering parts of her face.]
>
> Eliane: Qué te pasó? (What's up?)
>
> Sonia: [Sonia just continues to smile shyly.]

It seems clear that Eliane, despite her lack of familiarity with the experience Sonia is trying to share, makes every effort to meet Sonia in the story and to understand something about why it is meaningful to her. But with each unsuccessful attempt Sonia makes to explain herself, she becomes reluctant to say more. Eliane goes back and forth between Spanish and English, trying to find a way to make it easier for Sonia to speak. Sonia uses the Spanish word for priest (sacerdote), but Eliane still does not understand her and reads Sonia as sounding confused. In fact, she does sound a bit confused when she describes the sacerdote as "a priest, but above the priest." One possible interpretation of what Sonia is saying here is that she is trying to distinguish the roles of two priests in her church. In the Roman Catholic tradition, each church or parish has one priest who is appointed pastor. All other priests in the parish would be considered associate priests. To Sonia, the pastor may, in fact, be seen as the priest "above" all other priests. Eliane, however, appears unfamiliar with this tradition and therefore has no frame of reference to begin to make sense of what Sonia is saying.

This disconnection between Eliane and Sonia leads to Sonia's shutting down both verbally and physically. Sonia becomes quiet, moves herself back in her chair away from Eliane, and even covers her face with her hands. Although the action of covering her face suggests that Sonia was embarrassed or felt a sense of shame in this particular exchange, it remains unclear whether or not her embarrassment was simply related to her struggle to explain herself or if she felt exposed or perhaps even judged in some other way that we cannot see or know. What is clear is that Eliane's reaction to Sonia's story somehow triggered a response that created distance between them.

One of the most fascinating and perhaps revealing moments in this exchange occurred when Eliane asked Sonia if she just wanted to "skip the whole thing." Obviously, Eliane is trying to help her out of a difficult situation, and yet Sonia shakes her head "no," indicating that she does not want to stop talking about this experience with Eliane; however, in actuality she does "stop talking," at least in the physical sense of the word. In a way, what she is saying is that she wants Eliane to understand her, but she is now using silence instead of words to communicate.

What exactly led to the downward spiral in Sonia from speech to silence is something about which we can only speculate. What we can know, however, from a close reading of this exchange is that this movement tells us something about the importance of Sonia's connection to Eliane. When Eliane could not follow Sonia's story, when she had no words to fill in those that Sonia could not find, Sonia may have sensed that their connection was in danger. The more she spoke, the more distance she put between them. When Sonia stopped speaking, Eliane had to work harder to reconnect with her. In response to this perceived vulnerability in their relationship, Sonia may have chosen to speak in a language of silence as her way of preserving their connection.

Knowing Together:
Connection and the Limits of the Sayable

Because our project focuses on children's relationships, the relationship between interviewer and interviewee serves as both the medium through which information about relationships is elicited and the most salient relationship about which we have data. We have come to understand the crucial nature of the processes of negotiation inherent in building such a relationship. Our interest in knowing the range of children's relationships, including those that are supportive as well as difficult, disturbing, and perhaps traumatic, leads us to explore how children might signal a willingness or reluctance to speak about difficulties in relationships. Through this process, we have become intrigued by how children signal the edges of their ability to speak and to know what we have called the limits of the sayable.

These limits on what is sayable can take many forms: limits within the speaker to know, limits within the listener to hear, and limits within the context that affect both speaker and listener. By limits within the speaker, we acknowledge that at any given moment in the course of an interview, some experiences may not be consciously accessible to the speaker. By limits within the listener, we recognize that there are often conflicting demands that can impede the interviewer's ability to be fully present, ranging from managing the technical aspects of the interview to monitoring his or her emotional responses to what is heard. By limits within the context, we take into account that every interview is bound by unique constraints of time, place, mood, prior experience, and expectations. Each of these limits is subject to revision or renegotiation within the interview; what might be unsaid, unsayable, and even unspeakable at one point in an interview may become sayable at a later point.

In addressing and affirming the complexity of what is said and what is not-said in interviews, however, we also hope to understand more fully what is said and what is sayable. Our articulation of an interpretative poetics of languages of the unsayable is intended most deeply as "a new beginning, a raid on the inarticulate" (Eliot, 1943, *Four Quartets,* p. 31). Through this approach, we reach toward the artistry of poetry to hold the inarticulate, while facing the challenge of evidence in the practice of research. In Virginia Woolf's (1927/1955) terms, we are actively seeking an ideal of artistry and good research:

> Beautiful and bright it should be on the surface, feathery and evanescent, one colour melting into another like the colours on a butterfly's wing; but beneath the fabric must be clamped together with bolts of iron. (p. 255)

Notes

1. The four dimensions of an interpretive poetics are (a) a restorying of texts around inquiry (crafting stories), (b) recognition and disconnection in research relationships (creating an annotated transcript and tracing the dynamics of the relationship throughout the interview), (c) an interpretive poetics of figurative thought (through language contrasts and an exploration of metaphor, metonymy, and irony), and (d) an interpretive poetics of languages of the unsayable (missing information, erasures and revisions, smokescreens, and silences).

2. William Faulkner (1936/1964) provides an especially clear and powerful example of this process at the end of *Absalom, Absalom!* After listening to Quentin Compson's tortured and tortuous account of the events of the novel, Shreve, his roommate at Harvard says, "Now I want you to tell me just one thing more. Why do you hate the South?" For Shreve, Quentin's whole narrative has expressed his hatred of the South. Yet the novel ends with Quentin's response:

> "I don't hate it," Quentin said, quickly, at once, immediately; "I don't hate it," he said. I don't hate it he thought, panting in the cold air, the iron New England dark; I don't. I don't! I don't hate it! I don't hate it! (p. 378)

References

Bachelard, G. (1994). *The poetics of space* (M. Jolas, Trans.). Boston: Beacon. (Original work published 1962)

Brown, L., Argyris, D., Attanucci, J., Bardige, B., Gilligan, C., Johnston, K., Miller, B., Osborne, J., Ward, J., Wiggins, G., & Wilcox, D. (1988). *A guide to reading narratives of conflict and choice for self and moral voice*. Cambridge, MA: Harvard Graduate School of Education, Center for the Study of Gender, Education, and Human Development.

Brown, L. M., & Gilligan, C. (1992). *Meeting at the crossroads*. New York: Ballantine.

Budick, S., & Iser, W. (Eds.). (1987). *Languages of the unsayable: The play of negativity in literature and literary theory*. Stanford, CA: Stanford University Press.

Eliot, T. S. (1943). *Four quartets*. New York: Harcourt, Brace.

Faulkner, W. (1964). *Absalom, Absalom!* New York: Random House. (Original work published 1936)

Freeman, D. (1996). "To take them at their word": Language data in the study of teachers' knowledge. *Harvard Educational Review, 66,* 732-761.

Gilligan, C., Brown, L., & Rogers, A. (1990). Psyche embedded: A place for body, relationships, and culture in personality theory. In A. Rabin, R. Zucker, R. Emmons, & S. Frank (Eds.), *Studying persons and lives*. New York: Springer.

Herman, J. (1997, February). *Trauma*. Lecture in colloquium series, Harvard Graduate School of Education, Cambridge, MA.

Langer, S. (1942). *Philosophy in a new key*. Cambridge, MA: Harvard University Press.

Maxwell, J. (1996). *Qualitative research design: An interactive approach*. Thousand Oaks, CA: Sage.

Maxwell, J., & Miller, B. (1996). *Categorization and contextualization in qualitative data analysis*. Manuscript submitted for publication.

Miller, B. (1988). *Adolescent friendships: A pilot study*. Qualifying paper, Harvard Graduate School of Education.

Rogers, A. (1992). Marguerite Sechehaye and Renee: A feminist reading of two accounts of a treatment. *Qualitative Studies in Education, 5*(3), 245-251.

Rogers, A. G. (1993). Voice, play, and a practice of ordinary courage in girls' and women's lives. *Harvard Educational Review, 63,* 265-295.

Rogers, A. G. (1994). *Exiled voices: Dissociation and the "return of the repressed" in women's narratives*. Wellesley, MA: The Stone Center, Wellesley College.

Rogers, A. G., Brown, L. M., & Tappan, M. (1993). Interpreting loss in ego development in girls: Regression or resistance? In R. Josselson & A. Lieblich (Eds.), *The narrative study of lives* (Vol. 2). Newbury Park, CA: Sage.

Rogers, A. G., Casey, M., Ekert, J., Holland, J., Nakkula, V., & Sheinberg, N. (1997). *An interpretive poetics: The artistry of figurative thought in qualitative inquiry*. Manuscript submitted for publication, Harvard University Graduate School of Education.

Showalter, E. (1985). *The new feminist criticism: Essays on women, literature, and theory*. New York: Pantheon.

Stevens, W. (1954). *Collected poems*. New York: Knopf.

Taylor, J. M., Gilligan, C., & Sullivan, A. G. (1995). *Between voice and silence: women and girls, race and relationship*. Cambridge, MA: Harvard University Press.

Woolf, V. (1955). *To the lighthouse*. New York: Harcourt, Brace, Jovanovich. (Original work published 1927)

5

Gender, Generation, Anxiety, and the Reproduction of Culture

Wendy Hollway

Tony Jefferson

Introducing the Walters

We start with 70-year-old Ivy, mother of nine and grandmother of 32, talking about two of her children, son Tommy and daughter Kelly, who live close by on the public housing estate in northern England where she has spent the last 34 years:[1]

Ivy: Oh I were crying on er, Tuesday morning.

Interviewer: Yeah? What was that about?

Ivy: Well she phoned me, Kelly. And she said er, "I'm going to doctor's with Jonathan again, 'e's ever so poorly." So I said—she said "is our Tommy 'ere?" And our Tommy were dressing our Gary [Tommy's son]. So I said "yes." So she said "well will you tell 'im I want 'im." Well I came in 'ere and I said "Tommy, Kelly wants yer on phone." He says "I don't want to talk to 'er. I don't want to talk to 'er." I said "Tommy she wants ya." 'e says (..) "mam I don't want to." So I 'appened to say "'e don't want to talk to ya." She said "'e's nowt but a eff-ing fat b" and 'e 'eard 'er. He says "you know 'er? If I see 'er up at school, I'll 'it 'er." I said "oh, don't, you mu'n't." He said "I will." He says "she's getting too big for 'er shoulders, 'er." And I thought, oh, if 'e sees 'er up at school. But 'e didn't. But I were crying all Tuesday morning when Joan come on, who lives with our Tommy. They're not married you know. (Interviewer: Mmm.) And er, she said "what's the matter." I said "oh, it's been shocking this morning." She said "'e'll ger 'er, 'e'll ger 'er in 'is own time." She said "don't upset yourself about 'er." I says "well I do when she's calling 'im that." She called it me three weeks since.[2]

There are a number of reasons for starting with this upsetting moment of family discord. First, it introduces the three family members, mother, son, and daughter, whom we interviewed and whose relationships, practices, and meanings, and the way gender and generation underpin these, provide our chosen case history. Second, it illustrates family discord, both between son and daughter and between mother and daughter, beneath the family's close-knit appearance. Third, the upsetting features of this incident implicate emotional, rather than cognitive, processes underlying behavior. Ivy knows that Tommy does not get on with Kelly, a knowledge no doubt strengthened by her own difficulties with her daughter, yet she still finds it deeply upsetting. This level of distress points toward unconscious emotional dynamics also fueling and affecting cultural transmissions. There are no isolated external events to explain these hostilities; only a deeply embedded history and the unconscious dynamics implicated therein. In what follows, we intend to demonstrate the importance of positing, not rational, unitary subjects whose accounts can be taken at face value, but anxious, defended ones for understanding the complex dynamics—including love, hate, envy, guilt, blame, jealousy, and shame—underpinning the "reproduction of culture" in one family. In doing so, we shall show that what gets unconsciously transmitted, through projection, introjection, and identification, is more significant than the conscious component.

Arguably, the reproduction of gender difference is the most important phenomenon to explain in any account of the reproduction of culture. To the extent that men and women invest in traditional notions of masculinity and femininity—which are produced by the splitting of human capacities into polarized forms—structural changes, for example, in the availability of "men's work," do not lead to rational reallocations in the gendered division of domestic labor. Only psychoanalysis has shed light on the complex ways that a genderless infant may come to invest in the polarized world of gender difference. Here we want to track the meanings of gender difference and their unconscious effects in practice, particularly through Ivy's different relations to her sons and daughters. We shall see how differently the girls and boys are regarded in Ivy's inner world and the results of the workings of gender difference in how differently the cultures of respectability and respect signify for one of her girls (Kelly) and one of her boys (Tommy).

Mother, Sex, and Respectability

Once we are alert to evidence of irrational preoccupations in the text, we notice when an interviewee has inserted something in the text that is extraneous to the narrative. For example, Ivy explains to the interviewer who Joan is—Tommy's partner—and immediately interjects, "They're not married, you know." What is the significance of this aside? As we shall see when we explore the cultural transmission of respectability in Ivy's family, it is a major organizing theme in this family's dynamics; dynamics that, in their turn, help to explain the vicissitudes of the reproduction of this particular aspect of culture.

Earlier in this (second) interview, Ivy has told the interviewer that she was never married to the man whom she refers to as her husband, whose name she took, and by whom she had nine children. The revelation occurred as an apparent non sequitur when she was talking about her father.

> Ivy: I've never been married me, you know.
> Interviewer: Ah ha. I didn't know.
> Ivy: I meant telling ya last week. No. I got in with Albert when I were 18. And I stopped—'e's the only man I've ever 'ad. And they didn't like it, me mum and dad, because I weren't married.[3] But I changed me name by deed (..). I 'ad it all changed and all me kids is in Walters and I'm in Walters. But I weren't bothered about that, we were 'appy. And 'e were good. But the trouble was, 'e was already married (..) And 'e never 'ad any children to 'er. And I 'ad 9 to 'im didn't I? But I don't regret it, don't get me wrong. But no I've never, ever been married. And I'm not ashamed on it.

This revelation informs the understanding of numerous references to Ivy's concern for her daughters' sexual reputations and of how Kelly's relationship to sexuality and respectability was forged out of her mother's own history. In other words, it establishes a significant starting point for tracing the reproduction of culture where respectability is concerned. That Ivy's parents were opposed to her relationship with Albert is not, sociologically speaking, surprising because he was 15 years older than her and already married. This was an epoch (the 1940s) where marriage was the core of a woman's reputation. In this light, it is not surprising that Ivy changed her name to that of her common-law husband and, in effect, masqueraded as married. This history is particularly significant, however, when we pay attention to the emotional repercussions on Ivy and on her feelings as a mother of daughters. The shame was deemed sufficient that only two children knew of this family secret, which was kept throughout the period when Ivy's two elder daughters became pregnant without first being married themselves, the first at 16, the second at 14,[4] within about 6 weeks of each other. The second daughter, Fiona, had the baby without getting married. This would have been in the mid-1960s. Ivy's account of how she felt about this is contradictory, and to us suggests unresolved emotions:

> Ivy: And I used to say "oh, I'm not going out, people will be talking about me, 'er being pregnant." He [Albert] used to say "let 'em talk about you, while they're talking about you, they're leaving somebody else alone."
>
> Interviewer: (laugh). Is that one of the reasons you didn't like to go out?
>
> Ivy: I weren't frightened 'cos I used to show off if anybody said owt. I mean when Fiona were took in 'ospital, er, I 'ad a right go at one of doctors there. (..) And when she were in 'ospital, when she'd 'ad our Jonathan—I went—she wouldn't—I couldn't keep away. I 'ad to be there all the time. And I went in one day and she were crying. I said "what you crying for?" She said er, "two of women have just said—aye that's 'er what's not married."

Ivy got her daughter moved. Ivy's identification with this daughter is evident in the fact that she couldn't keep away from the hospital (she describes this as a force outside her control) and that she fought her daughter's battles concerning being stigmatized as an unmarried mother. Although she asserts more than once that the stigma didn't bother her (as she asserted four times that it didn't bother her that she was not married), the association that began this part of her account tells a different story: before her defenses were mounted, she states that she didn't like to go out because people would be talking about her. Although Albert appears unperturbed, she minds—either hiding in the house or fighting back—reactions that seem to be emotionally charged because she identifies her own unmarried status with that of her daughter.

At around this time, Ivy had a nervous breakdown, after which, she says, "I were frightened to go out. Before me 'usband died. I wouldn't go out and peg a, a pair of socks on line." (Before this, she "used to go out seven nights a week.") Although she first recounted the event as if she had no clue as to why it happened, twice subsequently in the interview, Ivy associated this breakdown with Fiona's pregnancy. According to psychoanalytic theory, such symptoms as agoraphobia can express a deeply felt contradiction that cannot be rendered conscious because it is extremely anxiety-provoking. By being stricken with agoraphobia, Ivy achieved the result of not having to expose herself to the shame of being talked about by neighbors who, she imagined, were maligning the family for their lack of respectability because of having an unmarried daughter.[5] Jonathan's illegitimate status is even now routinely evaded: He is referred to as a brother by Kelly and Tommy.

Kelly was the youngest of the three daughters and the only one to marry before becoming pregnant. Her mother's preoccupation with her daughters' respectability had a profound effect on her as a teenager. In response to a general question about things earlier in her life that worried her, she does not hesitate in coming out with three issues that turn out to be inseparable:

> Kelly: I think I've always worried about things. I've worried about boyfriends, er, I've worried about what me mum thinks. Er, I worried about becoming pregnant early. (..) Wo—wo—worried about boyfriends because er, like (..) er, I'd got—got two sisters (..) who'd got pregnant quite early. My sister were married at 16 and my other sister

were like 14 when she were pregnant and 15 when she 'ad 'er baby. (..) And I can remember 'aving a kiss with someone and I were worried sick that I were 'aving a baby. (..) there were no sex involved at 'ome or anythin'. (Interviewer: Yeah.) Er, never saw any sex or any cuddles with my dad at that time, what I can remember of 'im er, so sex were a dirty word to me mother. And I can remember laying awake at night thinkin' I were pregnant.

Interviewer: And you couldn't ask her.

Kelly: No. (Interviewer: mm) No. Couldn't ask.

In consequence, while Kelly's peers were having sexual relationships before marriage (this was in the late 1970s), Kelly remained a virgin until marriage at 18 and symbolized this with a white wedding:

Kelly: I got married in white and that were me virginity, and I lost it when I—on me wedding night (..) and that were because my Mum 'ad dug it into me 'ead that much, because my other two sisters 'ad let me Mum down and shamed 'er, as it were called, shamed and God knows what else.

Even then, however—the only daughter to have succeeded in the respectability stakes—Kelly felt that sex was wrong: "You know, and I used to feel guilty when I went to me mum's. (..) I used to think she knows I'm married and she knows I'll be 'aving sex. (..) Used to worry me stupid."

Later, Kelly left her husband and had two children by another man before getting married to her present husband, but her mother imagines this daughter as highly sexualized: "She's 'ad some men our Kel, Kelly, don't worry." This fantasy is echoed in Kelly's difficult feelings about how her Mum views her (and is reflected in the complicated structure of the factual part of the following account):

Kelly: I don't know what she thinks of me. (laugh). I real, I really don't. I—I—I often—I can lose sleep about it actually. 'Cos I often think, I wonder what me mum does really think. You know like, 'cos I'm like 34 and 'ad like—I've got three children to two different men and like—I'm like married again, so I've like—from being like 18 to like 6 year ago, I've like been married twice sort of thing, do you know what I mean? But like 'ad three relationships where children 'ave been involved in two of them and like me marriage now. And I often think I've—that is the first thing what comes into me 'ead, *I wonder what me mum thinks.* (Interviewer: Mmm.) (..) But I daren't ask 'er. (laugh). That sounds silly now, don't it? 'cos I'm like 34, but I daren't ask 'er what 'er real feelings are because I think I'd be embarrassed, of 'er feelin's.

Kelly's associations after this are to whether her Mum loves her ("She'll not tell ya that she loves ya. *Never.* Like I tell my children.") and to the fact that her Mum adores Kelly's oldest sister. The feelings that arise with her mother about sex are rendered anxiety-provoking because they are experienced in the context of a wider trauma, which is her feeling of never having been loved by her mother ("after my dad died, my life changed altogether, because there were no one there to love me").

The evidence from Ivy and Kelly demonstrates the influence that Ivy has on Kelly's feelings about her own sexuality. Ivy's frequent refrain is "'e's the only man I've ever 'ad"[6] and we have seen how Kelly's worries about her own sexuality were constructed out of the comparison. Because Ivy's construction of her daughter's sexuality bears little relation to Kelly's actual sexual behavior—a clue that points to the way different aspects of Ivy's own unresolved sexuality are getting projected into her daughters—an explanation in terms of unconscious intersubjective dynamics is required. Kelly, the only one to be a virgin on marriage, occupies in her mother's fantasy the position of having "'ad some men, don't you worry" (the tone conveys a prurient interest that is not consistent with criticism by a mother who believes in monogamy). Fiona, by contrast, the reprobate daughter whose illegitimate son Ivy took into the family, and who has never married her partner, has her sexuality exonerated by Ivy with the words "But I can honestly say this, she only 'ad (..) our Jonathan to that lad and she's only 'ad Denny for 'er other seven children. She's 'ad nobody else since." Likewise, the oldest daughter, Sally, could do no wrong, despite getting pregnant at 16. She was Ivy's "best lass." According to Kelly, "my eldest sister were like my Mum's eldest sister."

Sally, by mothering the younger siblings, looking after the house, and being adored by her father, took Ivy's position as the good woman; a fit made all the more easy by the fact that Ivy herself was her mother's oldest daughter (of three). Kelly describes the relationship as being more like sisters, which captures the way that the generational difference has been erased in the unconscious identification. That Sally has a maternal position in relation to Ivy is evidenced by the fact that Sally is the only one who can induce her to leave the house (Ivy does as she is told).

In Fiona, Ivy identifies her deviant, unrespectable side, possibly an earlier self: the one who, like Ivy, fought, didn't get married, insisted on going out to "fly 'er kite," even when she had a baby to look after, and has almost as many children as Ivy (more if her miscarriages and the cot death are counted). This identification is facilitated because both, in different ways, are mother to Jonathan. That these identifications predated any developed characteristics of Fiona herself is evidenced by Ivy's feelings about Fiona when she was a baby: "I don't know why (..) I just couldn't take to 'er." Fiona came soon after Sally, whom Ivy loved, and she must have been the recipient of Ivy's hate; that is of her failure to hold together in one object her feelings of satisfaction and frustration at having to care for her babies.[7]

> Ivy: She used to say "lift me up." I used to say "go away I don't want you. I'm not nursing you." And she were only one I said it to. She once sup, supped, drank some Sanizal [toilet disinfectant]. And our Sally come to tell me. I said "oh, let 'er drink it, let 'er drink it, let 'er die."

Later, when Fiona was getting into constant trouble with the law, Ivy again acted out her defensive hate upon her daughter: "They used to come at night, police, and say 'we've got somebody 'ere what belongs to you.' And I used to say 'if it's Fiona, don't drop 'er off 'ere, go and drop 'er in river.' " Unsurprisingly, this daughter is still preoccupied with her mother's love.

Ivy's wider feelings about her daughters once they were adolescents dictate her perceptions of their sexuality and, to generalize from a great deal more evidence than is provided above, Ivy idolizes her eldest; exonerates Fiona, the middle one, out of guilt; and denigrates the youngest, Kelly. The paradox that Kelly is the one who is denigrated by Ivy may be explained by Ivy's envy at the daughter who has achieved respectability and wider sexual experience (in Ivy's fantasy).

Ivy herself had lied about her marital status in her effort to achieve respectability. She had eight of her nine children in quick succession and, by the time that Kelly was growing up, slept in separate beds from her husband and was never seen to be physically intimate, not only with her husband, but with her children. Since her husband died when she was 49, she has not entered into another relationship, a fact that she repeats with pride, but no hint of regret: "'e were a good un. I've never 'ad anybody since. Nobody can come and do that on me, and that's a lot to say." In this claim, Ivy's pride appears to be linked to the fact that nobody could accuse her of unrespectable sexual behavior. Here we glimpse Ivy's habitual defense of splitting:[8] love and hate, good and bad. Whereas Ivy makes much of her monogamy, she appears to project onto Kelly the unacceptable part of herself, which had, or would have, desired other men.

Projection (the unconscious depositing of unaccepted parts of oneself into another) does not, of itself, secure the transmission of certain cultural values, however; the other part of the process is how the daughters receive these unconscious dynamics. In Kelly's case, the irrationality of her feelings about her sexuality, and how these are bound up with her mother, are demonstrated by the fact that, after her marriage, she was still experiencing her sexuality as unacceptable in her mother's eyes. This remains true 15 years later, when she is ensconced in a respectable marriage. Although it would be too embarrassing to ask her and has never been talked about (although Ivy evidently communicates her feelings about sexuality through other channels), Kelly thinks her mother would be shocked. Because we have evidence of Ivy's fantasies about her daughter's sexuality, we know that Kelly's feelings are accurate; they show that she is in touch with her mother's feelings about her sexuality; that is, they have been introjected by Kelly. To the extent that she identifies with her mother's projections—and her guilt about being sexually active suggests she does—her own sexual identity is affected, precisely because the dynamics are largely unconscious and therefore not amenable to rational evaluation and choice.

There is also evidence that Kelly has introjected Ivy's anxiety and her characteristic splitting defenses. For example, Ivy's agoraphobia involves panic attacks on the rare occasions she goes out, such as when she was taken to a nearby shopping mall and had to leave almost immediately (much to Sally's frustration). Kelly feels anxious there, too, and although it doesn't stop her going, she only uses the level that provides access to the exits.

Family, Territory, and Respectability

We have portrayed the sexuality of this working-class mother and daughter in the light of the wider theme of respectability. Later, we will show how respectability has a very different meaning for Kelly's brother, Tommy; one that does not implicate sex at all. First, however, we follow the issue of respectability through a web of meanings that connect sexuality to family and to territory, from Kelly's perspective. Here, we maintain a focus on her family relationships (both family of origin and current family) and show how the family's unconscious intersubjective dynamics reproduce in Kelly a version of respectability that mother and son construe as bigheaded.

As we have seen, at 18, Kelly achieved respectability by having a white wedding. She went to live off the estate, and by the time she was 20 had a daughter with her husband. Three years later, however, she was living with, and pregnant by, another man who was "the bee's knees, 'e were *everything* I wanted" and she was "besotted" with him. Their 4-year relationship was characterized by escalating violence from him, particularly during her pregnancies; so much so that her son was born 7 weeks prematurely and she miscarried during the second pregnancy. She finally left this man after he had put her in the hospital with horrendous physical injuries (he got a 12-month sentence after she pressed charges).

It had been impossible to conceal this violence from her family, and Kelly's lying about it must affect the significance to her family of any lying she still does: "They knew I was suffering violence. They— they knew I'd got black eyes. And I used to lie and say that one of kids 'ad 'it me in face wi' a toy (..) They knew what was 'appening. They—they—they're not, they weren't stupid."

Ivy's account provides different emphases:

> Ivy: I 'ad a lot of trouble wi' 'er round corner. She lived with this black man. Because they are 'alf-caste (..) She weren't married to 'im. She lived [off the estate] with 'im. And er, she 'ad it rough with 'im. Really rough. And one night er, well one day, 'e beat 'er up, really. And I mean really beat 'er up. 'E broke 'er jaw and everything. (..) She was in 'ospital for 4 days. She came out. I 'ad 'er for 7 months, 'er and three kids and never took as much as that off 'er. She—and our Colin [another brother] come on a Saturday when she'd come 'ome, and 'e went on his 'ands and knees,—and 'e sobbed and sobbed. Said "Kelly, don't ever go back to 'im." She said "no I'm not now, I've finished." (..) He got on verandah to throw 'er off, Blackie. I call 'im black sambo. But she got 'ell of a lot of money. (..) But you know Kelly, I did all for 'er. She said "when I get me money through I'll treat ya." I never got as much as a box of matches.

In addition to the racism through which Ivy viewed Kelly's disastrous relationship, Ivy's theme reveals itself before she finishes this story: after all the support from her mother that Kelly made use of after she left this man, Ivy got nothing financial from it, even though Kelly's compensation was substantial.

It was important for Kelly to return to the estate and thus to her family: "I wanted to come back and move to my family and to start a new life." When she left hospital, she depended on her mother primarily, but also on some of her brothers. She was "a total wreck" and also very frightened, particularly of men she didn't know. Her weight was down to a dangerous 6 stone (now it is 11 stone: "through contentment, I think"). After living with her mother (in the house where she was brought up), she got a house very close by, and her mother continued to look after all three children while Kelly went to work. Her son continued to live there for a year and still visits every day. More than violence, she feared that she would want to go back: "I just didn't want to fall in love with this man again, 'aving peace of mind, 'aving a little job, going to my Mum's, kids bein' 'appy."

During this period, in her family's eyes, Kelly must have been the least respectable member of the family: a single mother, with children (two of them mixed race) by more than one man; and known to have stayed in a violent relationship with a black man who subsequently went to prison. Like Ivy and Fiona, she feared what people would think of her; by which she meant her respectability: "[I were] very paranoid, very very paranoid. I used to think people were looking at me and talking about me and you know, everybody's finger were pointed at me and it wasn't."

Then she met Jim, whom she subsequently married. ("I never thought anyone else would love me and my children.") Jim was from off the estate. Kelly's feelings about the estate changed such that, after a year or so, "I couldn't wait to move again, 'cos it were—it were getting bad (..) it wasn't the place where I wanted to stay." Although she describes the problem in terms of the estate's decline due to strangers moving in, stealing off their neighbors, and using drugs, her account of getting a transfer quickly implicated Jim and her identification with his respectability:

> Kelly: And er, I were quite fond of Jim. I were, you know, like really really fond of Jim. But I weren't fond of like people what were about me any more. Because they were like wanting to know all what, all what were going off. Jim used to like—I suppose brainwash me into like saying "oh, it's a right estate." You know like "blah, blah, blah, what's a nice girl like you doing on estate" even though I'd been brought up on it, I was still condemning 'im for pulling the estate down, because—because I were an insider sort of thing, I couldn't see what that outsider saw.

Through Jim's eyes, she learned to construe her family and her territory as unrespectable: by the time Kelly moved, her attitude had changed from being "my territory" to a place where "I don't fit in their territory." Here, she positions as the "nice girl" of Jim's discourse. Although she had moved only half a mile away, to a house which geographically was central to the estate, and although her children still went to the same school, in her eyes she had moved off the estate;

from "little Belfast" to "paradise," from rough to respectable. Her anxiety about respectability leads her to polarize her past and her present, to construct a unique geography of the estate, and to harbor fears about the street where she lived, such that, when she visits Tommy, who still lives in "Little Belfast," she pips rather than get out of her smart, red Mercedes—even in broad daylight. She has achieved respectability by escaping from her family of origin. "If I'd 'ave stayed on estate, I'd 'ave been in a worse state (..) and probably still a one-parent family." It is in the context of Kelly's rapid social mobility that we later decipher Tommy's comment that lately Kelly has got "too big for 'er shoulders" and Ivy's complaint that, although "'er round corner"[9] has more money than she has ever had, Ivy still has not been recompensed for looking after the children. However, to understand why Kelly behaves in this way, we need to return to her relationship with her mother as she was growing up.

Kelly's older sister Sally was 13 when Kelly was born and was already looking after the children and doing domestic tasks: Certainly, she appeared to act as mother to Kelly. Then Sally married and left home (although she remained close by) and, very soon after, Ivy took in Fiona's baby, Jonathan. In Kelly's memory, she connects the miserable years that followed to her dad's death, when she was 12: "I loved 'im very much."

> Kelly: And then all of a sudden 'e's not there any more. (Interviewer: Mmm.) And then your mum who is there, bringing (..) another baby up. So once again I got me nose shoved out for this baby to be in place. Which belonged to my other sister. And I didn't get—any love at all. Er, and then I—I—I became like at 12, 13—this mother to this little boy. Because my mum were getting on. My sister didn't want 'im, and I used to 'ave to take 'im everywhere I went. (Interviewer: Oh right.) (..) I used to 'ate 'im. Literally *ate* 'im because I *knew* I 'ad to take 'im with me.[10]

When this theme was taken up in the second interview, Kelly expanded on the domestic and childcare obligations of her teenage years:

Kelly: Yeah. I used to 'ate 'im, and I resented me mother very much for it. Because em, I weren't allowed out, you know like and I 'ad no freedom and no break at all. (..)

Interviewer: Did you have Jonathan so that your mum could go out?

Kelly: My mum never went out. My mum never left the house.[11] (Interviewer: Mmm.) My dad 'ad died, er, my mum 'ad 'ad a right bad time with my sister who Jonathan belongs to. Er, and I just semt to be resented for everything what 'ad gone off.[12] (Interviewer: Mmm.) (..) I can remember 'aving to clean kitchen floor and wishing me mum were dead. 'Cos I used to 'ave to do everything. (..) And then like see to Jonathan sort of thing. (..) I used to go to bed with 'im as well. I used to 'ate 'im. I've never—I've never, ever in my life wanted to 'urt a child as much as I wanted to 'urt 'im. (..) But I used to 'ate me mum as well. I used to wish 'er dead. When she used to make me do things. And that is why I think I don't let my children do things. My children don't wash dishes or anything (Interviewer: laugh) 'cos I always 'ad to do it when I were younger. And I don't want 'em to resent me for it.

Not only has her own experience made Kelly consciously want to save her children from domestic chores, but it has had a lasting effect on her feelings about her mother, and especially her mother's child care: Because her childhood was spent looking after Jonathan, and because her mother had never even looked after her, now her mother can look after her children, while she has some freedom from child care. It is probable that these feelings affect financial transactions too: In Kelly's unconscious, her mother can never pay enough in recompense for Kelly's misery as a child. Moreover, Kelly is bereft of any other proofs of her mother's love, so much so that she has suggested to Ivy that perhaps her parents weren't her real parents, because that would explain Ivy's lack of love.

Indicative of their incapacity to communicate what they feel to each other is Kelly's description of a typical visit to her mother's: "She don't show me any feelings whatsoever. I can walk in now, she'll go 'what?' You know like, I'll go 'what?' You know. And then like if you say 'well I'll not bother coming round,' she's alright. You know." Yet, the interviewer's experience was of Ivy being preoccupied with the possibility of a visit from Kelly.

A further reason for Ivy's quite sadistic treatment of Kelly might be the fact that she was the apple of her father's eye: "she were ruined, though, 'er. 'Er dad spoilt 'er to death." From Kelly, we know that she went to the club with her dad, that he waited for her outside school, that she was cuddled on his knee and slept in his bed, and that he mended her doll. In contrast to his wife, who never accompanied him out and was physically distant with him, he was close to his daughter, who loved him. There is a hint of jealousy in Ivy's sadistic attempt to make Kelly feel guilty by projecting her own blaming of Kelly onto her dead husband: When a photo of Albert constantly fell off the wall, Ivy said to Kelly, "'e's coming back to haunt you, for what you've done to me." The likelihood of jealousy is also suggested by the fact that, on his death bed, Albert didn't want Ivy, only his children. Ivy would have known how that felt from the other side, because her own father had wanted her and not her mother on his deathbed.

If Kelly is escaping from the unrespectability of a "problem family," it seems predictable that the opposite—what encapsulates her image of respectability—is to be a "proper family." It is this image that she strives toward, in reality and in fantasy. What it means to be a proper family is derived not so much from her own experience of being a problem family, but by emotional traces etched into her memories of growing up without a proper family. Below, she talks as if she had no parents:

> Kelly: Looking back and talking to other people, they've 'ad like a better life than what I've 'ad. Because they've 'ad parents. Because they've 'ad mum and dads. And that's what I try to do for my children. Even though Jim's not their dad, they've still got a better life than what most kids 'ave 'ad. (Interviewer: Mmm.) They've still 'ad—they've 'ad more than what I've ever 'ad. (..) Er, we—we go out as a family, and I feel nice. I never 'ad that. We never went out with me mum and dad. I always went out with somebody else's mum and dad. (Interviewer: Mmm.) (..) I wouldn't allow any of my children to go away wi' anybody else.

A proper family here consists of "mum and dads"; that is, mum and dad as a couple, not "mum" and "dad." Now she has achieved that for her children—and for the child in her that she has projected onto them.

Kelly's fantasies too revolve around the proper family and a move off the estate altogether. They are also dominated by projections of success onto her children (rather than her own future) in which her children have benefited from the education that she was deprived of:

> Kelly: I've got what I want with my 'usband and my children and I'd still like more. More—not only for me—I'd like more for my children. And I'm 'oping sooner or later that we'll not always be 'ere. I'm anxious to move as well. (..) So I'm anxious to like move on, and see them doing something better. (Interviewer: Right.) I live in future instead of like living for today. (laugh).

What this insatiable investment in a rosy future suggests is a terror of her past; a desire to escape from a big, rough family that robbed her of her childhood, and from her own decline into unrespectability. Yet, her desire is on the children's behalf, while she and Jim are positioned as "just prepared and ready to wait" for them (rather like Ivy does, never going out to them). This is what drives Kelly's need to replace her family of origin with her current, respectable family and explains her ambivalent relationships with her mother and siblings— using them and keeping a distance. On one hand, she still wants their support as proof of a love that is contradicted in so many unspoken ways; on the other, her defensive distance from them not only secures her respectability but protects her from their hate. Ivy mirrors this position, preoccupied with Kelly's visits but professing not to care whether she comes or not.

In summary, Kelly's desires—which we have traced historically in broad outline—produce what it means for her to be a proper family, and the relation to her own family of origin is refracted through a series of unconscious intersubjective family dynamics. In this example, then, there is no smooth transmission of the cultural meanings and practices of family life.

Father, Community, and Respect

The theme of respect emerges early in our first interview with 42-year-old Tommy. Wondering why he has not been a victim of crime in his 33 years on the estate, all of them spent on what is unanimously acknowledged to be the "rougher" end, he suggests it is "Because we're well respected. We've been well respected on this estate ever since we've moved up."

Later, in the second interview, Tommy uses identical terms to talk of his dead father, unsurprisingly perhaps, given the importance for family respectability of a father's reputation in a traditionally gendered household.

> Tommy: Can you imagine your parents you've lived wi' and one 'as got to leave you. And the one I loved. I did, I loved 'im. I love me mam. But I loved 'im, because I 'ad some laughs wi' 'im. (..) He were, he were well respected chap. (Interviewer: Mmm.) They still talk about 'im in club where we go into na. "There were nobody, there were nobody better than your dad, your dad were fantastic.

As well as learning about his father's good name in the community, two other things of significance for our purposes should be noted. First, Tommy has stronger feelings for his father than his mother, evident in "the one I loved," the somewhat guilty sandwiching of "I love me mam" between "I loved 'im" and "But I loved 'im," the indicative "but," and in the way he is able to concretize his love for his father ("I 'ad some laughs wi' 'im"). Second, Tommy uses the term *fantastic* to describe his father. This, as we go on to show, is highly characteristic. The importance of these revelations we return to below.

Subsequently, Tommy introduces the notion that he personally is well respected on the estate and is therefore safe from crime.

> Tommy: I don't think anything will 'appen to me while I'm on this estate. (Interviewer: Right.) cos I've, I've confidence I've, I've got, I've got respect. I respect everybody on this estate. There's, there's kiddies all o'er this estate all call me by me first name. (..) It's brilliant.

(Interviewer: Mmm.) Wherever you go "hi ya Tommy, alright Tommy?" I love it. But I don't fear. I don't fear, fear anything. Nobody 'll touch me. (Interviewer: Right.) I'm well respected. And I respect, I respect all families on estate. I know, I know what they are, but you can't do anything about it. All you do is, you go and see their parents."

Interestingly, Tommy talks not only of being respected but of respecting "everybody." Given that he knows "what they are," a reference to the rampant delinquency of many of the youngsters on the estate, this apparently universal respect seems defensive; as does the notion that kids calling him by his first name is "brilliant." Both, as we shall see, are connected to the idea of his "fantastic" dad. The personal basis of Tommy's respect, as opposed to being the member of a well-respected family or the son of a well-respected father, is his local community involvement. Since he met his current partner, Joan, he has become very involved in the local working men's club, where "[I] built meself up" and "got a reputation." Now, as life member and current president, he is well respected there.

If one basis of his father's being well respected was the fact that he worked 13-hour shifts in the local steelworks to support a large family and died too young to enjoy the fruits of his long labors ("never got (..) not even got 'is bus pass," as Tommy painfully remembered), this was to be denied young Tommy. He left school in the late 1960s, served a 7-year apprenticeship, after which the firm "went bust." Thereafter, a series of short-term jobs followed, each ending in redundancy, interspersed with a 2-year period of unemployment. His last job ended after 18 months, when the forge closed. He was in his late twenties. Although he'd "love to get a job," he's never worked since. So external changes in the world of work, with Tommy one of the early casualties of deindustrialization, can begin to account for Tommy having to look to community involvement rather than the (shrinking) world of work for sources of respect. It also helps explain his strong investment in family life, another potential arena for securing respect. This is of considerable importance to Tommy, captured most movingly in his proud response to being asked whether he would be "grandad" to his eldest stepson's first child: "And I went 'I'd love it.' I just broke down, 'im asking me. 'E's got 'is own dad. 'E said 'you've done more for me than what my dad's done, and I'd like you to be our Chris's grandad.' "

Later, he repeats the point, adding, "it were fantastic." Given the evidence that his father was deeply loved (by at least some of his children), Tommy's family mindedness could be seen as following in father's footsteps. Indeed, Tommy probably has more invested in family, given that Mr. Walters senior, working 13-hour shifts, was often physically absent from the family household: the traditionally absent father of the industrial age. But this information about the bases of Tommy's respect being family and community reveals at least three other points of significance: in contrast to Kelly, his sexuality is nowhere implicated; the important identification would seem to be with the father and not the mother; and, again in contrast to Kelly, Tommy's sources of respect are his family and community of origin, which are precisely what threaten Kelly's hard-won and new-found respectability, a respectability based on her (metaphorical if not geographical) distance from everything Tommy holds dear. In the rest of this section, we take each of these points in turn, explore their significance for Tommy, and spell out their implications for cultural reproduction.

Well-respected does not connote sexuality, either for Albert or Tommy. Thirty-three-year-old Albert was already married when he took up with the 18-year-old Ivy. Nine children later, he remained unmarried (to Ivy). But none of this appears to have affected his standing in the community. Tommy has never married. He lives with Joan, her two teenage sons, and their 5-year old son, Gary, and has three children (who do not live with him) from an earlier relationship. This history would appear to play no part in how respected he is, either in the community's or his own eyes (although his mother felt compelled to mention it, as we saw earlier). Where sexuality, marriage, and illegitimate births loom large in Ivy's conception of respectability, and have had profound effects on daughter Kelly, they provide none of the content of Tommy's concern with being respected. Here, then, in the different meanings respect carries for men and women in our culture, is one area where cultural reproduction, working through the vicissitudes of gender, charts different paths for boys and girls: respect versus respectability. However, to stop there is to suggest, in line with traditional cultural reproduction theory, that this process is somehow automatic, a smooth transmission. But once we attend to the psychic processes involved, particularly the way in which typical defense mechanisms affect the observable pattern of identifications, the picture becomes more complicated—and the results more surprising. Which brings us to the second point, namely, Tommy's apparently strong identification with his father.

All the evidence so far presented suggests that Tommy identifies with his father and all that he stood for. Further evidence only strengthens the picture of closeness underpinning these strong paternal identifications. The poignant story about his breakdown after his father's death secures this reading better than any claims of how close he was. Too frightened to kiss his dead father, he became "really, really upset" that he had been the only one unable to do what he "should 'ave done." He broke down severely enough to need 3 weeks off work. Then, on a day he'll "never forget . . . never," he was "visited" by his dead father, who forgave him with the words "I still love you, don't worry about it." Thereafter, he decided to make amends by having "a tattoo put on," even though "I 'ate tattoos." Now he constantly tends it: "I always give me arm a little rub and a little kiss. Go in bath and make sure I wash 'im alright. You know what I mean?"

We can contrast this with what we know of his relationship with his mother, to whom he claimed also to be "very close." Although he said he went to see her every day (a rather formal definition of closeness), Ivy said that his daily visits were of more recent origin, since her move to her new accommodation. Moreover, when they lived on the same road, "I saw too much on 'im then."

This claim of closeness is also somewhat compromised, if not contradicted, by his revelation, straight after saying "I'm very close to me mother," that "there's one thing I don't ever do to me mother. I've never give 'er a kiss." This apparently goes back to childhood: "I've never kissed me mam. (..) Even when I were young." It seems reasonable to conclude that, whatever he really feels about his mother, he was closer to, and more identified with, his father.

Yet there are ways in which he does identify with his mother; in particular, in the way they view Kelly as a liar and "a big 'ead." In exploring the significance for Tommy of this particular identification, we shed light not only on the social and psychic origins of Tommy's hostility toward his sister, but also on how they have come to hold such diametrically opposed notions of respect/ability: Tommy's centered in his family of origin and the estate he loves and from which he'd "never move"; Kelly's on putting as much distance as she can between the future that beckons and her past that threatens, between her family of origin and her new family.

Central to this difference between brother and sister is their very different memories of childhood. Where Kelly remembers only how unhappy she was, Tommy's memories are characteristically ebullient:

> Tommy: It were great (..) You know wi' us being a big family, and everybody, and all at school (..). We, we always used to race 'ome for cow pie,(..) big meat potato pie—that's when we 'ad coal fires as well. (..) They were the *best* fires that we've ever 'ad, and we all used to race 'ome at tea time, to see who got (laugh) biggest plate and everything. We used to 'ave some right arguments, to see who got (laugh) biggest plate! And "is there, any more, is there, is there any more?" It were brilliant. And sleeping arrangement—'cos it (..) were a three-bedroomed 'ouse, between 10 of us. (..) Well it were brilliant. (Interviewer: (laugh)). There were—one, one, two, there were six of us. Three in one double bed, no, two, two in each double bed. (Interviewer: Yeah.) And in, well, you know then, we were skint. (Interviewer: Yeah) In the '60s we were skint. (Interviewer: Yeah). And to get a, to get a blanket to get covered up were unbelievable. To get big, big, big overcoats. (Interviewer: Yeah, yeah.) What me mother used to do, you, you know plates in oven—she used to put some bricks in. Get bricks out—t' warm bottom, warm bottom of the bed. And get plate out of oven, wrap it up in a er, a, a, a sheet and put it in bottom of bed, so stretch your feet out. And it were, it were, it were 'orrible in the morning 'cos it were, it were freezing cold. (Interviewer: Yeah.) Y'know plate and brick. There were no double glazing, no central 'eating or anything. All we, all we lived for were coal fire. (Interviewer: Yeah.) And me dad used to get up every morning, make s-sticks out of paper. (Interviewer: Yeah.) About 6 o'clock. Used to get *fire* blaring out before we get up (..). Always used to run down for a cup of tea, run at side of fire.(..) They were tremendous years.

If we take this account at face value, it is a variation of the "we were poor but we were happy" story of life in a big, crowded household. But look a little closer, and the characteristic formulation is altogether more revealing. The interviewer's opening question is interrupted with "it were great," as if to preempt any suggestion to the contrary. Thereafter, the notion that "it were brilliant, unbelievable, tremendous," provides a running chorus to a story essentially about kids fighting for survival in a deprived, poverty-stricken household: racing home from school in order to get enough to eat, constantly "wanting more," fighting over blankets (or overcoats) to keep warm at night, and waking up "freezing cold" and running down to secure a (no doubt also contested) place by the fire. It is not that Tommy represses the "'orrible" memories; this extract is littered with them. But what is being denied is the emotional reality (the pain). What the upbeat refrain "it were brilliant, great," and so on does is to eliminate all contrary (negative or painful) feelings that the memory might otherwise evoke. It is a characteristic defense mechanism for Tommy.

Let us remember that in this large, poor family, not only food, warmth, and space were in short supply, so too was parental affection of a physical kind (Tommy could not remember being kissed as a child), although not physical punishment (Ivy: "they've 'ad some 'ammer off me—them I've got"). It is a family where mum was out every night ("I never stopped in once before I were ill (..) I used to go out 7 nights a week to bingo") and was both a fighter ("oh I used to fight. They take after me") and a drinker ("I used to be a big drinker. (..) I used to be drunk every night"), and where dad was either working nights, sleeping days, or also out drinking after the day shift ("'e went out for a drink you see when 'e came 'ome at night, which as you couldn't blame 'im"). Later, the girls' teenage pregnancies precipitated their mother's breakdown and subsequent agoraphobia, and at least four of the children got in trouble with the law, two seriously enough to warrant terms of imprisonment, one constantly ("I 'ad 'er [Fiona] put down three or four times"). Set in this context, the constantly reiterated "it were brilliant" seems not merely defensive, but a manic denial of anything difficult or painful.

Or take Tommy's portrait of his father. Although Ivy claimed she "did the 'itting" and that Albert didn't ("'e would correct 'em, but if they wanted 'itting, it were me"), Tommy remembered his father as "strictest," and being whacked with the belt:

> Tommy: Got a leather belt like that and a big brass buckle on end, and 'e'd say "if you're not in for 8 o'clock, you gets the strap. If you don't do as you're told, you'll get the buckle." And we 'ad to be in 'ouse for 8 o'clock. I was in bed for half past eight. (Interviewer: Mmm.) And any murmur up them stairs—'e used to run upstairs me dad. I thought, 'ere we go, get 'old, get 'old of blankets and get covered up, 'cos we're gonna get whacked with his belt. And 'e used to come up and whack us with his belt. (Interviewer: He did?) Oh, unbelievable, aye. But appreciated 'im for it because 'e knocked, 'e knocked, 'e knocked sense into us, not to do it. But er, I, we were growing up, growing up, we 'ad some laughs.

This is not an unusual tale of paternal beatings: We heard many similar in the course of our interviews. What is unusual is how, once again, all the pain of such memories has been successfully repressed. There is nothing in this memory moderated by ambivalence: of a father, tired after a long day's work, with money and other worries on his mind, wanting only a bit of peace and quiet and a pint with his mates, perhaps overreacting to the boisterousness of his large family settling down for the night or, sometimes, taking it out on them for reasons beyond the misdemeanor in question; no hint of cruelty, injustice, or punishment exceeding the crime; only gratitude ("appreciated 'im for it") and laughs. Tommy allows nothing to alloy his memory of his "fantastic" father.

Tommy is, however, able to recognize that his family is less than ideal in not being close-knit, a fact he finds puzzling yet compelling (he returns to the theme twice in the second interview, each time unprompted), because it contradicts his fantasy of what big families should be like:

> Tommy: You'd think families 'ud be close knit family wun't ya? You'd think they'd meet every weekend. (Interviewer: If they live close enough) Or go, or go on 'olidays every year wi' each other. Er, I 'aven't seen one of my brothers na for 18 month, and 'e only lives at [a place nearby] (Interviewer: Mmm.) (..) We *never* meet. And it is a big family. (..) Always every time we meet there's always a big argument. (Interviewer: Yuh) (..) You get these families—all these families what

'aven't seen each other. It's like, like a reunion. (Interviewer: Yeah.)
Let's all meet again and 'ave a good laugh. (Interviewer: Yeah. You're
not like that.) Our family's not like that. I've never known it. (..) If
your mother's 'ad all these kids, you should all be together.

In the second interview, he returns to the theme:

> Tommy: But we never seem to all click and all meet at one, all go to me
> mother's at one, at one time. Which to me is, is fantastic, everybody
> to come, to meet up and all go to see me mother. (..) We've 'ad some
> great times.

Even though this fantasy family get-together has never materialized,
it "is fantastic" (not "would be"—a mix up of tenses surely betokening
the unconscious fulfillment of a wish unfulfilled in reality). Most
people have come to accept the mixture of good and bad, love and
hate, envy and gratitude, that constitutes family dynamics. In Tommy's
case, his consistent denial of all the bad, painful emotions associated with family life leaves him either puzzled, as it does here, or with
only his one-sided memories of how great, fantastic, or brilliant it all
was.

   When the defense of denial is combined with the related defense
of splitting, puzzlement is replaced by denigration. This would seem
to be the clue to understanding Tommy's open hostility to sister Kelly,
"the only one in the family I 'ate [a point he makes three times]. I love
everybody else." Here the mystery of why their family does not behave
like big families should is abandoned in favor of a simple love
everybody else/hate her model of the family. This can be held without
disrupting his investment in the fantastic family through the idea that
all families have one black sheep: "There's always one in a family (..)
Like I've told you, there's my sister in my family."

   The stated reason for his hatred is that "she's grown up to be a big
'ead and such a liar." Only two specific examples of these claimed
faults are given (although it is worth recalling that Kelly herself
admitted lying to the family about the violence she was subjected to;
a demonstration, should one be needed, that lying is not necessarily a
"hateworthy" offense). In the first example, Tommy claimed "she's

forged my mother's signature to draw some money out of this bank book," which makes her an "evil woman (..) to do it to 'er own mother." Whether true or not, we do know that Kelly's relations with her mother are difficult and complex; we can suppose, therefore, that, if true, there is more to this story than Tommy knows, or is prepared to know. We can also suppose that Tommy's source for this story is his mother, with her own investments in imagining, and retelling, the worst about Kelly. So we should notice Tommy's preparedness to side with his mother, to recount only her version, and hence to believe the worst about his sister. His other specific gripe is that Kelly "takes 'er three kids round [to Ivy's], 'look after kids while I go to work' but she never gives 'er a penny." He, on the other hand, buys "'er stuff every weekend." We are familiar with the first part of this gripe, having learned of it earlier through Ivy; and, once again, we notice Tommy echoing his mother's complaint, seeing it only through her eyes. The other side of his sister's exploitation of his mother is his own generosity in this respect: where Kelly takes, he gives. Here, perhaps, a certain sibling rivalry or jealousy over Ivy's response to Kelly's child-care needs is fueling Tommy's hatred (even though, as we saw in the opening quotation, Tommy's son Gary gets to stop over, too).

Even if these one-sided accounts are true, and Kelly is now a bigheaded liar, hatred seems out of place, disproportionate. After all, Kelly is the little sister Tommy "learnt (..) to walk when she were a baby," who constantly looked after their youngest, Jonathan, sacrificing her childhood in the process (and still does now he is older and needs help with his drug addiction), who endured a horrendously violent relationship that almost killed her, and after which he and his brothers supported her. It also seems irrational when we consider his apparent ability to forgive all kinds of faults in others he is close to, even when these involve the sort of crimes and misdemeanors that would appear to pose a threat to the respect he holds dear. His sister Fiona, for example, with her troubled history of early pregnancy, constant delinquency, and spells of imprisonment, would appear to have done far more to damage the family's "well-respected" name than Kelly, but Tommy, even knowing "she just was a waste of time," still loves her. In her case, others get the blame: "she just went wi' wrong people."

Similarly, his neighbor Sean, a friend since school days, remains "a smashing lad" despite the fact that he deals drugs from the house, keeps three untaxed cars, has done time for burglary (with Tommy's brother, "they were right cow bags"), plays reggae music so loud that "you 'ave to turn that telly up," keeps his wife short of money ("'e don't gi' 'er a penny"), and "'ates kids" so much that he got somebody to burn the children's play area down "for about 10 quid" because the noise annoyed him.

In both cases, of course, Tommy is doing what he characteristically does: denying the negative, painful aspects of Fiona's and Sean's behavior. Why, then, is Kelly not also the beneficiary of such denying behavior, but rather the hated object? The answer is to be found in the very different emotional significance for each of them attaching to the term respect/respectability: Kelly's sense of respectability became located outside her family and community of origin (given what these had come to signify unconsciously in terms of unrespectability). It remains to say a little more about why Tommy's sense of respect is so firmly locked into what Kelly has come to reject, which means detailing Tommy's relationship to the estate.

Tommy loved the estate when they first moved there:

> Tommy: It were brilliant feeling, to move into—and to move into a big 'ouse, 'cos it 'ad got a parlor, parlor-type room. (Interviewer: Yeah.) It were fantastic. And I felt right, right cocky, (..) the estate were unbelievable. People coming out, "Do you want any 'elp? (..) Do you want a drink of tea?" (..) Leave your door open na, they're in straight away, take your television and video. To walk up on this estate, I felt right proud. Because it—it was a 10-year waiting list for a three-bedroom and a 5-year waiting list for a two-bedroom. Na they can't wait to get off estate and nobody wants to come and live on estate.

And 33 years later, he still loves the estate, "even though it's terrible" and nobody wants to live there anymore. The estate, for all its problems, is practically the only place he's ever known; it's where he is known and belongs, like his father before him; it's where he feels safe; it's where he's destined to remain ("unless I win pools"); and, as a long-term unemployed man with few prospects of meaningful work, it has to be his best prospect of achieving "respect." It is Fiona's failure to move out of such a milieu, although she has moved cities, that probably endears her to him. And surely Tommy excuses neighbor Sean's appalling behavior because Sean comes from a local family of 12, all of whom Tommy knows, and will sit out with him for hours, "'aving a drink, 'aving a laugh and everything, going back, going back to past."

In a world where the prospects of socially valued achievements are few, where deindustrialization and other changes are denying this generation of men their expected patrimonial inheritance, knowing others and being known is part of what being well-respected means. Sean's willingness to sit around chatting, laughing, and reminiscing constitutes part of Tommy's sense of self-respect, as does the local kids calling him by his first name. Saying "good morning to anybody (..) no matter who it is" and always getting a good morning back is part of being well-respected, as is talking to someone who knew his father. It is in this light that we can make more sense of his remark "I've got respect. I respect everybody on this estate." We have argued that it is symptomatic of Tommy's habit of denial (surely not everybody is worthy of respect). It can also usefully be read in terms of knowing and being known: Tommy has respect in the sense that everybody knows him; he respects everybody, meaning he knows everybody. In this discursive frame, respect signifies the opposite of getting on and moving out, as in Kelly's version of respectability.

Being unable to move, either geographically or socially, reinforces Tommy's habitual pattern of denying (manically if regarded cumulatively) the negative features of either his family or the estate. It also helps explain the importance of the known and the local to his sense of being respected. In other words, his sense of self-worth and respect necessarily implicate the very family and community that Kelly has been forced to reject, with the consequence that he cannot afford, either psychically or socially, to recognize why Kelly must embrace her particular version of respectability. Because the costs are too high, he pathologizes her choice, hating her for rejecting him, them, the estate. Her bigheadedness is just that: too big for these things he is invested in. Kelly must be not only rejected, but hated for aiming for what he does not have, and what he constantly denies himself, because he is unwilling to re-enter the pain of family that Kelly has had to confront. In this, in splitting off an unwanted part of himself and projecting it into his father's beloved daughter, he shows himself, unconsciously, to be as much his mother's son as, consciously, he is his father's boy.

Conclusions: The Reproduction of
Gender Difference in the Walters Family

We have tried to show that cultural reproduction is primarily achieved through unconscious communications, not through conscious learning processes and not smoothly, as if children would end up faithfully reflecting their parents' culture if it weren't for structural changes in their environment. We have emphasized how cultural meanings acquire their emotional resonances from the defenses against anxiety that the parents are unconsciously communicating. Parents' meanings are refracted in a myriad of ways, affected, of course, by real events (like Tommy's unemployment or Kelly's violent partner), themselves rendered uniquely meaningful in the context of that person's biography and the ways that they have evolved for coping with anxiety:

> The meaning of [family events] is always mediated by what
> is in the child's mind at the time something occurs. And this
> in turn is already a function of previous events and of the
> fantasies at the time of those earlier events. (Scharff, 1988,
> p. 74)

So, in Tommy's case, we saw how decisive for his way of coping with reality are the splitting defenses that are a central characteristic of his mother's mental structure.

Tommy's tendency to idealize echoes Ivy's idealization of the men in her family. Albert was "a really good 'usband. I couldn't 'ave wished for a better one (..) 'e were one in a million, 'im." Similarly, she repeatedly makes a general claim about her sons: "I 'ave got good lads."[13] Given the gendered criteria for boys' respectability, this means, "I've not 'ad no trouble with them lads of mine"; a claim she repeats regardless of the facts and regardless of having mentioned, for example, that "our Pete was a rogue." The function of the claim, as a defense against anxiety, is apparent when it follows the mention of an uncomfortable fact, something that would reflect on her lads in a less-than-ideal light; for example: "they don't all come together, though they used to. But (..) they don't na. But 'er, I 'ave got, I've got good lads."

Ivy's relationships with her daughters are no more reality based, as we have shown, but they are always differentiated: to the interviewer, she never talked about "my lasses" or said they were "good girls" (or bad). This, we believe, is because of the different processes of Ivy's unconscious identifications with her sons and daughters. Whereas the former are characterized by gender difference, which is otherness (in this case idealized), the latter, as we have argued, act as receptacles for unresolved parts of herself because gender sameness provides a ready-made route for unconscious identifications.[14] These unconscious, intersubjective processes will vary, depending on whether a person's defenses are predominantly of the splitting kind (what Klein [1988a, 1988b] called the *paranoid-schizoid* position) or the kind where the coexistence of good and bad in the same object can be acknowledged (what Klein called the *depressive* position). The consequences for the reproduction of gender difference will be profound, because it is through the unconscious motivations leading to splitting that gender difference gets reproduced in the face of structural changes that would otherwise set in motion changes in gender-differentiated practices and discourses. Yet, even in Ivy's case—a woman who, as we have shown, is highly dependent on splitting defenses—her projections onto her daughters, to the extent that these are introjected by them, ensure that their versions of becoming women differ both from each other and from their mother.

Ivy's projections, starting from when her daughters were babies innocent of gender, provided much of the material, unconsciously transmitted, for the inner objects out of which the daughters built their own multiple sense of (gendered) identity. Their lives apparently revolve around the same themes as Ivy's: family, male partners, sex, mothering, and respectability, but with different emphases, traceable to Ivy's differentiated projections into her three daughters. We have argued that her sons were not in receipt of equivalent differentiated projections from Ivy because they were boys (we do not know if there were equivalent dynamics between Albert and his sons). What seems to be the case however, at least for Tommy, is that, despite being free from much of the content of Ivy's concerns because they are gendered (for example, with sexual respectability), he has taken on her habitual splitting defenses and that these are a defining feature of his identity and relationships.

So far, we have focused on cross-generation but same-sex identifications.[15] We have even argued that gender difference has the effect of othering the children of the opposite sex, such that they are not the targets (nor ready receptacles) for projections. Recent feminist psychoanalysis problematizes the kind of Oedipal theory that suggests that the successful outcome of Oedipal dynamics in terms of securing an appropriate gender identity involves exclusive identification with the same-sex parent. Benjamin (1995) has argued for the survival, beyond Oedipal dynamics, of an earlier good relation between father and daughter (and mother and son), where that was available. She argues that identificatory love—identifying with likeness between oneself and another—of the father by the daughter, exists "before and alongside object love" (p. 56). Object love involves love of something (or someone) different. Variations in the rigidity of parents' gendered roles will have an effect on the availability of cross-sex identification. In Kelly's case, there is some evidence that the caring she received from her father, for example, being cuddled on his knee, provided a resource she did not get from her mother, and nonetheless informed how she is a mother with her own children. In the following extract, the train of Kelly's association runs from never having a cuddle on her mother's lap, to cuddling her own daughter on her lap, to remembering that this is what she had from her father as a child:

> Kelly: But I can't remember ever telling my mum that I love 'er either.
> (Interviewer: Mmm.) 'cos she's never said it to me. (Interviewer: Mmm.) And I've never—never 'ad—as a little girl, come and sit on my knee. Big as what my daughter is, I'll still pull 'er and you know,

> like, she won't sit on my knee, but I mean I like still pull 'er and say
> "let's 'ave a" you know, like a cuddle, or "give me a kiss" or whatever.
> She'll push me away and say "go on!" you know. But I can't *remember*
> *any time at all.* I can from my dad.
> Interviewer: Mmm. I was going to say what about your dad, even though
> you were only 12 when he died.
> Kelly: Em, (pause) I can—I can't remember 'aving any bad times with me
> dad. I can remember like good times.[16]

The chain of associations here demonstrates Kelly's identification
with aspects of her father's care for her as a child, which therefore are
reproduced in her own practice as a parent. It thus provides an
example of cross-gender (as well as cross-generation) identification.
Nonetheless, Kelly does not identify with the masculine-coded respect
that in Tommy's view characterized their father, but rather with the
caring or loving aspect, which is easily read as maternal; that is,
characteristic of women not men.

In focusing on unconscious intersubjective dynamics, namely splitting, projection, introjection, and identification, we have tried to
demonstrate the unpredictability of cultural reproduction. There is
plenty of evidence of unconscious transmission, but the result is never
a simple reproduction. Unconscious meanings are more powerful than
conscious ones, precisely because of the emotions they invoke: ful-
filled and/or frustrated desires and anxieties that can be exacerbated
or soothed. But no child is a passive agent in receiving these meanings,
which are sown in different emotional soils and are subject to active
fantasies whose unconscious purpose is to cope with anxieties and to
protect against the disappointments of unfulfilled desires. Within
these processes, gendered identifications with respectability and respect can be reproduced and changed in ways that are never entirely
predictable or controllable.

Notes

1. These interviews were undertaken as part of our ESRC project, Gender difference, anxiety, and the fear of crime (award no. L2102522018). Our interviewees were
found through knocking on doors and following up family leads on the estate. In this

case, we found Tommy first. He mentioned that his mother might also be interested. She, in turn, put us on to Kelly. In each case, two interviews were conducted, one week apart, using narrative interview method (Hollway & Jefferson, 1997).

2. In editing excerpts from transcripts, we are caught between the wish to present a concise picture and the recognition that a great deal of information is provided by repetitions, stumbling with words, and so on. Our guideline, when editing—indicated thus (..)—was to eliminate material only when we judged there to be no loss of significance.

3. Ivy's father treated his wife very badly, often violently, and also some of his children, including Ivy: "we 'ad a shocking life at 'ome with my dad." She was thrown out of home by him at 16, and so it is not surprising that, not long after, at 18, "I got in with Albert." At 33, he must have felt a bit like the good father to her: "'e were good bloke, 'e were a good 'un."

4. Ivy's account puts her second daughter's pregnancy at 16; it is Kelly—who would have less reason to overestimate—who puts her sister's age at 14. Likewise, there is a discrepancy in the age given by Ivy and Kelly for Kelly's marriage, Ivy putting it at 20 and Kelly at 18. Kelly's reason for getting married was, she says, that she couldn't wait to get out. This suggests a motivation for Ivy's inaccuracy here, too: that her daughter wasn't that desperate to leave (so leaving it, in her fantasy, until she was 20). Ivy's account is strewn with inaccuracies, and she frequently contradicts herself. In our method, we use such evidence of unconscious motivations and concentrate particularly on these aspects of the text (see Hollway & Jefferson, 1996, 1997).

5. At around this time too, one of her sons, according to Tommy, was imprisoned for burglary and other offenses. Due to the absence of precise dates, we cannot be sure whether this "shaming" event pre- or post-dated Ivy's breakdown. If the former, it was possibly another contributory factor. However, as we show later, Ivy's idealization of her sons probably protected her from the full shaming impact of such behaviors.

6. However, as we can see from her earlier account ("I got in with Albert when I were 18. And I stopped—'e's the only man I've ever 'ad"), this claim looks questionable.

7. See Hollway and Featherstone (1997) for an extended examination of maternal ambivalence.

8. "When confronted with a painful situation such as the recognition of failure, disappointment and loss, or by the need to accept suffering, the mind, instead of accepting the reality, may attempt evasion by deploying primitive defence mechanisms, typically splitting, manic denial, projection and projective identification" (Hook, 1994, pp. 125-126, note 6).

9. To the interviewer, Ivy rarely refers to Kelly by name, but uses a series of negatively loaded references such as "'er," "she," "'er round corner," even when the other sisters get names in the same sentence. It conveyed the opposite of "our Kelly," which she rarely used, whereas she used it all the time with the other family members, including Kelly's children.

10. Ivy told a similar story about having to take her younger sister everywhere with her, while her mother went to work. One day she refused and her sister was hit by a van and disabled for life.

11. Ivy still does not go out, and it remains Kelly's (and the others') responsibility to go to her.

12. In addition, Tommy and Sally had breakdowns during this period (see next section). It would seem that, when the containing influence of Albert was lost, the family went to pieces. Kelly is suggesting that she was the scapegoat.

13. Ivy's idealization of Albert is a familiar aspect of unconscious Oedipal dynamics in which, it is commonly argued, women may end up idealizing men (originally fathers or the men onto whom these dynamics are transferred) as a defense against disappointment with their mothers, who are the first love objects. Ivy's relationship with her 96-year-old mother is fraught with hate: She never sees her and only knows whether she is out of hospital if her younger sister phones. After a rift a few years ago, "She didn't want nowt to do wi' us. Said we were all two faced."

14. Scharff (1988, pp. 87ff) gives some clinical examples of identification with an earlier self, which is then related to as an object.

15. We do not have the space to look at same-generation identifications, but it seems likely that they were influential, especially for the younger siblings. Sally—12 years older than Kelly—seems to have been responsible for looking after her a lot of the time. For example, when a condom was found in Kelly's coat pocket (given out during a sex education lesson), it was Sally who was dispatched to meet Kelly outside of school to confront her on what was deemed an extremely serious event.

16. Kelly's inability to break away from her violent partner—because of her continuing and involuntary "love" for him—makes sense in terms of her idealization of her father. Like Ivy's relationship with Albert, evidence of the negative side of her partner did not modify her idealization, which, being a defense, was not based on reality.

References

Benjamin, J. (1995). *Like subjects, love objects: Essays on recognition and sexual difference.* New Haven, CT: Yale University Press.

Hollway, W., & Featherstone, B. (Eds.). (1997). *Mothering and ambivalence* London: Routledge.

Hollway, W., & Jefferson, T. (1996, June 13-16). Methodology, narrative, and the defended subject. In *IX International Oral History Conference Proceedings,* Goteborg University, pp. 834-843.

Hollway, W., & Jefferson, T. (1997). Eliciting narrative through the in-depth interview. *Qualitative Inquiry, 3*(1), 53-70.

Hook, R. H. (1994). Psychoanalysis, unconscious phantasy, and interpretation. In S. Heald & A. Deluz (Eds.), *Anthropology and psychoanalysis: An encounter through culture* (pp. 114-127). London: Routledge.

Klein, M. (1988a) *Envy and gratitude and other works 1946-1963.* London: Virago.

Klein, M. (1988b) *Love, guilt, and reparation and other works 1921-1945.* London: Virago.

Scharff, D. (1988). *The sexual relationship: An object relations view of sex and the family* (2nd ed.). London and New York: Routledge.

❦ 6 ❦

The Recruitment of Women
Into the Academic Elite in Israel

Anna's Narrative

Beverly Mizrachi

$\mathcal{A}$ large number of studies on recruitment into national elite positions in Western industrial societies have focused on the sociodemographic characteristics of these elites (Giddens, 1974; Higley et al., 1979; Porter, 1973). This research has shown that these elites are recruited from the relatively privileged segments of their societies. However, these studies have also shown the existence of differential recruitment patterns to the various elites, that is, institutional spheres differ in the extent to which they draw upon groups possessing the preferred sociodemographic characteristics to fill their elite positions (Giddens, 1974; Higley et al., 1979; Porter, 1973).

Studies on Israeli national elites have also focused on the sociodemographic characteristics of these elites and have concluded that they, too, are characterized by an accumulation of advantages that provided them with preferential access to their elite positions (Etzioni-Halevy, 1993; Horowitz & Lissak, 1989; Weingrod & Gurevitch, 1977). These advantages derived from an interaction between the European-Western, relatively modern ethnic origin of those filling elite positions, their veteran status in the country, their level of education, occupational-professional attainments, and incomes (Eisenstadt, 1967;

Lissak, 1970; Matras, 1965; Yogev & Shapira, 1987). However, these studies also revealed that Israeli institutions vary in the extent to which they draw upon groups possessing these preferred traits for their elite positions (Etzioni-Halevy, 1993; Horowitz & Lissak, 1989; Schecter, 1972; Weingrod & Gurevitch, 1977). Thus, studies on national elite recruitment in Israel suggest that this process resembles that in Western, industrial societies.

While these studies on national elites in both Western, industrial societies and in Israel have focused on the sociodemographic characteristics of these elites, especially on their socioeconomic traits, they have neglected other sociodemographic characteristics that may be related to national elite recruitment. For example, the sociodemographic variable, gender, has generally been neglected as a research variable, even though social scientists regard gender as a primary criterion of differentiation in the allocation of social roles (Acker, 1973). Steinmatz maintained that this tendency to overlook women in social science research has resulted in a large amount of biased data that casts doubts on the validity of the findings of such studies and on the theory building that has evolved from them (Steinmetz, 1974). This research bias is evident in theories on elite recruitment. Because most of the research on elite recruitment has neglected women and focused primarily on men, these theories present mostly men's patterns of elite recruitment, or a "hegemonic model" (Personal Narratives Group, 1989, p. 7). By studying the recruitment histories of women, this research can suggest a "counter hegemonic model" (Personal Narratives, 1989, p. 7), that is, a model that applies to the recruitment of a nondominant group, women.

Thus, to expand our knowledge about the recruitment of women into national elite positions, I studied the sociological factors related to the recruitment of women into these positions in Israel. I was interested in learning whether a group of common factors were related to the recruitment of women into these positions, so that I could talk about general recruitment patterns, or whether different factors were related to their recruitment into the different elites, so that I could talk about differential recruitment patterns to the various elites.

The group of women included in this research consisted of women in strategic national elite positions in different institutional spheres in Israeli society. I chose to study strategic elites because, within the hierarchy of elites, these have "a general and sustained social impact" (Keller, 1963, p. 20). I focused on those strategic national elites whose positions were available in an open elite marketplace, that is, in theory, they were open to members of all social groups and not only to members of social groups that possessed certain characteristics, such as a particular gender. In other words, I wanted to study strategic national elite positions that were open to both men and women. This criterion meant that certain strategic national elites in Israeli society were excluded from the research. Specifically, the military and religious elites were excluded because, either due to regulations or tradition, their elite positions were not available in an open elite marketplace, that is, they were not open to women (Goodman-Thau, 1981; Israel Defense Forces, 1993). The political, cultural, and trade union elites were excluded from the study because of methodological considerations. Therefore, the study concentrated on the women in strategic national elite positions in academia, the civil service, and the economy.

Methodology

Like researchers of national elites in Western industrial societies (Giddens, 1974; Higley et al., 1979; Hoffmann-Lange, 1987; Porter, 1973), I used the positional approach as the operational definition of national elites: I regarded as elites those people who filled the top positions in organizational hierarchies in the various institutional spheres I studied.

I acquired the data by using the qualitative research methodology of life history interviewing. This methodology seemed especially appropriate for the study for several reasons. First, this methodology is especially suitable for studying topics about which little is known, such as women in national elite positions, in order to generate concepts and theories about them (Faraday & Plummer, 1979; Glaser & Strauss, 1971; Walker, 1985). Second, the life history method, which is a holistic approach, enables the study of lives as a whole and not just periods or episodes in them. Because I was interested in studying processes and patterns of recruitment to national elite positions, this methodology could reveal the consequential series of events or processes that appeared to be related to these women's recruitment into national elite positions. Third, life history narratives reveal the interviewees' subjective reconstruction of life events that he or she considers relevant to the topic being studied (Widdershoven, 1993). Because I wanted to learn these women's understandings of the life events that led to their recruitment to elite positions, the self-interpretive information supplied by life history narratives was precisely the type of data I sought. Finally, the life history methodology helps us understand the social aspects of the recruitment of both men and women because it places individual lives in a social context of time and place. As Rosenthal (1993) stated, biography is "a social construct comprising both social reality and the subject's experiential world" (p. 60). Thus, the life history methodology is another method for connecting individual phenomena with social phenomena or for connecting the micro with the macro.

I conducted three taped interviews of 2 hours each with each woman, for a total of 6 hours, and then transcribed the interviews. In explaining the topic of the research, I told the women that I was interested in studying how they achieved their elite positions and that learning about their backgrounds, their parents and siblings, their school and university experiences, their spouses, their children, the development of their careers, or anything else they might want to tell me, would help me do that. I asked specific questions only when the interviewees' narratives were too general or unclear to be useful for analysis. The women spoke freely about their lives.

To find the patterns and processes that were related to their recruitment to their elite positions, I conducted a content analysis of the women's narratives. The data provided by this analysis revealed three recurrent broad topics, suggesting that three sociological categories or factors appeared to be systematically related to these women's selection to their national elite positions. These were sociodemographic, sociopsychological, and career structure factors. It seemed that among the three different elites I studied, socioeconomic factors were related to socialization patterns toward achievement and types of nonstereotyped gender roles and that these factors were related to the career structures of the institutional spheres in which these women were employed and their elite recruitment. Thus, I could identify general recruitment patterns. However, I found that each of the different elites came from different socioeconomic backgrounds, appeared to have been socialized to different types of achievement goals and nonstereotyped gender roles, and chose different institutional spheres in which to attain elite status. Thus, I could identify differential recruitment patterns, as well. Because the data showed a relationship between these three factors, it seemed that they formed a conceptual framework for analyzing the recruitment of women into the national elite positions.

In this chapter, I shall present the findings on the academic elite, that is, on tenured full professors. I chose this elite because they were the largest group of women in elite positions in Israeli society at the time of the study and because they were the most articulate, providing me with much rich data for analysis. According to the advisers on the status of women at all seven universities and two major research institutes, there were 86 women tenured full professors in these institutions at the time of the study. This number constituted 8% of all tenured full professors at the time. Of these, 49 (57%) were in the natural sciences, 28 (33%) were in the humanities and social sciences, and 9 (10%) were in medicine. Within the natural sciences, the largest group was in chemistry and chemistry-related fields. The women in the humanities and social sciences were divided more or less equally among the various disciplines making up these two faculties. The distribution of these women professors among the various faculties and disciplines corresponded, more or less, to that of American women professors in American universities (Morlock, 1973; Patterson, 1973). I chose 13 women for inclusion in our research, a number that constituted about 15% of the 86 women in this elite at the time of our study. The group consisted of 8 women from the natural sciences and 5 from the humanities and social sciences. The women were selected by random sampling.

In presenting the data, I have focused on Anna, one woman in the academic elite, whose recruitment to her position seemed to demonstrate the normative and dominant recruitment pattern of the group as a whole. Both Shostak and Mead have discussed the validity of using one subject as a representative of an entire group (Mead, quoted in Langness & Frank, 1981; Shostak, 1989). The discussion, of course, centers on the extent to which one can claim that any individual is representative of the society or group to which she belongs. Stated differently, one can ask how, in conducting research, one limits the biases or distortions that may arise from drawing conclusions about a group on the basis of idiosyncrasies inherent in any individual's life. Shostak (1989) dealt with this issue by being the sole interviewer and interviewing all her subjects in an identical fashion. Mead claimed that "any member of a group, provided his position within that group is properly specified, is a perfect sample of the group wide pattern on which he is acting as an informant" (Mead, quoted in Langness & Frank, 1981, p. 53). I have maintained the validity of using one subject as a representative of the group of women in the academic elite by being the sole interviewer, interviewing all the women in this group in as an identical fashion as their narratives permitted and by constantly comparing the one woman's characteristics, Anna's, with those of the others so that the ways in which she resembles the group (is representative of it) or deviates from it is clear. Therefore, the reader may assume that those characteristics and analyses that are presented as applying to Anna are representative of the group as a whole, unless stated otherwise. Thus, although I have preserved the individualistic elements of Anna's life history, I have also tried to show how it is typical of the group to which she belongs.

Findings

Sociodemographic Factors

Anna was a professor of anthropology. She was in her mid-fifties at the time of her interview. In recalling her family's background, she told me, her parents had immigrated to Israel from Germany in the 1930s, before the Holocaust, and settled in Tel Aviv. "Both my parents were physicians and both worked full-time, even my mother, which was unusual at the time. . . . My parents had only two children, my sister and myself. We lived a comfortable existence."

There seemed to be a clear connection between Anna's socioeconomic characteristics and her recruitment into her position in the academic elite. Judging by any of the separate components of socioeconomic divisions in Israel (country-ethnic origin, length of residence in the country, education, occupation, or income), or all these components together (Eisenstadt, 1967; Lissak, 1970), Anna's narrative suggested that she was recruited from a relatively privileged sociodemographic base within Israeli society that gave her preferential access to elite recruitment. She had parents who were of European origin and were veterans in the country. Like half of the mothers and fathers of the other women in the academic elite, Anna's parents had a university-professional education, worked in middle-class professions and earned middle-to upper-class incomes within the circumscribed economic structure of the society during the pre-State period and during the approximately two decades following the establishment of the State of Israel in 1948, which was the time when Anna was growing up in her parents' home. Also, Anna came from a small family whose economic resources did not need to be divided among many children and could be invested in Anna and her sister. One expression of this investment was her parents' payment of tuition to the high school she attended and later to the university. Because attendance in high school was essential to entering a university, and a university education essential to entering the academic elite, Anna's parents' financial ability to pay these costs provided her with her initial access to elite recruitment.

Whether because of personal needs or out of conformity to the familistic norms of Israeli society (Peres & Katz, 1981), or both, Anna married. In marrying, she was different from American "highly productive" female academics and other women professors, who tend to marry less (Astin & Bayer, 1973; Davis & Astin, 1990; Morlock, 1973) than do Israeli women professors. In telling me about her marriage, she said,

> I married when I was 23 and still studying for my BA. Marriage was important to me because I wanted a husband and a child, a family of my own. My husband came from a background similar to my own. He was 2 years older than I. He was also an anthropology major and was planning an academic career.
>
> When we married, my parents bought us an apartment and, later on, bought us a car.

In marrying an academic, as did half of the women in this academic elite, and a future university professor, Anna resembled a notable percentage of highly productive American academic women (Davis & Astin, 1990), who also choose spouses from academia. Anna's husband was similar to his wife in his other sociodemographic characteristics. Like her, he was born to parents of European ethnic origin who were veteran settlers in Israel and who could be considered as belonging to the middle-class sector of the society. Thus, Anna's husband brought to the marriage socioeconomic resources similar to hers. Upon marriage, Anna and her husband pooled the financial resources each had brought to their union and accrued joint resources that enabled them to maintain their middle-class status and to enhance it. These joint resources were formed through two developing and interacting cycles; the career cycle and the family cycle.

Looking at the career cycle, Anna's narrative revealed that her husband finished his most advanced degree, his PhD, during the early years of their marriage, whereas she completed hers 7 years later. Because he began his career cycle earlier, he began earning a professional income before she did and enjoyed an increased income as he progressed in his career.

The long preparatory period required for attaining three academic degrees before embarking on the path to elite recruitment in academia (receiving a PhD) meant that Anna's earnings were limited during the early years of marriage. Once she completed her PhD, her income also increased as she advanced in her career, until it became more or less equal to that of her husband when she acquired professorial status.

However, Anna's husband always earned more than she did. Thus, whereas the couple was a single economic unit who pooled their economic resources, the contribution of each spouse was not always equal: The relative contribution of each varied according to their advancement in the career cycle and their concomitant salary increases.

While the career cycle was developing, the family cycle was developing, also. Anna and her husband had three children, which was the average number among women in this elite. Thus, she resembled American and other Israeli women professors, who have more children than do women of lesser academic rank (Astin & Bayer, 1973; Toren, 1991).

Anna and her husband's one constant and expensive item of consumption throughout the family life cycle was the employment of full-time (8 hours a day, 6 days a week) domestic help. This help was directed primarily toward child care, then toward cleaning and cooking. Anna recalled that the full-time housekeeper

> took care of the children and was superficially responsible for seeing to it that they did their homework when they came home from school. When they needed help with their homework, they asked my husband or me. When the children were sick, either the housekeeper stayed with them or my husband or myself—whoever was free at the time. She also cleaned the house.

Anna's narrative revealed that she and her husband hired household help from the time their first child was born and continued with this help for about 20 years. It was difficult to calculate the exact cost of such help, although studies have shown that one of the largest work-related costs among dual earner families is child care and baby-sitting (Hayghe, 1982; Hunt & Hunt, 1982). Hanson and Ooms (1991) wrote that, "Dual earner families spend as much as eight times more than single earners on baby-sitting and day care" (p. 632). When household help was no longer necessary for child care, the couple continued hiring help for housekeeping, which was also expensive.

It seemed that the allocation of such considerable joint financial resources to home management enabled both spouses to develop their careers. However, the allocation of these resources to home management was most crucial to the progress of Anna's career, particularly in the early stage of the family life cycle: It enabled her to "buy time" (Aisenberg & Harrington, 1988, p. 42) to complete her PhD, the prerequisite for the beginning of her academic career, and relieved her of home management responsibilities throughout the elite recruitment process.

It appeared that Anna's husband's financial contribution to his wife's career was a critical factor in her embarking on the path to elite recruitment into the academic elite. Even while she was working part-time while she was studying and, therefore, contributing to the couple's economic resources, it was probably the husband's higher income that enabled the couple to hire the domestic help that gave Anna the opportunity to begin her academic career and pursue it during the early years. Thus, although much research has maintained that marriage—and, therefore, husbands—may be a liability to the careers of wives (for example, Cooney & Uhlenberg, 1989), Anna's narrative suggested that for wives in the academic elite, husbands may be an asset, certainly an economic asset, particularly for wives who have children. This contention received support from the fact that there were no divorced mothers or widows who had supported children alone in this academic elite.

Anna's current relatively privileged socioeconomic status derived from economic advantages accumulated in two stages: first, in her family of orientation, both during childhood and during stages of her family life cycle (buying an apartment and, later, a car) and, second, in the family of procreation she and her husband established. Therefore, it seems that a theoretical approach to understanding the affect of socioeconomic resources on married women's (mothers') elite recruitment into the academic elite should include the concept of aggregate socioeconomic resources, that is, the sum total of the financial resources amassed in families of orientation plus those in the family of procreation. Anna expressed her perception of her relatively privileged socioeconomic status when she commented,

> We are certainly not as rich as the people one reads about in newspapers who build villas that cost a million dollars. I suppose that from the point of view of property and salaries, they are richer than we are. Actually, it is a privilege of academia that academics can live a quality of life—a lifestyle—that is higher than what they earn from their salaries. From a material point of view and from an intellectual point of view, we live on a higher level than our salaries would actually permit. We travel abroad for conferences, we interact with the international scientific community. All in all, we live extraordinarily well. I have no complaints on that score.

Sociopsychological Factors

Anna's narrative suggested that her socialization might also be a determining factor in explaining her recruitment to her elite position. This socialization appeared to be a consistent, continuous, and integrated process composed of four components: her parents' socialization toward individual achievement through excellence, her socialization toward nonstereotyped gender roles, her high school's socialization toward individual achievement through excellence, and her extracurricular activities, which taught her organizational and interpersonal skills important to her selection to her elite position.

When asked about her parents' expectations of her (defined as socialization goals), Anna mentioned two kinds: those that could be realized as children and those as adults. Anna recalled that during childhood, her parents expected high achievement measured by excellent performance in school, which they rewarded. She told me, "Both my parents expected excellence from me and high achievement, and they always reinforced my excellent performance. I was my parents' pride."

Anna's comments exemplified McClelland's (1961) contention that parents' socialization practices instill a need to achieve in their children that is expressed in a striving toward excellence for the intrinsic satisfaction that such achievement provides. In a sense, her parents could allow themselves to motivate their daughter to this type of achievement goal: Having acquired instrumental financial security for themselves and their children, they could sanction noninstrumental, intrinsic goals such as self-fulfillment. Although McClelland's study on acquiring the motivation to achieve was carried out on middle-class male college students, more recent studies (Delamont, 1989; Mickelson, 1989) conducted on middle-class females, such as Anna, supported McClelland's findings on the association between parental motivation to achieve and high achievement.

Anna's parents' expectations regarding their daughter's adult roles included giving equal priority to family and career roles. As Anna recalled,

> My parents expected me to marry and have children. I was very influenced by my parents, but especially by my mother. She was a professional woman, and it was clear to me that I would have a profession and a career. It never occurred to me to sit at home. I never even considered it.
>
> As far back as I can remember, my mother used to tell me and my sister that it is important for a woman to have a profession, a career. She would always say, "I want you to marry and have a career—not a job—a career. I want you to marry and have children and a good husband, but a woman must have a profession of her own." My sister and I used to hear that sentence all the time. My mother drummed that into our heads from the time we were very young. It was a dominant theme in our home. She, herself, loved her work and so we gave her a lot of support.
>
> The truth is, I thought about a career from the time I was 12 or 13, I had very ambitious professional plans. I didn't

see any obstacles. I don't remember having such clear plans about a family. I just took it for granted that I would have a family because I didn't know about any other options.

In my view, parental socialization toward integrating the traditional female (homemaking) and the traditional male (career) roles or combining feminine and masculine characteristics (Lieblich, 1991) into a single gender role for women constitutes nonstereotyped gender role socialization. In explaining the determinants of parental socialization toward nonstereotyped gender roles, my data support those studies (Call & Otto, 1977; Ginzberg, 1971) that found that parents who themselves had high educational and career achievements, as did Anna's parents, tended to socialize their daughters to such accomplishments, also. Furthermore, Anna's narrative also supported those studies that found that mothers seemed to be the more dominant parent in socializing their daughters toward what I termed nonstereotyped gender roles. Thus, my data and that of scholars such as Baruch (1972), Elder (1972), and Tangri (1972) found that mothers who were highly educated and had high career aspirations, as did Anna's mother, tended to have daughters with similar accomplishments.

Apparently, Anna's parents' emphasis on achievement through excellence was internalized and translated into academic achievement in school because she was accepted into a selective, elite academic high school. This school continued and fortified her parents' stress on achievement through excellence. Adler (1970) noted that academic high schools, like the one Anna attended, were, indeed, characterized by an emphasis on "quality" and "high standards" that lent them an "elitist flavor and orientation" (p. 293).

In describing her school years, Anna said,

> I went to a demanding, prestigious elementary school and high school. I loved school and it was important to me to excel. I liked being able to apply myself and to achieve high goals. I loved to excel at every subject. I got good grades and

I was highly reinforced at school. School was the dominant
factor in my life while I was growing up.

Anna's narrative reiterated the importance of prestigious, elite academic high schools in the recruitment of women into elite positions
and coincided with previously documented research (Delamont,
1989; Maxwell & Maxwell, 1984) that showed an association between the socialization practices in these types of schools and the
selection of women into these positions.

From Anna's narrative, I learned that she had been active in an
extracurricular organization, a Zionist youth movement, during many
of her school years. The ideology of these movements represented that
of the political and cultural elites in Israeli society at the time. They
advocated their members' joining collective pioneering settlements,
such as a kibbutz, after graduation from high school. In talking about
this activity, Anna stated that "I never really intended to join a kibbutz,
but my activities in the movement taught me a lot about getting along
with people, organizing projects, and being a leader."

As an agent of socialization, the youth movement in which Anna
participated during her school years seemed more important for the
skills it enabled her to develop than for its success in achieving the
goal it espoused. This concurs with Jencks's (1979) contention that
leadership and social skills acquired through extracurricular activities
during adolescence contribute to "getting ahead."

Anna's narrative suggested that her socialization toward achievement and nonstereotyped gender roles was conducive to the development of an ideology of egalitarianism that, in marriage, was expressed
in a desire for an equal division of domestic labor between her and
her husband and for equal opportunities for career development for
both. Thus, her narrative supported other research that has documented a trend toward this ideology among career women (Smith &
Reid, 1986; Vannoy-Hiller & Philliber, 1989; Yogev, 1981).

Anna's narrative exemplified this ideology when she told me,

Even before the women's movement, my husband always
shared the household and family responsibilities. He was
very proud of the fact that we had an egalitarian relation-

> ship. The schedule for running everything was my responsi-
> bility—I was the chief manager of the household—but my
> husband was very responsible about carrying it out. He dealt
> mostly with the financial matters and the maintenance of the
> home and car.

It appears that, in spite of their egalitarian ideology and their equal
division of domestic labor, this labor was divided into the traditional
gender spheres: Anna was responsible for home management, while
her husband was responsible for traditional male activities, such as
mechanics and repairs. It should be noted that while all the women in
this academic elite espoused an egalitarian spousal relationship, only
one quarter of the women implemented such a relationship in the
division of domestic labor. The majority practiced a more moderately
egalitarian, traditional, gendered division of domestic labor.

Anna and her husband were actually less burdened with domestic
labor than it appeared because, as I mentioned previously, they employed a full-time housekeeper for about 20 years. Thus, both the
absolute and the proportional amount of domestic labor, certainly of
housekeeping, reportedly performed by both spouses did not seem to
have impeded their professional achievements.

It seemed that Anna and her husband regarded the hiring of
domestic labor as a mechanism they implemented to express their
egalitarian ideology. However, this option was related to both the
sociodemographic (income) and sociopsychological (need for achievement and definition of nonstereotyped gender roles that stressed an
egalitarian spousal relationship) characteristics of this couple. It was
an option that required not only economic resources available only to
the middle- and upper-income strata, but also the willingness to
allocate these resources toward implementing their values of egalitarianism in the division of domestic labor.

Anna felt that she had an opportunity for career achievement equal
to her husband. She considered her husband to be highly supportive
of her career. In discussing this support, Anna recalled,

> My husband was always very supportive of my career in
> words and in deeds. He has had the greatest influence on my

life because I could always discuss my concerns and projects with him. He has been my sounding board and created a very supportive atmosphere. I never felt guilty toward my husband because of my work because he was so supportive. Actually, he likes women who are his intellectual equals.

Perhaps one expression of Anna's equal opportunity for career achievement was the way in which she and her husband dealt with the career conflict that could have ensued around the topic of taking sabbaticals. In discussing her sabbatical, Anna said,

When we went on sabbaticals, we looked for places that would take both of us, so we started by writing together for joint positions, universities that would be interesting for both of us. There was only one exception—when he was offered a very prestigious position and scholarship, so we went there. His was a paid position, but mine was not.

This policy of attempting to plan sabbaticals together gave both spouses an equal opportunity to advance their careers and avoided potential role-marital strain.

The critical importance Anna attributed to her husband's support in her elite recruitment, as well as findings in other research (Astin & Davis, 1985; Josselson, 1990), suggest that egalitarian husbands are clearly a career asset. If, in discussing her sociodemographic characteristics, Anna demonstrated that husbands were a financial asset, in discussing her husband's attitude toward her career, she demonstrated that husbands were a psychological asset, as well.

Anna's marriage seemed very satisfying, supporting other research (Crosby, 1987; Vannoy-Hiller & Philliber, 1989) that contended that a multiplicity of roles among career women was conducive, not detrimental, to satisfying marriages. This led us to suggest that among women in this academic elite, egalitarianism in the division of family labor and in the opportunity to achieve in their careers may be a contributing factor to their satisfaction in marriage.

Career Structure Factors

It seemed to me that Anna's choice of an academic career was not a random one: She chose a career that rewards the type of achievement to which she had been socialized: excellence.

In telling me about her career advancement, Anna focused on the characteristics of the academic career structure in universities. She stressed the importance of time and pace of career advancement, career continuity, the critical turning point in her career. In recalling the development of her career, Anna told me,

> When I graduated high school, I decided that I wanted to go to the university to study anthropology. I remember saying to myself as I walked the corridors, "I really love it here. I am going to stay here. My life is here." I really fell in love with the academic life from the very beginning.
>
> I did very well in my BA studies and immediately went on to my MA. I also worked part-time as a research and teaching assistant. When I finished my MA, I continued immediately with my PhD
>
> When I finished my PhD, my husband and I went abroad for a post-doc. When we returned home, I received my first formal appointment. From then on, things have gone smoothly. I was appointed instructor; one year later I was appointed lecturer; then, five years later, senior lecturer. I was appointed assistant professor nine years after that and full professor four years later. I have 46 publications—mostly articles in professional journals, but also books. It was important to me to publish my first book before I was 40 and to have it well-received. I did that. I have never had a strategy for developing my career—I just do the best I can every day.

Anna's narrative revealed that time was a dominant characteristic of the structure of the academic career in regard to her elite recruitment: She had to comply with a prescribed time schedule in her career development in order to reach elite status. Toren (1993) substantiated Anna's perception of the importance of time in academic careers when she differentiated between two different types of time. One was actual "physical" time and referred to the formal time determined by universities for remaining in a particular rank. The second type was social time. This referred to the culturally and socially acceptable time-in-rank for the subsequent statuses in the academic career hierarchy and is determined by one's academic peers. Failure to comply with the formal, physical time prescriptions of the university results in one's being dismissed from the university, whereas failure to comply with social time results in one's being considered incompetent by one's colleagues. Perhaps Anna revealed the pressure of time in academic careers best when she said, "If you ask me for money, I'll give you money—as much as you want. Just don't ask me for time. The only thing I can't give you is time—I don't have any."

Several factors seemed to be associated with Anna's ability to adapt herself to the time impositions required to achieve an elite position in the academic career structure. One appeared to be a connection between Anna's sociodemographic characteristics (her financial resources) and the institutional sphere in which she had chosen to build a career. Although these resources, described above, can be helpful to any married mother developing a career, they are particularly crucial to women in a career structure that imposes strict time-in-rank prescriptions for advancement to elite positions. For example, they enabled Anna to hire the help that freed her from domestic duties so that she could commit herself to her professional advancement.

A second factor seemed to be her socialization toward high achievement, which showed a link between her sociopsychological characteristics and the institutional sphere in which she had chosen to develop a career. As evidence of her high motivation toward achievement, when I asked Anna to place herself on a motivation to achievement scale that ran from 1 to 10 (10 being the highest), she placed herself in a high position on the scale. She explained, "Actually, I think I am a nine and a half. I want to do excellent work. My criterion is not external recognition, but the internal satisfaction of knowing that I have done excellent work."

Likewise, her socialization toward a nonstereotyped gender role construct that placed equal priority on family and career roles also enabled her to make the demanding commitment to a greedy career structure and legitimized that commitment. This socialization eased the role conflict that could have arisen from a gender role construct that placed first priority on family roles and second on career roles.

Another factor that helped Anna adapt to the time schedule imposed by the academic career structure was *strategies of productivity* (Astin & Davis, 1985). One such strategy was related to the planning of major family life-cycle and career-cycle events to minimize the conflict between them. Because the career cycle was a given, dictated by the demands of the academic career structure, particularly in regard to time and advancement, the family life cycle, such as children's births, were usually planned around the career cycle, rather than vice versa. In recalling the birth of her children, Anna stated,

> I planned to have the first child after I got my B.A. I was so happy with my husband that I wanted to complete the family by having a child. We discussed it and decided that we could have a child and continue our studies. I had had a good model from my mother, who had a profession and had worked while she had children, and decided that it was possible, so we had our first daughter. I didn't feel the need for another child for 4 or 5 years. I was working and working, coming home at 5 o'clock every day. After I finished my Ph.D. and post-doc, I felt some relief from my career pressures, so we had our second child, a daughter. When I was approaching 40, I wanted another child and with the feeling that I had really achieved a lot in my career and that I now could do what I wanted, I decided to have my third child, my youngest son.

This tendency to plan all their children's birth may be a specific characteristic of the women in the academic elite that differentiates them from other professional and academic women (Smith & Reid, 1986). The fact that Anna planned the births of all her children did not necessarily mean that they did not affect the development of her career, but that their disruptive effect was kept to a minimum. Other research also found that the family life cycle, specifically marriage and motherhood, did not significantly affect academic women's research performance and the number of their publications (Astin & Davis, 1985; Cole & Zuckerman, 1991; Toren, 1991).

An additional factor that enabled Anna to comply with the demanding time requirements of an academic career involved maintaining career continuity. The formal and informal time-in-rank prescriptions for each status in the academic career structure and the requirement for passing through each status in a consecutive order, dictated that Anna remain in the career structure on a consecutive basis, rather than on an interrupted basis. Working about 12 hours a day, it took Anna approximately 19 years to achieve her elite position. Almost all of these adaptations to the demands of the academic career structure may be regarded as gendered adaptations by which women compete with men in the academic recruitment pool for elite positions because they indicate how women respond to the demands of this career structure while manipulating cultural role definitions for women.

Anna mentioned her appointment as instructor, and its accompanying tenure, as the critical turning point in her career. If career achievement can be regarded as a transition from one status to another, then the appointment to instructor may be regarded as a transition from the status of an aspirant to that of an acknowledged professional. Trice and Morrand (1993) likened this transition to a rite de passage and, apparently, Anna regarded it as such, also.

In evaluating her performance in her three major roles, that of career woman, spouse, and mother, Anna considered herself very successful in her career role and in her spousal role, although somewhat less successful in her parental role. She tended to attribute her success to her personal efforts, rather than to external forces, such as luck. In talking about her success in her academic career, Anna explained, "My success in my career is a result of my talent and my hard work." In explaining her success as a spouse, Anne said, "We feel romantic toward each other, and we try to be good to each other. I work hard at my marriage."

Anna considered herself only fairly successful as a parent. She explained,

> Rearing children is a day-to-day thing. I try to maintain good communication with my children, to listen to them, to be sensitive to them. My first daughter was rather individualistic and stubborn. We had problems with her, so we went to counseling. My second and third children were easier. Being a parent is a difficult job. You can never really know whether you have been successful. That has been said by people wiser than I. It is a big pleasure to see children grow and to be with them in their good moments, and it is very demanding to be with them in their crises and to feel that you are doing the right thing.
>
> My work was never a problem for my children. They never knew a different reality. They grew up knowing that mother worked and father worked. The mothers of the other children in their environment also worked. If I had felt that they were suffering because of my work, I don't think I would have stopped—I just would have tried to solve the problem in a different way. I never felt guilty toward my children about my work. I often felt pressured because of time, the management of time, but never guilt.

Anna's tendency to perceive herself as successful in her various roles is a nontraditional feminine gender characteristic. Scholars have noted that women tend to devalue their success and attribute it to external factors, whereas they tend to attribute their failures to their own internal factors because success (achievement) is inconsistent with the traditional feminine identity (Wiley & Crittenden, 1992). Apparently, Anna did not feel that her feminine identity was threatened by her achievements: She acknowledged them and took credit for them. This was another aspect of her nontraditional gender role, and I attributed it to her socialization toward achievement and toward nonstereotyped gender roles.

In concluding the interview, I asked Anna to sum up her life, then at mid-point. She reflected for a moment and then said, "I have the kind of life I want."

Conclusions and Discussion

While this analysis has focused on the life history narrative of one individual woman in the academic elite, as a sociologist, my intent was to analyze a group as a whole. Specifically, I was interested in studying the sociological factors related to the recruitment of women into the academic elite. My data suggested that certain sociodemographic, sociopsychological, and institutional career structure factors may be related to this process. The narratives of these women in the Israeli academic elite revealed that they came from relatively privileged backgrounds. They were socialized to strive toward the achievement of excellence for the intrinsic satisfaction this type of achievement provides and to nonstereotyped gender roles that placed equal priority on career and family. They chose to achieve their elite positions in academia, which rewards their specific types of socialization and requires their particular type of socioeconomic resources. In fact, the data suggested a systematic relationship or "fit" between these factors. Thus, this research adds to our knowledge about national elite recruitment in that it proposes a more inclusive analytical-conceptual framework for studying elite selection than has been used previously and suggests the factors that should be included in this framework. This systematic configuration of characteristics among the academic elite I studied implies that the recruitment pattern to this elite constitutes a distinct recruitment pattern.

While studying the sociological factors that explain the recruitment of women into the national academic elite was the primary focus of this research, the data drew my attention to a secondary theme: the elitism of the academic elite in Israeli society. In examining the sociodemographic characteristics of these women, the data revealed that the overwhelming majority came from a socially preferred ethnic and socioeconomic background in Israeli society. It is almost a tautology to say that they made up the educational elite in the country. These women's sociopsychological characteristics also contributed to their elitism: Their parents and schools socialized them to strive toward the best, toward excellence, an elitist value. The extracurricular activities in which the overwhelming majority of these women participated, Zionist youth movements, were identified with the political and cultural elite of the period. They chose to develop careers in academia, a meritocratic institution that rewards excellence. They also perceived that they lived a privileged lifestyle. Furthermore, this group's elitism was fortified by their belonging to an "aristocracy of culture" (Bourdieu, 1984). According to Bourdieu, although academic titles guarantee that their bearers possess formal competence in their fields, these titles also guarantee that they possess a general culture that qualifies them for membership in this aristocracy and creates symbolic boundaries that separate them from nonacademic elites and nonelites. Together, these characteristics bestowed a "collective eminence" (Granfield & Koenig, 1992, p. 517) on these women that, together, constituted elitism.

I am convinced that the life history methodology, more than other methodologies, enabled me to gain access to the in-depth data that led to the construction of an analytical-conceptual framework for analyzing the recruitment of these women into the academic elite. But did these narratives teach us something about women's narratives, per se? In analyzing life history narratives of women, Chanfrault-Duchet (1991) noted three types of narrative models that she defined as feminist approaches to the life history methodology of women: the epic model, which "reveals an identification with the values of the community"; the romanesque model, which presents "the quest for authentic values in a degraded world"; and the picaresque model, which reflects "an ironic and satirical position in relation to hegemonic values" (p. 80). These three models seem to have a common denominator that characterizes them as feminist models: They all represent narrative forms of protest against the status of women in society. It was interesting to note that none of the narratives of the women in the academic elite I interviewed fit any of these three models. None expressed protest against the status of women in society.

What explains this lack of feminist protest in these narratives? Considering the small percentage of women in the Israeli academic elite at the time of this study (8%) and the minority status of women in the academic elite that has been depicted in the literature on this topic (Aisenberg & Harrington, 1988; Astin & Davis, 1985; Lie & O'Leary, 1990; Zuckerman, 1991), one could have expected such protest in these narratives. In one explanation, this lack of protest among Israeli career women has been attributed to various cultural factors in the society (Lieblich, 1991). I would like to propose an additional explanation on the more individual level. Perhaps one of the most striking characteristics of these women's narratives was their individualism. As was mentioned previously, these women were socialized to a high level of individual achievement, both by their parents and their schools, which made high achievement appear to be a realistic goal for them ("I never expected any obstacles."). This striving for individual achievement was also supported by the significant person in their adult lives, their husbands. For the women I studied in the academic elite, this socialization and support appeared to serve as "a continuity of self" (Fiske, 1980, p. 259), a stable, core aspect of their identity as an individual that ran like a thread throughout their lives and gave their lives consistency and direction. In fact, this may be a unique characteristic of women in elite positions that distinguishes them from others who have careers, but who are not selected to elite positions. This does not mean that these women were unaware of the minority, marginal status of women in academia and in society, in general, and of the social factors that contributed to this status. What it does mean or suggest is that these women's individual orientation was more important than their group orientation, their orientation to women as a group. Simply, they did not think that the factors that were related to the status of women as a group applied to them. However, this does not mean that the narratives were not gendered, that is, that they should be considered gender-neutral. Perhaps one way of gaining insight into the more specifically gendered or "counter hegemonic" (Personal Narratives Group, 1989) aspects of these narratives would be to conduct life history research on the recruitment of men into the national academic elite and then to analyze and compare their narratives with those of the women in this study.

References

Acker, J. (1973). Women and social stratification: A case of intellectual sexism. *American Journal of Sociology, 78,* 936-945.

Adler, C. (1970). The Israeli school as a selective institution. In S. N. Eisenstadt, R. Bar-Yosef, & C. Adler (Eds.), *Integration and development in Israel* (pp. 287-304). Jerusalem: Universities Press.

Aisenberg, N., & Harrington, M. (1988). *Women of academe.* Amherst, MA: University of Massachusetts Press.

Astin, H., & Bayer, A. (1973). Sex discrimination in academia. In A. Rossi & A. Calderwood (Eds.), *Academic women on the move* (pp. 333-375). New York: Russell Sage.

Astin, H., & Davis, D. (1985). Research productivity across the life and career cycles: Facilitators and barriers for women. In M. Fox (Ed.), *Scholarly writing and publishing issues, problems, and solutions* (pp. 147-161). Boulder, CO: Westview.

Baruch, G. (1972). Maternal influence upon college women's attitudes towards women and work. *Development Psychology, 6,* 32-37.

Bourdieu, P. (1984). *Distinction.* Cambridge, MA: Harvard University Press.

Call, V., & Otto, L. (1977, February). Age of marriage as a mobility contingency: Estimates for the Nye-Barardo model. *Journal of Marriage and the Family,* pp. 67-79.

Chanfrault-Duchet, M. (1991). Narrative structures, social models, and symbolic representation in the life story. In S. Gluck & D. Patai (Eds.), *Women's words* (pp. 77-92). New York: Routledge.

Cole, J., & Zuckerman, H. (1991). Marriage, motherhood, and research performance in science. In H. Zuckerman, J. Cole, & J. Bruer (Eds.), *The outer circle* (pp. 157-171). New York: Norton.

Cooney, T., & Uhlenberg, P. (1989). Family building patterns of professional women: A comparison of lawyers, physicians, and postsecondary teachers. *Journal of Marriage and the Family, 51,* 749-758.

Crosby, F. (Ed.). (1987). *Spouse, parent, worker.* New Haven, CT: Yale University Press.

Davis, D., & Astin, H. (1990). Life cycle, career patterns, and gender stratification in academia: Breaking myths and exposing truths. In S. Lie & V. O'Leary (Eds.), *Storming the tower: Women in the academic world* (pp. 89-108). London: Kogan Page.

Delamont, S. (1989). *Knowledgeable women.* London: Routledge.

Eisenstadt, S. N. (1967). *Israeli society.* New York: Basic Books.

Elder, G. H., Jr. (1972). Role orientation, marital age, and life patterns in adulthood. *Merrill-Palmer Quarterly, 8,* 3-24.

Etzioni-Halevy, E. (1993). *The elite connection and democracy in Israel.* Tel Aviv, Israel: Siffriat Hapoalim. (in Hebrew)

Faraday, A., & Plummer, K. (1979). Doing life histories. *Sociological Review, 27,* 773-798.

Fiske, M. (1980). Changing hierarchies of commitment in adulthood. In N. Smelser & E. Erikson (Eds.), *Themes of work and love in adulthood* (pp. 238-264). Cambridge, MA: Harvard University Press.

Giddens, A. (1974). Elites in the British class structure. In P. Stanworth & A. Giddens (Eds.), *Elites and power in British society* (pp. 1-21). Cambridge, UK: Cambridge University Press.

Ginzberg, E. (1971). *Educated American women—Life styles and self-portraits*. New York: Columbia University Press.

Glaser, B., & Strauss, A. (1971). *The discovery of grounded theory*. Chicago: Aldine.

Goodman-Thau, E. (1981). Challending the roots of religion's patriarchy and shaping identity and community. In B. Swirski & M. Safir (Eds.), *Calling the equality bluff* (pp. 45-53). New York: Pergamon.

Granfield, R., & Koenig, T. (1992). Learning collective eminence: Harvard Law School and the social production of elite lawyers. *The Sociological Quarterly, 33*, 503-520.

Hanson, S., & Ooms, T. (1991). The economic costs and rewards of two-earner, two-parent families. *Journal of Marriage and the Family, 53*, 622-635.

Hayghe, H. (1982). Dual-earner families: Their economic and demographic characteristics. In J. Aldous (Ed.), *Two paychecks—Life in dual earner families* (pp. 27-41). Beverly Hills, CA: Russell Sage.

Higley, J., Deacon, D., & Smart, D. (Eds.). (1979). *Elites in Australia*. London: Routledge & Kegan Paul.

Hoffmann-Lange, U. (1987). Surveying national elites in the Federal Republic of Germany. In G. Moyser & M. Wagstaffe (Eds.), *Research methods for elite studies* (pp. 27-42). London: Allen & Unwin.

Horowitz, D., & Lissak, M. (1989). *Trouble in utopia*. Albany: SUNY Press.

Hunt, J., & Hunt, L. (1982). Dual career families. In J. Aldous (Ed.), *Two paychecks—Life in dual earner families* (pp. 41-60). Beverly Hills, CA: Russell Sage.

Israel Defense Forces. (1993). *Order of the High Command for women soldiers*, 2.0701. Tel Aviv: Ministry of Defense.

Jencks, C. (1979). *Who gets ahead?* New York: Basic Books.

Josselson, R. (1990). *Finding herself*. San Francisco: Jossey-Bass.

Keller, S. (1963). *Beyond the ruling class*. New York: Random House.

Langness, L., & Frank, G. (1981). *Lives*. Novato, CA: Chandler and Sharp.

Lie, S., & O'Leary, V. (Eds.). (1990). *Storming the tower*. New York: Kogan Page.

Lieblich, A. (1991). A comparison of Israeli and American successful career women in midlife. In B. Swirski & M. Safir (Eds.), *Calling the equality bluff* (pp. 90-99). New York: Pergamon.

Lissak, M. (1970). Patterns of change in ideology and class structure in Israel. In S. N. Eisenstadt et al. (Eds.), *Integration and development* (pp. 141-162). Jerusalem: Israel Universities Press.

Matras, J. (1965). *Social change in Israel*. Chicago: Aldine.

Maxwell, M., & Maxwell, J. (1984). Women and the elite: Educational and occupational aspirations of private schools females 1966-76. *Canadian Review of Sociology and Anthropology, 21*, 371-395.

McClelland, D. (1961). *The achieving society*. Princeton, NJ: Van Nostrand.

Mickelson, R. (1989). Why does Jane read and write so well? The anomoly of women's achievement. *Sociology of Education, 62*, 47-63.

Morlock, L. (1973). Discipline variation in the status of academic women. In A. Rossi & A. Calderwood (Eds.), *Academic women on the move* (pp. 255-313). New York: Russell Sage.

Patterson, M. (1973). Sex and specialization in academia and the professions. In A. Rossi & A. Calderwood (Eds.), *Academic women on the move* (pp. 313-333). New York: Russell Sage.

Peres, Y., & Katz, R. (1981). Stability and centrality: The nuclear family in modern Israel. *Social Forces, 59*, 687-705.

Personal Narratives Group. (1989). Origins. In Personal Narratives Group (Eds.), *Interpreting women's lives.* Bloomington: Indiana University Press.

Philliber, W., & Hiller, D. (1983). Relative occupational attainments of spouses and later changes in marriage and wives' work experiences. *Journal of Marriage and the Family, 45*, 161-170.

Porter, J. (1973). *The vertical mosaic.* Toronto: University of Toronto Press.

Rosenthal, G. (1993). Reconstruction of life stories: Principles of selection in generating stories for narrative biographical interviews. In A. Lieblich & R. Josselson (Eds.), *The narrative study of lives* (Vol. 1, pp. 59-91). Newbury Park, CA: Sage.

Schecter, S. (1972). *Israeli political and economic elites and some aspects of their relations.* Unpublished doctoral dissertation, London School of Economics.

Shostak, M. (1989). What the wind won't take away. In Personal Narratives Group (Eds.), *Interpreting women's lives.* Bloomington: Indiana University Press.

Smith, A., & Reid, W. (1986). *Role-sharing marriage.* New York: Columbia Univesity Press.

Steinmetz, S. (1974). The social context of social research. *American Sociological Review, 9*, 111-116.

Tangri, S. (1972). Determinants of occupational role innovation among college women. *Journal of Social Issues, 28*, 177-201.

Toren, N. (1991). Biological productivity and research productivity of women professors in Israel: Facts and perceptions. *Megamot, 2*, 285-300. (in Hebrew)

Toren, N. (1993). The temporal dimensions of gender inequality in academia. *Higher Education, 25*, 439-455.

Trice, H., & Morand, D. (1993). Rites of passage in work careers. In H. Arthur, D. Hall, & B. Lawrence (Eds.), *Handbook of career theory* (pp. 397-416). Melbourne, Australia: Cambridge University Press.

Vannoy-Hiller, D., & Philliber, W. (1989). *Equal partners—Successful women in marriage.* Newbury Park, CA: Sage.

Walker, R. (1985). An introduction to applied qualitative research. In R. Walker (Ed.), *Applied qualitative research* (pp. 3-27). Hants, UK: Gower.

Weingrod, A., & Gurevitch, M. (1977). Who are the Israeli elites? *Jewish Journal of Sociology, 19*, 66-77.

Widdershoven, G. (1993). The story of life: Hermeneutic perspectives on the relationship between narrative and life history. In A. Lieblich & R. Josselson (Eds.), *The narrative study of lives* (Vol. 1, pp. 1-20). Newbury Park, CA: Sage.

Wiley, M., & Crittenden, K. (1992). By your attributions you shall be known: Consequences of attributional accounts for professional and gender identities. *Sex Roles, 27,* 259-272.

Yogev, A., & Shapira, R. (1987). Ethnicity, meritocracy, and credentialism in Israel: Elaborating the credential society thesis. *Research in Social Stratification and Mobility, 6,* 187-212.

Yogev, S. (1981). Do professional women have egalitarian relationships? *Journal of Marriage and the Family, 43,* 865-871.

Zuckerman, H. (1991). The careers of men and women scientists: A review of current research. In H. Zuckerman et al. (Eds.), *The outer circle* (pp. 27-57). New York: Norton.

❧ 7 ❧

Powerful Stories

The Role of Stories in Sustaining and Transforming Professional Practice Within a Mental Hospital

Tineke A. Abma

$\mathcal{A}$ few years ago, Welterhof, a middle-size general mental hospital in the south of the Netherlands, started a vocational rehabilitation project. The aim was to train and assist (ex-)psychiatric patients to find a meaningful daytime activity to support their social integration back into society. The project started on a small experimental scale in the garden and greenhouse and was developed "along the way" by a specially formed, multidisciplinary task force composed of an ergotherapist, vocational therapist, psychologist, and social worker and chaired by the coordinator of the therapy units. The initiators of the project—an executive manager and the coordinator—and the members of this task force related its eventual success directly to the existing professional practice of the therapists. This practice was

AUTHOR'S NOTE: This article is based on the stories of a good many people whom I have had the pleasure of knowing. I would like to thank the psychiatric patients and therapists at Welterhof. Patricia Ritterbeeks made the rich stories suitable for narrative interpretation. My thanks also go to Jennifer Greene and Yael Oberman for their helpful feedback on an earlier draft of this chapter.

experienced as problematic, because it reduced patients to incompetent and passive subjects, and this, in turn, made social integration objectives less feasible. To realize the project's desired integration objectives, patients needed to take responsibility for their lives, make their own decisions, and show initiative. The existing professional practice prevented this from happening, and several therapists longed for change.

To facilitate the project, I was asked to conduct an evaluation. Together with an internal evaluator, I evaluated it *responsively*—a term that will be clarified in the next section—using stories as a vehicle for reflecting on and transforming professional practice.

By a story, I mean "an oral or written performance involving two or more people interpreting past or anticipated experience" (Boje, 1995, p. 1000). Boje's definition emphasizes that stories refer to *lived experiences,* to immediate sensations. To be able to live and understand the drama we call our lives, people give meaning to their experiences by telling stories. Without stories, our lives and practices would be meaningless. Boje's definition further stresses that stories develop, change, and are transmitted in *conversations.* Storytellers always require a cast of listeners. Storytelling is a socially and situated language *performance* (Boje, 1991). Stories imply actions toward others (claims, requests). Their aim is not primarily to describe a situation but to motivate people to act in a certain way so that a practice is continued or changed. Storytelling has a *sociopolitical* character, because of the diversity of interests and values of the actors. Different actors will make different claims as to what has to be done to sustain or transform a practice. Power inevitably plays a role in the struggle around stories (Mumby, 1993).[1] Some actors are allowed to tell their stories, and are skilled at making their stories plausible in a wide variety of social contexts. Other stories are not uttered or heard, and hence not validated.[2]

Another characteristic is that stories are never just a representation of experiences. Stories are *interpretations.* To interpret is to impose an order on the experiences and events that call for interpretation. In stories, events are connected by a plot. The plot is the basic means by which specific events are brought into one meaningful whole. This makes the interpretation of stories different from scientific descriptions and explanations: In stories, events are temporally connected; scientific theories or models use causal laws to draw connections. It is the *sequentiality* (temporal order of events) rather than the truth or falsity of story that determines the plot. Although a linear temporal ordering is a dominant form, different orderings are possible, and we should not make the mistake of excluding stories that do not follow this particular (masculine and Western) rationality (Bloom, 1996). As interpretations, stories contain an evaluative or moral framework. People tell each other stories to find out how they should act in certain situations, how they relate to others, and what their identity and role is. In telling stories, actors are involved in the act of generating *value*, judging the worth of their lives and social practices.

Stories frequently embed concrete, situated examples of action and the consequences of action that inform choices about behavior. As such, stories offer situated strategies for action, and every professional practice is guided by a set of stories that professionals have constructed for the constraints in their work. These stories are grounded in a body of more or less interdependent, enduring, and broadly sustaining standard stories. A *standard story* can be defined as a story that is repeated over and over again and gives stability to professional practice. The sustaining power of a standard story stems from its ability to set forth truth claims that are shielded from testing and debate. The standard story is so self-evident that its claim to validity outweighs the need for justification or proof. An example of a standard story about psychiatric patients who are institutionalized is the famous novel, *One Flew over the Cuckoo's Nest* by Ken Kesey (1962/1983). The story is located within the clean environment of a hospital where the regime is cruel. Psychiatric patients are portrayed as weak and vulnerable subjects who are dependent on the expertise, care, and protection of the arrogant and insensitive nurses and therapists. When a new nurse disturbs the daily routines, everyone in the institution gets upset. It takes a very long time, but in the end, some patients feel empowered to leave the hospital. They step out of the plots that ruled their lives and create a new story.

In Welterhof, many therapists no longer recognized themselves in the standard story that dominated the setting, and this created a vacuum: The standard story was no longer acceptable, but at that particular moment in time, there was no other story available to make sense of actions and give them meaning. We reasoned that the introduction and retelling of marginalized stories might alter therapists' interpretation of the situation, stimulating their imagination and, in turn, leading to transformations in their professional practice.

This is a chapter about the role of stories in sustaining and transforming professional practices, illustrated by an evaluation of a vocational rehabilitation project within a mental hospital. The setting was characterized by an asymmetrical relation between therapists and patients. This implies that this account generates specific insights into the relationship between stories, power, dynamics, and professional practices. Nevertheless, I expect that this text will offer a vicarious experience for those who are working in other professional organizations, within, for example, higher education or the public services. The outline of this chapter is as follows: After a description of the responsive evaluation approach and how it was carried out in this particular setting, I describe how the expert power of therapists manifests itself via a standard story (re)produced in interactions with patients. In the following section, I explore why therapists are beginning to doubt the worth of the standard story. I then examine how unheard stories stimulate the therapists' self-reflection and imagination, and finally, I reflect upon the transformative power of stories and my text.

Evaluating Responsively

> There is that uncontrolled marketplace with the sound of a thousand voices. But there is also something else: lonely voices and chirping, stories that nobody hears and nobody wants to hear. But they are there.
>
> Kerstin Ekman

The initiators of the project, who asked me to evaluate the reha-bilitation project, expected that regular feedback would stimulate the reflection on actions taken and eventually result in a transformation of the professional practice of therapists. To achieve this, we followed a responsive evaluation approach (Abma, 1996; Guba & Lincoln, 1989). According to this approach, human beings (including evalua-tors) are active interpreters of their world.[3] In the interpretation, we bring different experiences, biographies, and socializations into play. These different social, temporal, and historical contexts equip differ-ent interpreters with different experiential resources. A policy or program will therefore have diverse, sometimes conflicting, meanings for different people. A responsive evaluation takes this diversity as a point of departure for a conversation between authentic voices in order to enhance personal and mutual understanding. This can be done either directly, by bringing those who have an interest in a program together, or indirectly, via the evaluator as facilitator and mediator. The conditions required for a responsive evaluation were quite good in this case: Those with an interest in the project seemed to be willing to talk openly about their experiences, to place their standard story between brackets, to listen to other stories, and to readjust and change their stories on the basis of the conversations they had with each other.

In a responsive evaluation, people with an interest in a program are involved in the process of evaluation as active partners instead of information givers (Greene, 1988). They are given a voice in order to bring forward their interpretation of the situation and to influence the evaluation. One may try to involve as many people as possible, but circumstances often require that one makes choices and selects certain people. To create a power balance between those who have an interest in the program, Guba and Lincoln (1989) argue that an evaluator should deliberately try to give voice to those whose interests might be damaged. *Victims*—one could also speak of people who try to sur-vive—are often hard to identify. They tend to bend their head and to avoid eye contact. Victims do not have a face. They are nameless and often want to remain anonymous. With your head down, it is hard to raise your voice, to offer resistance. And if you dare to speak, it is even more threatening to do so in front of a powerful person. In this evaluation, it was the internal evaluator who was able to identify and to built a relationship with those who felt marginalized. Members of the task force considered her to be one of them. In private, they told her that their work remained invisible and that they feared sanctions if the project failed. Patients also shared their frustrations and fears with her. We decided to invest extra energy to create room for these voices from the margin (Abma, 1997c), but we also included those who initiated and managed the project (Abma, 1997a).

We started having individual interviews with the task force thera-pists. In qualitative interviews, most of the talk is typically not narrative but question-and-answer exchanges. This type of interview does not encourage storytelling (Reissman, 1993). To avoid this, we tried to listen with a minimum of interruption and to use silences as occasions for the respondent to speak. We asked open-ended ques-tions, such as "What does it mean to work with psychiatric patients?" and "What does it mean to be involved in this project?" And we expected that the combination of open-ended questions and the natural conversational style would be more likely to encourage story-telling than conventional interviews. The interviews were recorded on tape. In the transcription of the interviews, and also in the presen-tation below, we did not "clean up" talk to make it more readable, because we felt the meanings in the stories could in part be derived from asides, repetitions of words or phrases, and expressive sounds and silences. What deeply moved our respondents, what worried them, and what made them feel frustrated and angry became apparent in their way of talking. In addition to the interviews, we relied heavily on informal conversations during coffee breaks and lunch hours. It seemed as if respondents were less inclined to behave rationally and that the more interesting stories, those that came from the bottom of their heart, were told to us in these situations.

None of the stories were presented to us as discrete units with clear beginnings and endings that could be detached from the surrounding discourse. They came to us in bits and pieces, so we had to mold the narrative fragments from the diverse information sources together to derive meaning from what respondents wanted to tell us. We acted as *bricoleurs* (Denzin & Lincoln, 1994, p. 2), and this shows how deeply we were part of our analysis. To get an insight into the professional practice of therapists, as constituted by the stories of participants, our analysis was structured by the following questions: "How do respondents in interviews impose order on the flow of experience to make sense of events and actions in their lives?" and "What kind of actions are implied in the story?" We read the stories for content (what does the respondent tell us?), performative aspects (what kind of actions are implied?), and language (how is the story told?). Although we did not apply one theory to describe and interpret our findings, our analysis was guided by certain theoretical notions, such as Bakhtin's (1953/1981) conception of the hierarchical relation between discourses. To check the credibility of our findings and to facilitate conversation among members of the task force, we asked them whether they recognized themselves in our interpretations. After a discussion, we were asked to concentrate on the experiences of the patients, and so we did.

Interviews did not seem a very appropriate way to collect stories from patients participating in the project. Sometimes, respondents experience an interview as an examination. The interviewer then runs the risk of ending up with a scant amount containing relatively irrelevant information (Fortuin, 1994). To avoid this and to gain trust, we chose to work with the patients. We reasoned that the relationship and trust we had built up working 3 days with the patients would enable them to share their personal stories in each other's company. We came up with the idea of a picnic and hoped that the group and place (everyone loved being outside in nature) would give the patients a feeling of safety. According to Hopkins (1996), this is a necessary condition for storytelling. Also, we expected that the picnic would give them a feeling for the "specialness" of what was about to happen. To elicit stories, we used visual aids. Participants were invited to tell a story about themselves and the project with the help of two images. They could choose from a set of 40 images selected by us as evaluators. The set was as diverse as possible so the images would appeal to people with different interests; it contained photos, cartoons, drawings, paintings covering a wide variety of subjects (gardens, people, streets, etc.), and more abstract images. These *artful methods* were chosen because they can reveal hidden meanings and (internal) conflicts and are particularly appropriate when respondents find it difficult to express themselves verbally (Barry, 1996; Liebermann, 1996).

After conversations among the separate groups of therapists and patients, we wanted to start a conversation between these groups to contribute to developing a mutual understanding with regard to their diverse, and sometimes conflicting, experiences. Given the asymmetrical relationship between therapists and patients, we decided not to bring them together directly, but to use our draft report, which contained a collection of stories without conclusions and a summary as a vehicle for conversation. We expected that our working document would serve this purpose, because it was a collage of stories and not a scientific description of facts or a conclusive argument (Abma, 1997b). A relative advantage of the narrative (versus a logo-scientific or argumentative) mode of knowing is that stories are open to multiple interpretation (Bruner, in Czarniawska, 1997). The meanings embedded in stories are not fixed, and this creates an opportunity for social negotiation. At a working conference, the members of the task force and the managers of the project were asked which story touched them the most, to tell this story in their own words to the group, and to describe what effect it had on them. By telling another person's story in one's own words, the participants were invited to distance themselves temporarily from their own story. We assumed that this intensive and creative approach would create possibilities of living through stories and embodying them (Reason & Hawkins, 1988).

Stories Sustaining the Professional Practice

In this section, I am presenting a story to illustrate how stories sustained the professional practice of therapists in Welterhof. It is a story about a little shop in the hospital. The main characters are two patients, Zef and Trees,[4] and a therapist. The story is based on daily conversations and oral stories with the therapist who was responsible for the boutique as part of the rehabilitation project and the two patients who were working there. An extended and validated version can be found in our working document (Abma & Ritterbeeks, 1996). Our story is a tragic story, because it has a negative end (Gergen,

1994). Telling a tragic story can raise pity and concern, serve as an excuse for failure, lead to sanctions, or stimulate the search for improvements (Gergen, 1994, pp. 206-207). We presented this tragedy as part of our report to encourage therapists to improve their practice.

> When the vocational therapist of the Garden and Greenhouse proposed to smarten up the place, the boutique had been neglected for a long time. She persuaded her colleagues that it might be a good "training place" for participants in the rehabilitation project. The boutique was emptied, cleaned, and at the end of January, using minimal resources, underwent a complete metamorphosis. The walls were painted, old furniture replaced, the shop window redecorated, and all the products put nicely in place. On the 20th of March the boutique was opened in a festive mood. Since that day the "shopping street" that connects the meeting centre with the living apartments has been revitalized . . .
>
> Zef and Trees were the first ones to run the new shop. Both ex-psychiatric patients lived on their own and were looking for a meaningful day-activity. According to the therapists, they were "ready" for the rehabilitation program.
>
> One of the vocational therapists was responsible for their rehabilitation and the shop. In collaboration with him, Zef and Trees chose to adjust their product line to the needs of the residents of the hospital. They did not want to sell expensive things; the prices of most of the products varied between *f*2.50 and *f*5.00. And according to Zef, this formula worked: "People when they walk, automatically look at the attractively organized things. Some residents only want to chat, and that's OK too. But if they want to, they can buy a cheap present, for example." Zef was the embodiment of a market vendor. For him, the boutique was a market stall. He saw this visualized in a photograph of a marketplace presented during the picnic.
>
> Zef and Trees invested a lot of time and energy in their business. They found the work meaningful, nice, and varied. It was also instructive: "You can rediscover your possibilities, and learn a lot, like how to sell, make bouquets, change and

adjust the shop window to new themes. Buying things, handling money, estimating revenues, chatting with folks, that all is very important for me," said Trees. She had once owned a pub, and she liked the contact with people. "At home I only worry." At the same time, they experienced the work in the boutique as emotionally burdening. It confronted them with the pain and sorrows of the residents of the hospital. Sometimes they found this hard to handle. They identified themselves with the residents and took their problems very serious. Zef compared himself with a man who carries a big globe on his neck: "I see in this picture someone who takes too much on his shoulders. I also do that; I keep my head bent."

Right from the start the therapist at the garden and greenhouse had told them that the boutique was a "temporary working place" and that they should make plans for the time when they would have to leave. But when the training period was almost finished, Trees realized that she did not want to leave. "Why can't I just stay and work here?" she asked herself. She got the feeling that the therapist wanted to "dump" her and didn't understand why. "Don't I work well enough? Has something gone wrong with estimating what it costs to buy things? That's possible. Everyone can make mistakes. But for the most part everything goes quite well. I get along with my colleague Zef, and with the clients. The shop window always looks original . . . " Zef also worried about leaving the boutique and looking for a voluntary job outside Welterhof as had been agreed.

The therapist concluded that Trees had become too attached to the boutique. He saw this as a symptom of her illness. The "detachment" was the subject of a discussion between the assisting therapist, Trees, and her psychiatrist. The therapist reminded Trees of the appointments they had made for leaving the place and she was not behaving according to what had been agreed. He also said that she was in fact "too good" for the boutique. It would be better for her to find something outside the institution. Then she would be less confronted with the problems of the residents. The psychiatrist approved this. In a more general way, the therapist observed that other patients should also have a chance. And in addition, the therapist had to keep an eye on the "output" of the project. Especially because there were questions being raised that queried the existence of the project.

Trees felt misunderstood. After the summer, she was again admitted to the hospital. She could not deal with the situation. Afterward, she was informed about a plan for her future. In order to promote the "detachment," it was agreed upon that Trees should not go back to the boutique, but she would gradually begin within the garden and greenhouse. The "wound" still too fresh and not yet healed. . . . It was painful for her to see that another participant had, during her absence, taken "her" place. She rejected the suggestion that she begin as a host in the garden and greenhouse in preparation for a voluntary job in the "botanical garden." If she could not go back to the boutique, she would look for a voluntary place within Welterhof. Zef also left the boutique. He found a voluntary job in Welterhof's "social program."

In the above story, one may recognize a tension between the stories of the patients and the "story" of the therapist. I have put the term story in quotation marks, because one can hardly recognize the representations of the therapist as a story. The labels and clinical categories (detachment) and the narrowly descriptive and toneless language used by the therapist do not seem to refer to experiences. His case representation has the character of a scientific report.

The patients tell a biographical story. Their stories inform listeners about their lives. Like the onset of mental illness, rehabilitation can be seen as a chapter, a chronological chain of events. Getting back to work is considered an important life event. The biographies tell us that the personal lives of Zef and Trees have completely changed. They again feel like valuable members of society. Zef is full of pride in "his market stall." As a market vendor, he means something to the residents of Welterhof. For Trees, the boutique is a place where she can meet others. She returns to the role she previously occupied as a pub owner. The boutique has an *existential* meaning[5] in their stories. Working in the boutique touches their whole being; they are no longer objects but are becoming subjects. The existential meaning contrasts with the meaning of the boutique in the therapeutic story. In the account of the therapist, the boutique acquires meaning in the context of the project. It is a "training" or "temporary working place," and its meaning is primarily functional. The boutique is a means whereby the goals of the project can be realized and its existence can be justified in an organizational context that emphasizes tangible results. The valued endpoints of the patients' stories and the account of the therapist clearly differ. The patients regret the dramatic event in the light of their own personal future. The therapist worries about the further course of the project and the course of actions to be taken.

In stories, events are connected by a plot. In this case, therapists reopen a boutique as part of a rehabilitation program, two patients have to leave the boutique, and they feel misunderstood are the events that call for interpretation. These events are, however, organized around different plots in the stories of the patients and the account of the therapist. The life stories of Zef and Trees are structured by the significant, turning points in their life (Denzin, 1989, p. 22). Participating in the rehabilitation program offers new perspectives in their life. They get attached to the boutique and feel misunderstood because they have not had a chance to bring their story to the fore. The account of the therapist, on the other hand, is a report of a particular set of events worth relating for reasons that are other than biographical (Hunter, 1991). The account of the therapist must formulate an implicit argument for action. Its theme is a quest for diagnosis, and therefore, with perfect therapeutic soundness, the therapeutic account begins with a therapeutic observation (Zef and Trees are "ready" for the rehabilitation program). Time represented in this account is not the lived time of illness and rehabilitation but the plotted time of therapeutic discovery (the attachment and noncompliant behavior is a symptom of Trees' illness, and it is better for her to find work outside the institution). How to deal with the pain, disappointment, confusion, and frustration felt by the patients is a matter about which the therapist has little to say. Being primarily interested in the clinical experiences, she shows less interest in the personal life stories of patients.

The different interpretations of the situations resulted in a misunderstanding between the patients and the therapist. The patients experience the abstractions in the story of the therapist as a denial of their life story and existential questions. The therapist thinks that the patients are noncompliant, but the appointments and plans the therapist is referring to have no meaning for them. What is relevant and plausible in the account of the therapist is hardly relevant and plausible in the context of the stories of Zef and Trees. In the end, however, the argument of the therapist settles the matter and the decisions that were taken: The participants of the project had to leave the boutique.

This outcome can be understood in the light of the character of the therapist's account and the asymmetrical relationship between therapist and patients. The account of the therapist sets forth powerful and persuasive truth claims—claims about appropriate behavior and values—and these are shielded from testing or debate. The therapist does not have to prove or justify the assertions in his account. The scientific air and the fact that it is grounded in a standard story makes the account so compelling that it is difficult for listeners to question its content. To offer resistance is even more difficult for patients who feel marginalized. Although they try to bring their experiences to the fore, they could hardly develop their own stories. Zef obeyed the decision taken by the therapists.[6] Trees uttered her dissatisfaction, but her emotional outbursts were immediately interpreted in terms of her illness and, hence, reduced to the account of the therapists. This created a narrative imbalance. The asymmetry between the stories was further enforced by the hierarchical relation between the different languages; the professional jargon and the *Algemeen Beschaafd Nederlands* (General Civilized Dutch) spoken by the therapists and the common language and dialect spoken by the patients[7] (Bakhtin, 1953/1981). Ultimately, power differences led to a situation in which the stories of the patients could not develop. Their uncompleted stories were not heard and hence not validated.

The stories that were woven around the boutique show how the professional practice of therapists is repeated in stories and how these stories, in turn, sustain professional practice. The standard story about therapists and patients was reproduced, and hence, the existing practice in which the patients are dependent and passive and the professionals use their authority to solve conflicts. One patient resisted this by showing her anger, but she was not able to develop her story. As a result, no stories were developed in which the experiences and arguments of the patients could become meaningful. The relational and emotional patterns between therapists and patients were repeated.

The Standard Story No Longer Worked

To appreciate how the sustaining power of the standard story might be avoided, the experiences and stories of therapists will be examined in more detail for what they reveal or conceal and how the gaps in some situations give rise to the need for other stories. We gathered these stories by having individual interviews with the members of the task force, including an ergotherapist, a vocational therapist, a psychologist, and a social worker. In addition, we interviewed several therapists whom they considered to be experts on rehabilitation.

What did the therapists tell us about their identity as a therapist and their role in the rehabilitation project? First of all, they told us, it means determining which psychiatric patients are appropriate for the project. Much like the school teachers described by Weick (1976), the therapists in the mental hospital felt themselves caught up in the "business of building and maintaining categories" (p. 8). On the basis of the therapist's decision, patients could participate in one of the standard programs.

This categorization was considered to be a very difficult task. One ergotherapist, for example, said,

> No, you don't have that [security]. . . . You see them for 6 weeks. You observe the growth that an individual goes through. But sometimes it is marginal. Sometimes you wonder: Will he succeed? Isn't it too early? or Can they manage it? Someone may state that he is ready, but . . . well. . . . What you see contradicts the feelings the patient himself has. Who am I to say: Yes, I think he'll do fine. A colleague might think he isn't ready. It is all very subjective, isn't it?

In cases of doubt, therapists consulted the team of professionals treating the patient. The ergotherapist described this as follows:

> When someone is admitted to the hospital there is always the voice of the whole treatment team. If I am convinced that a patient is not ready and the psychiatrist and others go along with my assessment, well . . . even then it is still up to the patients to choose what they want.

As a professional, the ergotherapist encountered the limits of professional theories and networks (Rein, 1983). The abstract nature of a theory may serve as a generalization, that is, it explains what is common about a category of people, but it falls short as a means to explain the variation within that same group of people, that is, what makes them different from each other. Anecdotes and stories about particular cases may, in these instances, serve as a way of reducing uncertainty (Hunter, 1991). These were, however, absent in the case of the rehabilitation project. The therapists had no experiences and no case stories that could serve as an example or reference point.

The dramatic effects the categorization can have on the lives of patients in terms of their self-image, hopes, dreams, and aspirations (Deegan, 1993) made me wonder why therapists do this. I was more or less convinced that this was their way of establishing their power over patients, but the explanations the therapists themselves offered in their stories forced me to adjust my preconceptions. A recurring explanation in their stories was that they felt bound by the organizational context in which they worked. They characterized this context as one dominated by large numbers and a lack of time. The ergotherapist for example said,

> You have seven people in one group, but everyone needs help and then you often think "I should give them a task. The next time I will invent something new." But it is always like this and you end up never adjusting the activities.

Therapists also lacked the time to evaluate the individual progress of the people in their groups. The vocational therapist for example said,

"Your work is spread over several units. Very often, we have appointments at 12 o'clock. It has always been our wish to do evaluations, but in practice, it is hardly feasible." Within this organizational context, it was also difficult to realize innovations. In the words of the ergotherapist, "One needs time to develop good projects and at the moment we lack time, because we are continuously working with groups."

Given the organizational context, the therapists fell back on the routine solutions supported by the standard story of the therapist as expert. These, in turn, had several shortcomings. The ergotherapist, for example, claimed that traditional practice was not very effective in terms of her professional practice goals:

> I offer them several possibilities, and most of the times, they will get an idea of the kind of activities they would like to do. But often I have the feeling that people do not experience this as individual attention and that they have the idea that they are just filling in time instead of working on an individual program with certain goals.

The traditional practice also created a clinical distance between the professionals and the patients that, according to some, contributed to passive behavior on the parts of the patients. This, in turn, made social integration objectives unfeasible. To realize the project's desired integration objectives, the patients need to take responsibility for their lives, make their own decisions, and show initiatives. These potentials were lost the moment they were approached as sick and incompetent victims. The vocational therapist, for example, said, "People who are now hospitalized have not always been that way." The words of the vocational therapist also suggested that the authority in many situations was no longer automatically accepted by patients:[8] "The approach taken by the whole institution is in dispute, not only the one taken by the garden and greenhouse."

From time to time, the therapists began to feel subversive, lost, futile, disconnected, wrong, incompetent, or maligned. Their experiences no longer matched their image of self or their ideals, but the therapists took no action. When the therapists realized that their professional practice sustained their patient's dependent behavior, the standard story was no longer accepted as adequate. There was a longing for change, something that clearly differed from routine solutions. The vocational therapist, for example, began to raise the following questions:

> What actions need to be taken to prevent hospitalization? What do you have to do in order to avoid the situation in which people no longer express their own wishes, no longer utter their own will? We have a method, and we take responsibility out of people's hands. Of course, there are always situations when you need to take over, but to what extent? I think we need to invent something new.

The ergotherapist expressed her desire for change as follows:

> We offer them [the patients] things, but we need to be more serious in our approach and draw their attention to the responsibility they themselves can take within ergotherapy, and emphasize that they can determine and decide what they want.

Because of their feelings of frustration and poor adjustment to the goals of their professional practice, it soon became apparent that a new story was needed. There are similarities here with the observations made by Rein (1983):

> The stories, slogans, maxims, principles, and myths by which many individuals in a bureaucracy feel themselves welded together and harmonized, many people sharing one overarching rational and ethical purpose, all "slip" a little. There is still orderly action . . . the day-to-day routine goes on. But this complex structure of actions is partly unshielded and unjustified in an ideological and emotional sense. (p. 152)

It was these "leaks in the plumbing and the threadbare state of the
ideological fabric" (p. 153) that created the necessity to enrich the
standard story. The once so-strong texture had finally worn out, holes
had begun to appear in the fabric, colors had faded, and the usual
repairs no longer worked. Other stories had to be woven into the
existing texts to give color and solidity again. How this weaving took
place is the subject of the following section.

Transformations in Professional Practice

To gain more insight into the experiences of the patients and to be
able to confront therapists with their stories, we organized a picnic.
My colleague asked every patient to participate a week before the
picnic and again on the day before the event itself. Everyone had to
decide for him- or herself whether he or she wanted to join the group,
and we were happily surprised that everyone joined the event. Although there were initially some fears of speaking in public, these were
overcome after a while. As confidence grew, participants spontaneously began to respond to each other's stories. When Arthur, for
example, told us about his dreams for the future (getting a paid job),
Peter responded with his future fantasy (working in a monastery to
combine his love for philosophy with gardening) and his feelings of
uncertainty. Then Zef told us about his hopes and fears. Like Sche-
herazade's midnight tales, every story engendered another story, and
each time, other meanings were highlighted. The use of images also
proved to be very appropriate. All kinds of nuances that were hidden
in a story were dramatically expressed in the chosen images.

In some cases, the images presented fitted in well with the themes
that dominated the lives of patients. An abstract painting divided into
blue and yellow and chosen by Peter, for example, symbolized the
division he was experiencing:

> At this moment, I feel a little bit divided, because I see prac-
> tice and theory as two different things. Theory [points at the

> blue part of the picture] is easier for me, it does not domi-
> nate [the picture]. The yellow color refers to practice, it is
> dominant [in the picture], and I have more trouble with that.
> I would like to turn these two sides into one, a harmony be-
> tween what I want and what actually can be realized.

Arthur recognized Peter's feelings. He compared himself to an ele-
phant: "I have chosen that picture, because I think it is a beautiful
animal. Strong." The image referred to the energy and physical power
he felt. He could not use all his energy and power in the work of the
project. Instead of weeding, the most prominent activity of the project,
he wanted to work with heavy machines as a step toward joining the
Gardens Department of the Sheltered Employment Scheme: "I'm a bit
disappointed. They [Sheltered Employment] often work with machines. I think, if you want to go in that direction, you should learn
to use them." At the same time, he recognized himself in an image of
a boy sitting on a wall with his hands in front of his eyes: "I see myself
in that picture, because I experience difficulties and then I withdraw,
until I am completely alone. And then I wonder whether I will, in fact,
even succeed in getting back to work."

The patient's stories were full of ambiguities. On the one hand,
they expressed their doubts and fears about their abilities and, on the
other hand, they felt the professionals underestimated and underval-
ued them. Patients needed security and approval but also wanted to
be challenged and to have responsibility. Arthur's story is illustrative:
"I needed rest. All around me had failed. After talking about it, I
decided to go to the therapy group for a while. . . . A burden was lifted
from my shoulders." After a few weeks, however, this relief was
replaced by feelings of helplessness: "Because I am in the therapy
group, I don't feel like going to work. Sometimes I think to myself I'll
just stay home, but then I start to worry, so that isn't a solution either."
Arthur was not the only one who temporarily moved from the
rehabilitation group to the therapy group. It is quite possible that the
need for therapy does not stop when someone is ready to rehabilitate
and vice versa. Arthur's experiences raise the question of whether the

distinction between therapy and rehabilitation is at all relevant. Whereas therapists were involved in a discussion about this distinction, the stories of the patients showed that there was a need for groups to be supported by people who have therapeutic as well as job-related skills.

Furthermore, the stories illustrate that rehabilitation involves a painful process of acceptance. Peter said: "I am sometimes scared that I will always be in there [sickness disability regulations] and never get out. . . . I don't want to give up working on it. But it is almost impossible for me to think of work." He expected to be teased about his "psychic problems." The acceptance of personal limitations is painful. The stories also tell us that rehabilitation is not a process that brings large benefits with it. It is a process of small beginnings, proceeding step by step with falls and recoveries. Peter had, for example, tried to work in Sheltered Employment once before and failed. The present project gave him a new chance:

> They placed me once before in Landpark to see if that suited me. But it did not work, because I had several psychic problems. These aren't so dominant now. . . . The only thing I want to do is to go back to Landpark. But I should be patient and slowly start training to work again.

This project had given him new hope for the future: He saw it reflected in a picture of a white vase with a white orchid on a green background: "I have experienced lots of disappointments in my life, but I feel it is possible for something beautiful to grow up and begin to bloom again."

The patient's stories differ from those of the therapists. Patients say they want to be recognized by the therapists as grown-up people who are able to make decisions and to take responsibility for their lives. Categories that are important for the therapists (rehabilitation versus therapy) have hardly any meaning for them. Furthermore, the patients' stories illustrate that rehabilitation is a capricious process. Every journey toward recovery is full of ambiguities, pain, and frustration. It is a process of muddling through, and it is different for everyone. Hope and trust are essential to survival and recovery.

Reactions of Therapists

In the first instance, the therapists involved in the project were concerned about the plan to organize a picnic: "Watch out, they might become psychotic." This reaction can be understood as an expression of concern for the welfare of the patients. It is not an unusual reaction, as we can see from what has been described above. The behavior of patients was interpreted as pathological and symptomatic of the diseases from which they were suffering. However well-intended the care, it was a repetition of the belief that the professional knows what is good for the patients, better, in fact, than the patients themselves. Although the therapists were convinced of the correctness of their assessment, the effect of their professional attitude is that patients are deprived of the possibility of determining what is right for themselves and of making their own decisions, articulating their own boundaries, and being able to fail and to learn from this failure. This happened in the case of Trees. By reducing her emotional reactions to her diagnosis, her ability to resist her disease was undermined, and hence, her ability to recover and build up her own life was also threatened.

We organized a working conference with the members of the task force and managers of the project to confront them with the usually unheard stories of the participants in the project to stimulate their reflection and imagination. These stories were part of our working report, and we asked the participants to respond to the story that touched them the most, to tell this story in their own words to the group, and to describe what effect it had on them.

The coordinator of the therapy units started telling how she was moved by the story of the picnic. Reading that story was a painful confrontation. It was like looking in a mirror and discovering that your appearance is not so beautiful as you thought. She had always seen herself as someone who was convinced of the necessity of a "cultural shift," as a major proponent of the "rehabilitation philoso-phy." This story made her realize that she was no better than the "old-fashioned" therapists. It shocked her that her reactions were different from her own words: "I thought, this isn't right, you're saying something quite different from what you really do." She disliked this inconsistency in her behavior and openly admitted that she has underestimated the patients. Her story prompted a conversa-tion on the discrepancy between actions and words. The social worker:

> We have talked about it [the relation between the patient
> and the therapist] very often. We were going to give them
> [the patients] another name in the project; the patient then
> becomes a voluntary employee and the therapist a trajectory
> assistant.

The ergotherapist responded: "And it is a whole process! You can use other names, but really what you have to change is your own ap-proach." She compared this change of attitude with a process, suggest-ing that it is more complex than the replacement of an old attitude with a new one. Like the coordinator, she emphasized that it is relatively easy to change one's language. More difficult and important is to change one's actions.

Several others spoke, and then it was the turn of the ergotherapist. She was touched by the stories of Arthur and Peter. In their stories, she recognized the diverse and sometimes conflicting needs of many patients. Their stories helped her to articulate her own problem:

> How do I react in such a way that I give people a feeling of
> safety and care on the one hand, but on the other do not
> take so much out of their hands that people feel disempow-
> ered to start doing things themselves.

What is interesting is the notion of autonomy that is reflected in this quotation. Autonomy is not understood as the opposite of connection and caring, as it is in more traditional, masculine interpretations, but both autonomy and caring are seen as aspects that need to be balanced in a relationship; safety and care on the one hand, and freedom and encouragement on the other. The ergotherapist also emphasized that giving patients more freedom to make their own decisions does not mean that one does not feel any responsibility for the patient.

The Transformational Power of Stories

One of the assumptions that runs through this chapter is that actions of professionals are grounded in stories and that the standard stories that are reproduced in actions give stability to a professional practice. Transformations of a professional practice start with the confrontation of ambiguity that calls for reflection.

Stories play a powerful role in transformation processes, because they work as a mirror (Forester, 1993). In this particular case, the story of the picnic, for example, confronted the therapists with a discrepancy between their good intentions and their actual behavior. They began to see themselves differently. The story also helped them to see things more clearly; that they were no better than the old-fashioned therapists. The awareness grew that good intentions will only become more than rhetoric if they actually express one's attitude toward the patients. Another paradox that stimulated their reflection was that one cannot demand that patients become more independent and take responsibility for their lives. Therapists began to realize that demanding empowerment was a repetition of their expert role and hierarchical relationship with the patients. The unheard stories of the patients further reminded them of things to which they had developed blind spots in their work: the pain, fear, and frustration experienced by the patients. Retelling the stories of the patients enabled the therapists to live through the difficulties patients experienced during their process of rehabilitation.

Ambiguity calls for reflection and this creates an opening for transformations. Stories are powerful tools in change, because they are one of the most fundamental ways to order experiences and events. Because, in stories, events are not described in abstract terms but rather as experiences, stories can easily be assimilated. They are the means by which we construct our personal experiences. For this reason, we are influenced by stories. Development and changes in practice do not come from the rational application of formal abstract knowledge and information. Rather, development is rooted in changes at a more basic level, where someone is changed by new experiences (Kennedy, 1983; Stake, 1986). In this case, the therapists saw that it was possible to approach patients in a more equal way and that this did not necessarily lead to psychotic behavior. The stories showed that patients were willing and able to make decisions themselves and to give meaning and direction to their lives. As such, the stories offered those therapists who no longer believed in the standard story a meaningful context in which to act and to establish a new identity and role. Those who experienced the shortcomings of the standard story were willing to validate the experiences and stories of the patients and to weave the plot line into their stories. In concrete terms, this led to an adjustment of professional practice, because therapists redefined their relationship with patients as well as their own identity and role.

My Text—A Story?

In this chapter, I wanted to illustrate (rather than argue or demonstrate) that stories can sustain and transform the professional practice, and I felt I could do this only in and through the stories the patients and therapists told me, themselves, and others. I intended to write in a narrative rather than in an argumentative or a logo-scientific mode. This raises the question of whether I have succeeded in that attempt. Is my text a story? My text does contain narrative parts (the repeated fragments of stories told in the hospital and my story about how the evaluation was planned and carried out), but it also contains some arguments and generalizations. In a story, the events would be woven into a meaningful whole by a temporal sequence. My text is, however, organized by a certain claim or generalization that stories can sustain and transform professional practice. In that sense, I only partly succeeded in my attempt to show and tell, and this has made me even more aware of how the academic writing practice dominates us as scholars. Writing in a narrative mode is a challenge I want to face in the future, and I hope others will join me in that attempt, because stories are appropriate for conveying the complexity, concrete details, and context of lived experiences, they suit our common knowledge, speak to a public, and are open for social negotiation.

Notes

1. Power is considered here as the possibility of influencing and sustaining meanings in practices. Power is relational insofar as others can honor or resist attempts to influence and sustain stories; whether this resistance succeeds is uncertain.

2. Quite often, it concerns painful experiences of marginalized groups. The traumatic experience is (temporarily) banned from the consciousness, because the experience violates the identity (Mishler, 1991) or because the sociopolitical context doesn't allow the telling of certain events. Survivors of political struggle, war, concentration camps, and sexual cruelties silence themselves or tell a "pre-narrative": a story that does not develop in time and/or does not express what someone felt (Reissman, 1993). Telling unheard stories can have a therapeutic and healing effect (Danticat, 1996).

3. Responsive and narrative approaches have a dialogic conception of the subject: Human beings are continuously involved in the communication with others and have to rely on their response.

4. The names are pseudonyms.

5. Although the term *existential* does not refer directly to existentialism as a philosophical tradition, there are some connections. For example, Sartre's idea that an individual life "develops in spirals; it passes again and again by the same points but at different levels of integration and complexity" (quoted in Bloom, 1996, p. 184).

6. Obedience can be understood as a survival strategy. See Belenky and others (1986).

7. Zef and Trees speak a mixture of Limburg's dialect and General Civilized Dutch (Algemeen Beschaafd Nederlands) known as *Knoebele-Huilands*. This dialect is spoken in Heerlen and surrounding areas.

8. Questions are asked and sometimes "counter-power" is built up, for example, by consulting another doctor for a "second opinion," by the formation of interest groups, and by making complaints.

References

Abma, T. A. (1996). *Responsief evalueren, Discoursen, controversen en allianties in het postmoderne* (Responsive evaluation: Discourses, controversies, and alliances in the postmodern). Delft, Netherlands: Eburon.

Abma, T. A. (1997a, June 4-6). *Confusion of tongues in organizations: Evaluating responsively in a multi-voiced world.* Paper presented at the conference, "Organizing in a Multi-Voiced World: Social Construction, Innovation and Organizational Change," Leuven, Belgium.

Abma, T. A. (1997b). Sharing power, facing ambiguity. In L. Mabry (Ed.), *Evaluation and the postmodern dilemma: Advances in program evaluation* (Vol. 3, pp. 105-119). Greenwich, CT: JAI.

Abma, T. A. (1997c). Voices from the margins: Political and ethical dilemmas in evaluation. *Canadian Review of Social Policy/Revue Canadienne de Politique Sociale, 39,* 41-53.

Abma, T. A., & Ritterbeeks, P. (1996, April 5). *Al doende zoeken we de weg* (As we work, we search for the way). Eindverslag van een responsieve evaluatie van het project arbeidsexploratie en -rehabilitatie in Psychiatrisch Centrum Welterhof te Heerlen.

Bakhtin, M. M. (1981). *The dialogic imagination.* Austin: University of Texas Press. (Original work published 1953)

Barry, D. (1996). Artful inquiry: A symbolic constructivist approach to social science research. *Qualitative Inquiry, 2*(2), 411-438.

Belenky, M. F., et al. (1986). *Women's ways of knowing: The development of self, voice, and mind.* New York: Basic Books.

Bloom, L. R (1996). Stories of one's own: Nonunitary subjectivity in narrative representation. *Qualitative Inquiry, 2*(2), 176-197.

Boje, D. M. (1991). The storytelling organization: Story performance in an office-supply firm. *Administrative Science Quarterly, 36,* 106-126.

Boje, D. M. (1995). Stories of the storytelling organization: A postmodern analysis of Disney as "Tamara-land." *Academy of Management Journal, 38*(4), 997-1035.

Czarniawska, B. (1997). *Narrating the organization: Dramas of institutional identity.* Chicago: University of Chicago Press.

Danticat, E. (1996). *Krik? Krak!* New York: Vintage.

Deegan, P. E. (1993). Recovering our sense of value after being labelled. *Journal of Psychosocial Nursing, 31*(4), 7-11.

Denzin, N. K. (1989). *Interpretive biography.* Newbury Park, CA: Sage.

Denzin N. K, & Lincoln, Y. S. (1994). Introduction: Entering the field of qualitative research. In N. K. Denzin & Y. S. Lincoln (Eds.), *Handbook of qualitative research* (pp. 1-17). Thousand Oaks, CA: Sage.

Forester, J. (1993). Learning from practice stories. In F. Fisher & J. Forester (Eds.), *The argumentative turn in policy analysis and planning* (pp. 186-209). London: UCL Press.

Fortuin, K. (1994). Evaluatie-onderzoek in een paradoxale beleidscontext (Evaluation within a paradoxical policy-context). In A. Francke & R. Richardson (Eds.), *Evaluatie-onderzoek, Kansen voor een kwalitatieve benadering* (Evaluation-research: Opportunities for a qualitative approach (pp. 155-176). Bussum: Coutinho.

Gergen, K. J. (1994). *Realities and relationships: Soundings in social construction.* Cambridge, MA: Harvard University Press.

Greene, J. C. (1988). Stakeholder participation and utilization program evaluation. *Evaluation Review, 12*(2), 91-116.

Guba, E. G., & Lincoln, Y. S. (1989). *Fourth generation evaluation.* Newbury Park, CA: Sage.

Hopkins, B. (1996). Transforming tales: Exploring conflict through stories and storytelling. In M. Lieberman (Ed.), *Arts approaches to conflict* (pp. 275-295). London: Jessica Kingsley.

Hunter, K. M. (1991). *Doctors' stories: The narrative structure of medical knowledge.* Princeton, NJ: Princeton University Press.

Kennedy, M. M. (1983). Working knowledge. *Knowledge: Creation, Diffusion, Utilization, 5*(2), 193-211.

Kesey, K. (1983). *One flew over the cuckoo's nest: A novel.* Harmondsworth, UK: Penguin. (Original work published 1962)

Liebermann, M. (1996). Introduction. In M. Liebermann (Ed.), *Arts approaches to conflict* (pp. 1-6). London: Jessica Kingsley.

Mishler, E. G. (1991). Once upon a time . . . *Journal of Narrative and Life History, 1*(2 & 3), 101-108.

Mumby, D. K. (1993). Introduction: Narrative and social control. In D. K. Mumby (Ed.), *Narrative and social control: Critical perspectives* (Sage Annual Reviews of Communication Research, Vol. 21, pp. 1-12). Newbury Park, CA: Sage.

Reason, P., & Hawkins, P. (1988). Storytelling as inquiry. In P. Reason (Ed.), *Human inquiry in action.* London: Sage.

Rein, M. (1983). *From policy to practice.* New York: Sharpe.

Reissman, C. K. (1993). *Narrative analysis.* Newbury Park, CA: Sage.

Stake, R. (1986). An evolutionary view of educational improvement. In E. R. House (Ed.), *New directions in educational evaluation* (pp. 89-102). London: Farmer.

Weick, K. E. (1976). Educational organizations as loosely coupled systems. *Administrative Science Quarterly, 21,* 1-19.

❦ **8** ❦

Writing as Performance

Young Girls' Diaries

Barbara Crowther

*G*irls' personal diaries are, in the commonsense view, confessional writing: The reality composed in their pages is understood as truth, and the opinions expressed are seen as accurate and honest. Diaries are generally studied as social evidence or as historical commentary on everyday life, but in my investigation of young girls' diary-writing, I have been struck by how much more complex their discourse and their function is. They lead me to suggest that for many young girls, diary-writing also constitutes a performance, both a public and a private one. This might have considerable implications for the way diaries are treated in the study of lived culture, and—more provocatively—in forensic practice, where their status as confessional material means they are often presented in criminal cases as evidence. In discussing the performative dimension of diary-writing, I will be drawing not only on theoretical work relating to the psychological function of diaries, but also, centrally, on the reflections of a sample taken from 40 women whose diaries, written when they were 10 to 14, between the late 1950s and the early 1970s, form the basis of my broader research project.[1]

This group from whom I collected my initial data makes no claim to being socially representative; indeed, I know little about the background of the informants, although it may be indicative that most came in response to an advertisement in *The Guardian* (a left-liberal British newspaper). Others came via a Nottingham daily newspaper, or by word of mouth. Through a questionnaire, I gleaned the informants' position in the family (over half were the only girl and nearly the same number, although not all the same people, were the oldest child—these figures exclude the five children without siblings). I also found out about their diary-writing habits and other people's responses to them; who their influences or models were, if any; and their feelings about why and for whom they wrote. One of the aims of the larger research project—still in its early stages—was to study girls' early personal writing, when it is still relatively innocent of cultural expectations of the diary as genre, analyzing it as a discrete discourse.

From the sample of 40, a core of 15 emerged who (a) wrote regularly, (b) were prepared to give me access to their diaries, and (c) wrote throughout the age 10 to 14 period. These 15 have constituted the corpus of the research project and are the source for my main observations and suggestions in this piece. Their comments and reflections on their earliest diary-writing years have demonstrated to me that the diary can be an important site for playing out (as well as, occasionally, writing about) complex struggles within the family, society, and themselves, and that diary-writing can be a significant weapon of resistance as well as a tool in their subject formation as they "move from silence into self-narrative" (Smith, 1993, p. 4).

Of these 15, 3 representative diaries have provided some textual illustrations for my arguments about the performative aspect of diaries; these few glimpses are too scant to construct any interpretive reading of the lives of the three girls—nor are they intended to—but they may indicate something of the different ways their diaries were brought into play with the range of circumstances covered in their developing lives. Deborah (the oldest of three sisters) was very shy and underconfident but studious and good at school; Peggy (with two younger brothers) was an extrovert and very naughty at school; Jackie (who had a twin sister and an older brother) was somewhere in between. Jackie's home life, however, was rather unsettled (her parents later separated); Peggy's was stable but very strict, and she was often alone; Deborah, an unhappy girl, was very distanced emotionally from her parents. Some of these comments about the girls could largely be deduced from the diaries; others, without some prompting, could not. This distinction can, in part, be accounted for by the recognition that performance plays a significant part in diary-writing. It is the way we should understand diary-writing, rather than the light diaries shed on lives, that is the subject of this study.

Framing the Study

This investigation concerns a practice and a product of early adolescence, a time when, as girls' independence grows, a public face, and an acceptable one, is increasingly being demanded of them, but a public voice gets little encouragement. I have found very little contemporary academic work in either cultural or psychological studies that treats child diarists separately from adult diarists. Most references to diaries are made in the context of the historical silencing of women's voices, or they are discussed as a form of autobiography. I have found only one study that considers diaries by authors as young as 12 (Sosin, 1983, an article that contains a full review of previous relevant literature). Educational research (e.g., Gilbert & Taylor, 1991) has studied teacher-led diary projects, but such a context necessarily produces a rather different kind of writing.

Girls detect early that men's voices are heard more and culturally valued more than women's are. There are very few cultural texts or products that reflect and engage specifically with little girls' experience, before they are addressed by the ideologies of heterosexual teenage femininity and romance.[2] It is not hard for girls at this age to feel they don't count socially and culturally, especially when this feeling is compounded within the family. A statement from one of my informants, the second of four daughters, bears this out graphically: "My parents were preoccupied with marital strife and my siblings were very vocal"; she felt she wrote "to express my voice which could not be heard otherwise." Another informant recalls that "[her] words didn't describe the real feelings—they were a way of asking 'the world' to notice me." The diary, then, may offer some girls a way of "proving" they exist, that their experience matters.

Diaries are much more than daily entries. Wiener and Rosenwald (1993) point out that a diary is "at once an object, a place, and an activity" (p. 34). A diary exists without a word ever being written in it. As a book, whether a notebook or a commercially produced book with the days of the year measured out, it already has materiality. What individuates a diary, what makes a diary "my diary," is the creation of a text within it. "Keeping a diary" indicates not only ownership, but regular writing and commitment. In using the term performance in connection with these early-adolescent diaries, a term normally connoting public presentation, I am not claiming that they are anything other than thoroughly private writings. But often there is simultaneously some element of public performance in the keeping of them. Before turning to the private side of the performance and to the written text itself, I want to examine this public aspect.

Public Performance:
Keeping a Diary

Few of my informants (just 5 out of 40) kept the fact of their diary-writing secret. For most, their family members and some of their school friends knew that they kept a diary. Peggy, however, was one of the exceptions, and her experience, standing in harsh contrast to the generally tolerant attitude of families, may serve to illustrate the high degree of risk and of commitment that can be invested in diary-keeping. For her, it was "a big secret, something 'wicked' that I did privately." When her parents found her original diary (which consisted of lesson-by-lesson reports of her days at school, mostly quite pedestrian but peppered with pranks, and almost nothing about the evenings or weekends), they confiscated it, gave her a stern lecture and "Mum said that Dad had burnt it." She discontinued writing until by chance she came across the diary some months later and spent the next 3 days copying it all out before returning it to her father's drawer.[3]

Peggy's, however, is an unusual case. In general, a child's diary-writing seems to have been treated like any other interest, not perceived as odd. Making a daily entry (even if, for various reasons, it lapsed from time to time) was acknowledged as a regular commitment, on a par perhaps with going for a run or following a soap opera. Those that wrote found considerable satisfaction in this unintrusive activity. I want to consider their satisfaction not so much from the subjective standpoint of the diarist's psychology, her personal gratification, but in terms of her relationship to others, her growing autonomy, and her changing reality.

If no one knows, or no one is intended to know, what is inside a girl's diary, yet they know she keeps a diary, the writer is communicating to those close to her that she has something of her own to say—she has feelings, responses, opinions, or, at the least, a life worth recording. She does not want to tell all or any of it directly (although parts might get expressed elsewhere), nor let anyone read what she writes (save the occasional special friend—only three in my sample). She is putting on an act about her autonomously articulated life, communicating through an activity and through the maintenance of an exclusive and excluding relationship between herself and her unfolding text. Seen as a performed communication, largely about communication, it is a regular reminder to her close circle not only that she is able to communicate beyond those known social relations, but also that they are excluded from this special relationship, the first, perhaps, of many. (That girls quite commonly make this public gesture, and do so much more than boys, suggests they have more difficulties in communicating their autonomy and individuality, a theme I will come back to.)

Sometimes, the act of withdrawal in order to write the diary is quite histrionic, with Do Not Disturb signs, and (if disturbed) a hasty concealment of paper, drawing attention to the exclusivity of the diarist's world. Although girls may want their diary-writing acknowledged, the efforts and the risks they take to keep the contents secret suggest it is a site of considerable tension. Some of the diary-covers have warnings like *Strictly Private, No Entry* on them; others are disguised as school exercise books (one is labeled *THEOREMS. Ahem*). This risky play of exposure and concealment, prohibition and challenge is another face of the diary-keeping performance. Keeping the contents safe is not just about privacy but part of securing autonomy, independence and identity.

In assessing the safety and boundaries of self-disclosure, issues of trust are crucial. We can explore this by teasing out key words: diaries are confidential; diarists confide in them; they contain confidences, are used as confidantes. The root of these words is *fides*—trust. You entrust your feelings to the page and trust your family and friends not to intrude. But you can never be confident they won't sneak a look, and it is perhaps this risk-taking, this boundary-testing, that is part of the attraction (and the function) of diary-keeping. Some writers don't even dare give away the secret of keeping a diary. You trust your diary but cannot quite trust your family or friends any more.

A number of diaries I have seen testify to the fear and expectation of family members not respecting the rule of privacy. One informant who suspected her mother read her diary inserted messages on bits of paper warning her off. The inside cover of Peggy's "new" diary contains a warning: "Mum, Dad—If you get hold of this, before you swipe it, THINK. There's nothing *really* bad in it, IS THERE? *NO!*" Surprisingly, an entry in Jackie's diary (at 13) shows little respect for her twin sister's right to privacy: "I read Janice's diary and it was full of blokes she likes." Jackie, by her own account and the evidence of her writing, was a more conventionally moral girl than her rather rebellious sister. Within the next few months, as she turns 14, there is a marked increase in references to boys.

Another informant admitted that although she refused to let her family read her diary (she learned the danger by showing a "best friend" who later vindictively exposed the contents), she did tend to leave it lying around and wondered therefore whether her mother did read it. This is probably not uncommon: the outcomes of unconscious desires are hard both to establish and admit. Family therapists have sometimes found that in cases of severe problem behavior, where communication between the adolescent girl and her parents has completely broken down, the girl has used her diary to throw down a challenge to the parents (usually the mother), daring her to enter the world of her excessive feelings. She is in fact acting out, rather than saying, that there are important things that they are not talking about. Often, this comes to light when the mother, finding and reading the inadequately concealed diary, discovers a can of behavioral worms and seeks help for the daughter's "problem." The mother's inability to resist the impulse to read the diary confirms, and exacerbates, the communicative difficulty between them.[4]

In addition to concealment and disguise, it is interesting to look at the signifiers of secrecy. Some commercially produced diaries are designed with a kind of chastity belt—a lock and key, which may give young people a rare sense of control and security. Inside the book they sometimes reproduce the lock and key symbolically through a lexical code or system of euphemisms. My sample, disappointingly, contained no systematic code use (e.g., letter-by-letter substitution), but only isolated instances, usually to disguise references to specific people (often an initial or "it") or, very commonly, to having periods ("it" again or *, in addition to evasive terms such as "the curse," "coming on").[5] A code, however simple, may well help alleviate anxiety when you feel uneasy about your bodily or your emotional behavior.

By showing concern for concealment, young diary-writers are laying claim to a life that requires tight security, a secret and (by implication) exciting and perhaps transgressive personal life that remains closed—and undisclosed—to her family. This intimation alone may be a source of pleasure. It links her to a long tradition of diary-keeping, in which secrecy and codes are part of the *langue* and the mythology. The tradition has a strong female association, too: in earlier centuries, middle- and upper-class young women were encouraged to write diaries as a more acceptable form than novels or, worse, plays.[6] There are several positive models for fledgling female diarists, particularly Anne Frank, whom about one third (13) of my respondents named as a formative influence. Children's fiction, too, offers a number of positive representations of girls who write diaries.[7] Perhaps entry into the sisterhood of diarists is also part of the attraction and satisfaction for young girls and helps to confirm their gendered identity.

Some of my respondents' comments reflect the sense of gaining status by conforming to a culturally recognized model, if only because it was "a teenage-girl type thing to do." One felt "a sense of importance, pride that my grandmother (she gave me the diary) had taken me seriously enough to give me one as a present." Deborah, concerned at being a "misfit," felt "I confirmed my normality by keeping a diary," although, at 10, "the idea of having a secret, subjective life . . . was very foreign to me." Although diaries can thus offer girls an affirmatory position, an entry into one of the "provided subjectivities in relation to the regulative power of modern social apparatuses" (Walkerdine, 1986, p. 194), the gendered implications of this are more contradictory, less positive, even disturbing. Gift catalogs and the covers of many diaries sport clichéd images of traditionally feminine girls writing diaries—say, sitting in a demure dress under a blossom tree. Adolescent boys are certainly not given such cultural and ideological encouragement toward reflexivity nor any such formal recognition of the validity of trying to harness and express their complicated and amorphous feelings.[8] But the feminine associations of private diary-keeping and the symbol of the lock and key contrive to reinforce the ideological assumption that girls must have secrets and—importantly—that girls' thoughts should remain secret, their lives locked away, their problems and excitements not aired or shared.

For much of the time, there is relatively little in the content of these diaries that really warrants the secrecy. There are remarkably few moments of disclosure or potentially incriminating confidences, certainly in the younger years (say 10 to 12)—that is, before the entry of the phantom of romance, which seems to offer a paradigm for more prolonged moments of self-expression and exposure, the kind that provide—and reinforce—the common image of girls' diaries.[9] Even these moments are infrequent before the age of 14 in my sample, although without doubt, it is the fact rather than the frequency of any exposed emotions, however mild, that determines the fear of discovery. Many of my respondents noted that although they became "increasingly intimate" and more reflective over the years, they started off record-keeping, recording events, deeds, and routine—"My early diaries are immensely tedious records of the minutiae of daily life." The fear of exposure may indeed be augmented by fear of ridicule, at the banality of the entries or their style.

> Saint Patrick's Day. 'Tis top of the mornin' to ye. Answered telephone in office. Did experimental art. Melted Crayons on cardboard. Came in at 12.30 to do it. Sandy, too.
> Mr. Lieberman made us clean up desk. Got compliment on

darning by Mrs K. Switched notebooks. Cut out animal trans-
fers. (Deborah)

The fear of what may happen if any of this detail, so much of it
mundane, fell into unscrupulous or punitive hands testifies to the
insecurity of relationships of trust among siblings, parents, and
friends. It serves to remind us how tenuous these girls' control is over
their own affairs, how frail their self-confidence.

Performing a Function:
Filling a Need

Most diaries are, at any age, a mixture of chronicling and some
reflection. They provide a welcome ever-listening ear for thoughts and
observations, especially when other people can't be told, or won't
listen.[10] Part of adolescence involves easing up on the claim that
anyone should be interested in the minutiae of your life. Keeping a
private diary is a way of dealing with this, and it can be seen as a public
(or at least material) demonstration of growing autonomy. But it also
represents a private strategy for dealing with the complex of feelings
that are struggling to find recognition socially and in the family. In this
private face, there is a dimension of performance, too; before turning
to this, however, I want to broaden the discussion to include a
psychoanalytic view of the role of diaries, through D. W. Winnicott's
(1953) work on object relations theory. This is in no way intended to
pathologize diary-writing; like other habits and routines, diary-writing
meets some children's needs and not others', although its appeal to
girls rather than boys may have some psychological roots, a point that
will be picked up later, when Winnicott's ideas are supplemented by
reference to (post-)Lacanian analyses.

The key issue for us in Winnicott's (1953) theory of child development is the importance of the transitional object, perhaps a teddy
bear or comfort blanket, that helps infants manage during the first
stage of separation from the mother, when they have to recognize that
she is not always or exclusively there. Diaries, as Deborah Sosin (1983)
has pointed out, have many of the same functions for adolescent

children that Winnicott ascribes to toddlers' transitional objects. Adolescence is, of course, the second significant phase in human development, when issues of individuation and separation are brought sharply into play, as the emotional ties and securities of childhood are slackened and severed. A closer look at Winnicott's argument will demonstrate the links between diaries and transitional objects, lending support to more radical approaches to the study of diaries.

Winnicott's (1953) approach is to see individuals as both producers of and products of symbolic communicative acts. Young children, as part of the development of their individuality, attach themselves to objects, possessions that take on a symbolic dimension in their attempts to master the social world. These objects represent the security of the mother or mother-figure (and the breast) and offer a place of comfort that both recalls this security and simultaneously confirms the child's separateness from the mother, bridging the space that is opening up between mother and child.

> The use of objects for self-soothing during the normal separation-individuation process enables the child to tolerate ambivalence and to differentiate between the "me" and the "not me." When all else fails (i.e., mother is not available), the transitional objects tolerate the discharge of both negative and positive affects, thereby helping the child's developing sense of self. (Sosin, 1983, p. 95)

In endowing the transitional object with symbolic value the infant's first creative acts occur, the first engagement with culture, a preliminary step toward separation and becoming a social subject. The cherished object provides the child with the means to explore the boundaries between *me extensions* and *not me,* to test reality and to start to exercise the imagination in play and fantasy. It is not difficult to see how this connects with early teenage diary writing. Sosin (1983) points out,

> In an effort to substitute for the exclusive tie to the parent, adolescents may form intensified relationships to abstractions such as ideas, nature, or religion, or to inanimate

> objects such as cars, drugs, or books. . . . The teenage diary becomes a safe, private, all-accepting partner—a transitional object—which facilitates the passage into adulthood. (p. 93)

Two particular features of Winnicott's (1953) account of the transitional object are also worth noting. First, it is at moments of crisis or strong emotion that the transitional object is turned to, or when separation is most obvious and unavoidable: bedtime is the classic moment. Diaries are conventionally written in bed: considered rationally, this is the best and most private time to reflect on the day, but there may also be a residual memory of night-time separation that makes it the most comforting time. This can be seen as a self-soothing mechanism, the diaries being used as "actual and symbolic manifestations of particular mental operations having the aim of establishing the sense of mother at a 'not-mother' time" (Downey, 1978, cited in Sosin, 1983, p. 95). Second, Winnicott comments on the ownership or possession of the transitional object and the creative process involved in making it one's own. Although it exists before you and without you (it is often a gift), it is nonetheless created by you. The ownership of a (working) diary also involves authorship; the diary becomes an extension of the self and a separate product; the distinction between the subject and the object, me and not-me, is complex.

One of the values of the object relations approach is that it recognizes that diaries are not merely passive containers for feelings and emotions ("a repository for secrets," in the words of one of my sample); they function interactively with the developing individual. The relationship between the child and her diary is a central factor in her struggle for differentiation. (We shall return to the latent gender issue here.) If part of the work of an early diary is to help the transition between the known world and the unknown (as transitional objects do), the recording of routine and daily minutiae can be understood as confirming the known, while the expressive and reflective aspect helps make sense of the unknown. As the selection and articulation of material defines and anchors personal priorities and attitudes and pulls inchoate feelings into focus, so the very process of writing contributes to the construction of identity. Indeed, seeing what one has written, seeing the subject made object, and noticing (even unconsciously) the distance between one's sense of oneself and the self projected on the page, may subtly affect the composition of future entries. This leads us to the private performance angle; the approach here will involve treating the diary more as a text than as an activity.

Private Performance:
Inventing an Audience

A performance, almost by definition, assumes an audience—yet there is no immediate audience for personal diaries, certainly not one that can respond. However, an underlying tenet of modern discourse analysis and rhetorical study (e.g., Leith & Myerson, 1989) is that all utterances, all communications, have an addressee, so it is worthwhile reflecting on the address of diaries. My suggestion is that young diary writers conjure an audience (or addressee) in their text and then "play" to them, interact with them, enter into an imaginary dialogue with them.[11] One aspect of this implied audience, I suggest, is their own self, and some of what is going on in diary discourse is a kind of performance in front of a mirror, seeing how things look, trying out poses and voices.

It is important to recognize the conceptual distinction between a reader of a diary and its audience. By audience, I mean the constructed reader of the communication, the addressee. It is not necessarily an imaginary persona who will one day read the text—often there is none intended. (As an academic researching diary-writing, I was never the intended audience for anyone's diary, yet I am their reader.) The audience (in this context) is an idealized listening voice, a disembodied "you," a position inscribed in the text through the (unconscious) choices that inform the writing.[12] Because the ideal "ear" for different types of communications change, there can be considerable modulation in the address, even within a short space. Few young diarists exhibit the "settled" voice associated with mature diarists, who are more conscious of generic and literary traditions. Their diaries cover a range of experience even in a single entry: chronicling a day in detail; logging variations in routine (e.g., bedtimes, meals); noting, describing or commenting on events; reproducing dialogue; expressing feelings; articulating desires and fantasies; exhorting or admonishing oneself—the list could go on.[13] Some are predominantly in logging mode, others more reflective, but all contain a mixture of these elements.

> [Brother] Richard's first day at work as an apprentice char-
> tered accountant, he's done fairly well, he thinks. Played vol-
> leyball in gym, had dinner. Went to Christine's to deliver a
> film to be developed, with Mum. Went to the fair, Richard
> won me some dolly mixtures. Went on the big wheel. Rich-
> ard started rocking it. I haven't got a head for heights! I
> think Heather's going off with Cas, certainly from the way
> she treats me. I don't really mind as much as I used to; her
> and Cas have a lot more in common anyway, and they both
> like boys. From what Heather's said about me to her friends,
> I'd never be able to lift my head up again! (Jackie)

In part the modulations in voice, which are carried in the sentence structure, vocabulary, punctuation, and the degree of summary, signaling the distance of the addressee, are determined by (and determine) the different orders of communication, which can range from the remote ("had dinner") to the intimate ("I don't really mind . . . ") The addressee becomes anything from a record-keeper to a confidante, a confessor, a skeptic, a moral judge, a peer or a parent (critical or admiring), one's "better self," and so on. These imaginary positions (as it were) ask questions (such as, What did you do then?) and embody responses (e.g., That's not nice for you, is it), to which the writing "replies." With each modulation of address, the writer is involved in putting on a slightly different performance, presenting different readings or inflections of the same life, different manifestations of the self. It involves no greater versatility than talking about oneself to a number of different people using different registers, but diaries concentrate the process, providing the appropriate listener for any utterance, and in a communicative context determined by the diarist alone. They thus give the opportunity not just for self-expression but, more important, for self-creation and "trying out new role identifications" (Blos, 1962).[14]

Although it would be mistaken to place too much emphasis on intentionality, it is instructive to note what or who the diarists in my sample claim they were writing for.[15] Only a handful claimed there was "no sense of an audience." Most of the other replies were "for myself," or more specifically a "future self," my "other self," or an "observer self." A few saw a friend or confidante as interlocutor, or, as one said, "a reader who would 'see' me clearly." The rest testified to some sense of posterity, mostly their offspring (one hoped they would "be read by grandchildren or great-grandchildren—but not my children") or family ("of some historic interest to my family in about 50 years time").[16] A more public posterity was envisaged too: One informant "imagined my diaries being discovered in 100 years' time and being a source of social and historical interest"; another "included comments for posterity—I intended my diary to be read in a couple of centuries' time and taught in schools like Pepys's diary." This figure of self-in-posterity suggests a reassuring belief in continuity, an optimism about the process of growth and change, distinctly different from the picture of underconfidence and uncertainty suggested by many of those who say they wrote solely for their present selves. This latter group might be said to write for the process of writing; we might call it therapeutic writing. It is important nonetheless to think of it as an interactive relationship, the diary encouraging and noting the expression of the self, the recording of a life.

The concept of an "implied" reader is applicable even to writing that claims to have no sense of a possible "real" audience. Stylistic items such as corrective phrases ("Stephen L. has broken his arm or at least a bone in his wrist, which is the same thing"—Peggy) and deflecting phrases ("It'll sound awful to say this but . . . "—Deborah or "I was mad—probably unreasonably but, well!"—Janice) are enough to testify to the writer having a sense of audience.[17] Written words become permanent and truth-bearing, and there may be a reluctance to commit to paper an inaccuracy or an ignoble or unjustified feeling. The writers' own values and manners infuse their writing, and they construct an address that assumes shared standards and desires and shared cultural norms. Forms of self-regulation operate unconsciously. For example, "free" expression may be constrained by the fear of feeling disloyal or despicable by admitting certain things, or of seeing yourself voicing some opinion that "out loud" might be felt to demean you. The dialogic activity in a passage Jackie wrote suggests a certain unease, about the acceptability of her appearance, perhaps, or possible suggestions of vanity: "I sent her [a new pen-friend] one of those letterettes. Oh, and also a photo of me, which, as Janice would say, is enough to put anyone off! Charming!"

Again, if you are discouraged socially, as children are, from boasting, it should be legitimate to blow your own trumpet in the privacy of a diary; but it appears that moments of personal pride are often recorded evasively, either told through the responses of others or reported without much comment. You don't, perhaps, want to hear yourself bragging.

> They were all very complimentary about my dress. (Jackie)

> Sinton said my paraphrase was very good! ~~Am flattered!~~
> Twill turn my mutt! (Peggy)

Social proscriptions are deeply ingrained; a better self often determines or corrects the tone. Deeply upsetting moments may also be underexpressed to make them personally bearable (and culturally more acceptable). A large number of my informants recognized they deflected their distress: One notices such episodes are "baldly recorded as incidents, without saying that I had been upset," another "downplayed feelings of hurt and humiliation"; others mentioned not wanting to admit to family rows, "being bullied," and "issues I found agonising"; indeed, "the more painful things were the less I wanted to write about them." Deborah's diaries, for instance, give no indication of the deep unhappiness and unkind treatment she remembers much of the time. Some pain is too uncomfortable to replay, even to yourself let alone another. The following incident, for example, displays admirable good-humor and bravado but betrays little of how it felt for 13-year-old Peggy:

> Tests back, and Cor blimey if Schwartz hasn't forked out for prizes! Clifford (1st) got a Cliff Richard calendar 1963!
> Sandra and Pauline (2nd =s) got photos of Elvis and Kooky!

> Me, clever clot, as per usual, got 37%. Bottom in class! But the old boy had got a booby prize for me!!!!=A peice of oily rag folded in polythene, and stapled to a peice of paper, and on the paper written this "To M. H.—The Booby Prize consisting of one piece of rag soaked in midnight oil which should be burned nightly until examinations" So, come next term, and a week before exams, I shall swot by a nightlight made of Schwartz's *vest, and his oil for his Volksvagen!!!*

In articulating their experiences, diarists develop strategies (which may involve some degree of self-censorship, if not actually of denial) so that they feel satisfied with the version of themselves the diary projects. Both the self and the events are objectified in the writing of them and thus are representations that have had to pass muster as acceptably representative of the experience she wants to record and of herself as actant.[18] The sense of a diary's audience, however nebulous or unacknowledged, is bound to have some bearing on the writer's selection and focus.

Watching the Performance:
The Diary as Mirror

In this process of self-representation, it is clear that the writer is contributing to a perception of herself as she feels others should view her. Wiener and Rosenwald (1993) call it "creating an impression" (p. 39), a necessary part of "managing emotions" (p. 38). They suggest a diary needs to be seen not only as an object and a space but as a mirror, whose function is "the observation of the objectivated self" (p. 43). They too, like Sosin (1983), discuss the connections between diary use and infant development, concentrating on the concept of the "mirror stage," described as the moment when the child first realizes that "the self is not merely a sensate fragmented body but something that can be viewed as an integral object" (p. 44). Their theory goes beyond Winnicott's position, as it involves an advanced imaginative operation of putting oneself in the place of one's reflection and gazing back:

By writing about oneself in the diary one creates a picture of the self as a whole. One may also become aware of the self as divided into subject and object, the experiencer and the observer of experience. Beyond the transitional object function of the diary, which serves to help the self differentiate from others, this mirror function of the diary helps to distinguish not only the "me" from the "not-me"; it also embodies the division between "I, the subject" and "me, the object" of reflection. (Wiener & Rosenwald, 1993, p. 44)

These authors, despite noting the female bias of diary writing, do not pursue the gendered implications of the mirror stage, which, associated particularly with Jacques Lacan (1966) and Julia Kristeva (1974), has a particular significance for gender and the adoption, through language, of patriarchal values, "the law of the father." But the gender implications are explored by Nancy Chodorow (1978), whose revision of Lacan provides a possible explanation for why many more young women than men keep personal diaries. Little boys, she suggests, find it easier to differentiate and separate themselves from the mother (the primary caregiver in a patriarchal society, where the father is often a more distant figure) because their gender identity can clearly be perceived as not-mother. However, girls' primary identification with the mother is less easy to deny or repress, the similarities and continuity between them confusing the act of differentiation, which can cause them to have more problem with separating and emotional autonomy.[19] This seems an area that could well repay further consideration, but it is outside the scope of this study.

The diary-as-mirror, then, can offer the possibility of "creating an impression," not just in the regulation of self-representation but, inversely, in trying out different poses, experimenting, taking communicative risks. It is clear many young writers use their diaries in this way from time to time—many of their owners are conscious that they did this. One of my respondents comments on the "sense of performance" she detects in her diaries; others speak of their "melodramatic exaggeration of emotions," and "exaggerated tone and terminology," of being "provocative," of restructuring personal responses to public events (e.g., Churchill's death) and "telling myself what I wanted to hear." Asked if they were always honest and truthful in their diaries, one fifth of my sample replied no.[20] In needing to find out how it feels to give voice to other feelings, to hear themselves say them, young diarists may sometimes (with no deliberate intention) exaggerate, lie, make outrageous statements, and experiment with terms and expressions and even styles. Where else could they take such risks safely?[21]

This, I think, is one of the most salient and overlooked aspects of diary-writing—not something all diarists do, or have done, but common enough to be significant. This is performing to oneself, not one's better self, maybe one's worse self, a performance they themselves can watch, as it were, in a mirror. At the transitional stage of adolescence—when both one's subjectivity and one's style are unsettled and maybe open to experiment—it must help in the development and strengthening of identity, not only "defining the self by objectivating and then observing it" (Wiener & Rosenwald, 1993, p. 45) but extending and manipulating its boundaries too.

Conclusion:
Diaries as "Evidence"

The suggestions I am making about the self-monitoring and performing functions of diaries, although based only on a small sample of young diarists, may well be applicable to older writers, too. The use made of personal writing is clearly far more varied and complex than commonly assumed, and a number of commentators (as we have seen) attest to its importance in developing identity and in making sense of one's own life, shaping the stories that help define one's experience. The popular confessional myth about diaries as bearers of the truth has tended to dominate the understanding of them and their status in academic cultural study. This tendency is particularly important when, as they often are, personal diaries are used as forensic evidence. Notable in feminist mythology is the case where an entry in a woman's diary, snatched by an estranged partner, was used to "prove" her unsuitability for being awarded custody of their children because she expressed some negative feelings about motherhood and the children.

In murder trials (or the media coverage of them, certainly), diaries are often treated unproblematically, as straightforward reportage of true events and pure feelings (which remain valid until actually contradicted), without adequate consideration of a performative dimension. In 1991, there was the case of Rachel McLean, an Oxford student murdered by her boyfriend and concealed under the floorboards of her house after she taunted him about having other lovers. "Pretty Rachel, 19, bombarded him with love letters which declared her undying love for him. But her diary revealed her secret heart and mind" (Coles, 1991). In her diary, she referred to him as a "sick, childish bastard" and wrote of "the vampire-like way he leeches my affection," sentiments that contradicted his story of a devoted reciprocal love and weakened sympathy for him, as if he were not telling "the truth" about their relationship. In a confused emotional state, she may have used her diary to test out different feelings, or to hear herself saying things she sometimes felt but would not say to him, but these should not be seen as her only authentic emotions. She herself recognized the element of performance in her direct communications with him—"I just wrote John's Valentine card. Full of sweet, pure words. Words that I shovelled out from some fountain inside me. A fountain which has dried and cracked." While we acknowledge spoken hypocrisy, we are loath to accept that there could also be inauthenticity or insincerity in diary entries. Again, when two sisters, Michelle and Lisa Taylor, stood accused in 1992 of murdering Alison Shaughnessy, the wife of Michelle's former lover, Michelle's diary entry that "my dream solution would be for Alison to disappear" was held up in court virtually as a confession to murder, intention rather than fantasy, and contributed to her wrongful conviction (later overturned).[22]

Failure to recognize the potential for performance, fantasy, and inaccuracy in diary-writing could also be risky in the context of Britain's (1992) Children Act, which has allowed greater value and credence to be ascribed to a child's testimony in cases of custodial dispute. It would be dangerous if the myth and mystique of a young girl's diary afforded it special status as material evidence, without reference to the range of possible activities besides record-keeping and self-expression involved.

As a strongly gendered site of personal commitment, involving a small but substantial proportion of young girls at any time, diary-writing as a process of "creating a self" (in one informant's words) deserves closer examination by feminists. Also, most important, we need to recognize its value as a mechanism girls can call on to help in the process of separation and differentiation, when their relationship to gender and identity is psychologically and materially different from boys' (Chodorow, 1978). The burning of diaries after adolescence is a common ritual that uncharitably destroys the very evidence my research wants (they always seem to be irredeemably burnt, never just thrown out). This act of consigning them to flames is perhaps the ultimate act of separation for diarists, and their last great performance.

Notes

1. My occasional use of the generic feminine pronoun is an acknowledgment not just that my informants were women, but that at this age regular diary-writing is predominantly (although not exclusively) a female activity. All names of diarists have been changed.

2. The comics and magazines targeting the 8 to 12 age group (like the monthly Bunty and Debbie and Mandy "libraries" that have been publishing strip-picture stories for decades in Britain in almost unchanged form) run stories of girls in exceptional circumstances—with extreme advantages (talent) or disadvantages (poverty), or a frequent combination of the two, orphanhood.

3. After the entry on Friday 13th July 1962, it jumps unexpectedly to

> October 7th 1962: In the evening Dad went out. I mooched about, and suddenly beheld my beloved diary, in the bottom drawer of his file! I swiped it fast, and immediately settled down and copied the Whole Lot into this. Then on, Oct 10th, I finished copying, and put it back. Now I intend to carry it on. DAY OF TRIUMPH!

4. Catherine Crowther, personal communication. The mother's curiosity featured strongly among my informants. One "suspected" her mother read it; another realized her mother might have done so, as she read her brother's diary; others knew their mothers did because of specific behavior changes or oblique references to things they had kept to themselves, so (as one said) "I had to be much more careful about what I wrote." The parents of another, so worried by what they read when they found her diary, sent her to a Child Guidance Clinic.

5. Jackie's code is merely a shorthand, however, in her interestingly graphic account of period problems—and myths—at 13 in 1971:

Tuesday February 16

Today I started a *, which meant that I can't go swimming with the form tomorrow, so I decided to buy some Lil-lets, but I bought the wrong size, the super, instead of regular, and they wouldn't fit, it was agony! Anyway, Linsey lent me a couple, and I managed, after about an hour and a half's effort, and I at last got it to fit! I'm really pleased now because I can Go tomorrow.

Wednesday February 17

(. . .) Rachel couldn't swim though because her mum had T.B, she can't use Lil-lets until she's at least 16, because of it, which is an awful pity.

6. Girls are still encouraged to write diaries. Although most of my informants remember little response from their families, 10 of the 40 felt their diary-writing was positively encouraged by their parents, as "something pre-adolescent girls were supposed to do," although it was sometimes regarded more as record-keeping than expression of feelings. The encouragement came particularly from their fathers, from whom many received their first diary. Begos (1987) demonstrates how fathers have often been the prime motivator of young diarists (Anne Frank's diary, for instance, was a gift from her father).

7. As models, my respondents recalled Dodie Smith's *I Capture the Castle,* Louise Fitzhugh's *Harriet the Spy,* Susan Coolidge's *What Katy Did,* and Louisa May Alcott's *Little Women*—and even an American comic-strip heroine, Little Lulu, recently reclaimed as a proto-feminist.

8. Boys seem to be encouraged at this age to focus their energies on more extroverted or externalized activities and sport, where there is some measure of display or goal, and boys, much more than girls, tend to make systematic collections of material things like football magazines. (See Begos, 1987, p. 69; Sosin, 1983, p. 94.)

9. For example, Deborah claims she was unable to articulate her feelings of unhappiness and inadequacy throughout puberty but found a locum and a model for self-expression in the discourse of romance. At barely 13, her mundane fact-dominated diary contains an uncharacteristic reflection: "I'm finally making some progress on Jack. I kind of experience all popular love songs." Ten months later she can (but rarely does) write more expansively:

Life is so complicated and my insides are restless and unsatisfied. Parents are no help at all . . . Does Jack like me? Why am I so different than other girls? . . . The grown-up side of me says this is silly to be worrying, but my adalescent self disagrees.

10. The claim that no one cares or there's no one to talk to is common in adolescence. Phrases such as "My mother didn't understand me, I felt a misfit, misunderstood, an outsider, and lonely" occur frequently in the questionnaire replies.

11. Mikhail Bakhtin (1981) centers his theory of language on dialogism and proposes that meaning is essentially argumentative. Likewise, Leith and Myerson (1989) claim the idea of dialogue is central to interpreting texts. The questions "Whose words

are these?" and "To what is this voice replying, to what are these words replying?" provide (they suggest) a valuable way of "interpreting by asking questions and by using the idea of address to focus the questioning constructively" (p. 152).

12. In his introduction to his book (subtitled *People and Their Diaries*), Thomas Mallon (1984) examines his own diaries and raises the question of address in a different way:

> Who is this "you" that's made its way more and more often into these pages in the last few years, this odd pronoun I sometimes find myself talking to like a person at the other end of a letter? Sometimes when I'm writing on the right-hand leaf of a notebook I catch sight of a spelling or grammatical mistake I made on the left one the night before, and I correct it. For "you"?

> I can say without a trace of coyness that I have no idea who "you" is . . . Whether or not they admit it, I think all the purchasers of the five million blank diaries sold each year in this country have a "you" in mind as well. Perhaps in the backs of their minds, or hidden in the subconscious strata, but there. Some people are certain who that pronoun is . . . But most [. . .] would deny that they have anybody in mind but themselves. I have to say that I can no longer believe them. (p. xvi)

13. Mallon's (1984) chapter headings catalog (via their functionaries) the various functions of a diary—Chroniclers, Travelers, Pilgrims (covering self-discovery, comprehending the world, etc.), Creators, Apologists, Confessors, Prisoners. Each category is kept separate, and, despite the range, adolescent girls are only mentioned in the confession chapter (most of which is given over to the sexual confessions of male diarists).

14. One of my respondents took this exercise in constructing identity to extreme lengths: "I was constantly writing stories, and sometimes used the diary in connection with these—i.e., taking on the persona of whatever heroine I was writing about at the time."

15. I have tried to distinguish their sense of the "project" of their writing from the personal conditions that may have spurred them to write. My question was "Who or what did you think it was for? Did you have an audience in mind?" Stylistically, the major difference between the sense of a public or a private audience is in the explanation of background. References that seem "obvious" to the writer become impenetrable even to the same diarist years later, let alone an outsider. Not surprisingly, few entries make much concession to the reader-in-posterity.

16. Jackie had a very specific objective: her diaries became

> a deliberate attempt to put down on paper the agonies rather than the joys of being my age . . . so that, first, I wouldn't forget how I felt at that age if I ever had my own daughters and second, that if my daughters ever doubted I felt like them, there were records to prove it.

17. This sense can, indeed, be inhibiting. Rebecca Hiscock records the words of Emily Shore who, at 18 in 1838, having written a journal for 7 years, admits to feeling "without my being often aware of it, cramped" by the notion that her journal

may some future day when I am in my grave be read by some individual. . . . I have by no means confessed myself in my journal; I have not opened my whole heart; I do not write my feelings and thoughts for the inspection of another—Heaven forbid!—but I imagine the vague fear I have above mentioned has grown into a sort of unconscious habit, instinctively limiting the extent of my confidence in ink and paper. (Hiscock, 1986, p. 156)

18. Valerie Walkerdine (1984) illustrates the difficulties girls face having models of "good girls" to live up to, and so few acceptable ways of dealing with anger and aggression:

In pre-teen girls' comics, the heroines convey an overwhelming sense of loss, which is resolved by its investment into the selfless service of others. . . . Difficult feelings about that loss are dealt with in these comics by locating them in the "bad" characters . . . We are not all "good girls" who are selfless, and who have repressed anger. Some of us are and were angry, jealous, horrid. But bad girls are punished. . . . Being a naughty boy and a naughty girl is a very different matter. (p. 180)

19. A useful discussion of female identity as process, and of the integrated individual in fiction as a male construct, and how this may affect the difference in the forms of male and female writing, can be found in Gardiner (1982).

20. Marge Piercy (1987) recognizes that diaries may not be truthful chronicles but have performance functions too, in her novel *Small Changes.* Her heroine reads through her adolescent diary and

What struck her so sharply . . . was how different, how exactly different her memories were from what she had written in the diary.

She had lied to herself. She had lied by omission and by alteration of the truth, constantly, daily, fervently, with many exclamation points. . . . Things were supposed to be a certain way, and in her diary always she tried to pretend that they were. Never did she admit on paper more than kissing. Everything coarse and painful was censored from her life. Her diary was the record of how it was all supposed to be. (pp. 29-30)

21. The reflections of Michelle Fine and Pat Macpherson (1994) on the quality of the conditions of their ethnographic research with four adolescent girls testify to the rarity of conditions of such collective trust. Yet, they fully recognize that all participants "occluded the 'truth' in cultured ways" and adopted "mobile positionings." The performance dimension in self-presentation is acknowledged in their description of their fieldwork sessions as "an ideological dressing room in which the six of us could undress a little, try things on, exchange, rehearse, trade and critique" (p. 242).

22. Criminals have also, of course, fabricated alibis and emotions in their diaries to deflect suspicion away from them. (See Sosin's footnote, 1983, p. 167, on the Rudgely poisoner.)

References

Bahktin, M. M. (1981). *The dialogic imagination: Four essays* (M. Holquist, Ed.; C. Emerson & M. Holquist, Trans.). Austin: University of Texas Press.

Begos, J. du P. (1987). The diaries of adolescent girls. *Women's Studies International Forum, 10*(1), 69-74.

Blos, P. (1962). *On adolescence: A psychoanalytic interpretation.* New York: Free Press.

Chodorow, N. (1978). *The reproduction of mothering.* Berkeley: University of California Press.

Coles, J. (1991, December 4). Rachel's secret diary of torment. *Daily Express,* pp. 1, 5.

Downey, T. W. (1978). Transitional phenomena in the analysis of early adolescent males. *Psychoanalytic Study of the Child, 33,* 19-46.

Fine, M., & Macpherson, P. (1994). Over dinner: Feminism and adolescent female bodies. In L. Radtke & H. Stam (Eds.), *Power/gender: Social relations in theory and practice* (pp. 219-246). London: Sage.

Gardiner, J. K. (1982). On female identity and writing by women. In E. Abel (Ed.), *Writing and sexual difference* (pp. 177-191). London: Harvester.

Gilbert, P., & Taylor, S. (1991). *Fashioning the feminine: Girls, popular culture, and schooling.* Sydney: Allen & Unwin.

Hiscock, R. (1986). Listening to herself: Women's diaries. In G. McGregor & R. S. White (Eds.), *The art of listening* (pp. 152-168). London: Croom Helm.

Kristeva, J. (1974). *La revolution du langage poetique.* Paris: Tel Quel.

Lacan, J. (1966). *Ecrits.* Paris: Editions du Seuil.

Leith, D., & Myerson, G. (1989). *The power of address: Explorations in rhetoric.* London: Routledge.

Mallon, T. (1984). *A book of one's own: People and their diaries.* London: Picador.

Piercy, M. (1987). *Small changes.* London: Penguin.

Smith, S. (1993). *Subjectivity, identity, and the body: Women's autobiographical practices in the twentieth century.* Bloomington and Indianapolis: Indiana University Press.

Sosin, D. A. (1983). The diary as a transitional object in female adolescent development. *Adolescent Psychiatry, 11,* 92-103.

Walkerdine, V. (1984). Some day my prince will come: Young girls and the preparation for adult sexuality. In A. McRobbie & M. Nava (Eds.), *Gender and generation* (pp. 162-184). London: Macmillan.

Walkerdine, V. (1986). Video replay: Families, films, and fantasies. In V. Burgin, J. Donald, & C. Kaplan (Eds.), *Formations of fantasy.* London: Methuen.

Wiener, W. J., & Rosenwald, G. C. (1993). A moment's monument: The psychology of keeping a diary. In R. Josselson & A. Lieblich (Eds.), *The narrative study of lives* (Vol. 1, pp. 30-58). London and Thousand Oaks: Sage.

Winnicott, D. W. (1953). Transitional objects and transitional phenomena. *International Journal of Psycho-Analysis, 34,* 89-97.

❧ 9 ❧

Ding Ling and
Miss Sophie's Diary

A Psychobiographical Study
of Adolescent Identity Formation

Dora Shu-fang Dien

$\mathcal{D}$ing Ling (1904-1986), a well-known Chinese writer, wrote a short story entitled *Miss Sophie's Diary* (*Shafei nüshi de riji*), which was published in 1928. It brought her fame and notoriety. In Feuerwerker's (1986) words, it is generally seen "as an audacious revelation of a young woman's contradictory sexual feelings," although it can also be read "as a metaphor for, or as a dramatization of, the 'liberated' individual's struggle to define an authentic self" (p. 115). During her years of political persecution in the late 1950s and throughout the 1960s, this controversial work was repeatedly cited as evidence of her bourgeois inclinations because the accusers identified her with the female protagonist, Sophie, who is preoccupied with self-gratification in her fantasy rumination about sexual desires. Ding Ling strenuously denied that Sophie reflected her own persona.

Interestingly, *Madame Bovary* (Flaubert, 1857/1959), which appears to have had a major influence on Ding Ling's development as a writer and as a young woman, also led to the famous trial of the author, Gustave Flaubert, in 1857, "for outrage to public morality and religion"

(LaCapra, 1982, p. 7). However, Flaubert openly told his readers, "*I am Madame Bovary*" (Cowley, 1959, p. vii), and the "hysteria" shared by Emma and Flaubert has been seen as a key link between the content and creation of the novel (Heath, 1992).

Ding Ling's denial that Sophie is herself is quite understandable, given the harassments she had to endure time and again. However, from my study of her life, I have come to see Sophie as a reflection in important ways of the author at that time, although Sophie is unquestionably a fictional character constructed out of various models drawn from literature, of China and of the West, as well as life, which both Feuerwerker (1982) and Li Daxuan (1991) have ably documented in their respective scholarly analyses. Focusing on the period of transition from childhood to adulthood, what is known as adolescence and young adulthood in Western psychological literature, I wish to show how her writing of *Miss Sophie's Diary* helped Ding Ling progress into adulthood, much as B. F. Skinner's writing of *Walden Two* helped him resolve his midlife crisis (Elms, 1994, pp. 85-100).

Psychobiographical Case Studies

In 1982, Runyan noted how the study of life histories had been relegated to a marginal status as the quantitative scientific paradigm gained ascendancy in the social sciences. He saw a steady increase in the amount of work related to the study of lives since the mid 1960s; however, much of it was associated with aggregate studies of the life course. He made a strong case for the value of the individual case study approach. As he points out, psychologists are interested in three levels of generalities in studying human lives, that is, universals, group differences, and particular individuals, and that these levels are not mutually exclusive, each illuminating the others.

Having made an impressive array of such psychobiographical studies, Elms (1994) concludes,

> Psychobiography is not only a way of doing biography; it's a
> way of doing psychology. Most psychologists have been
> trained to stay as far as they can from looking at one whole

human being or one life at a time. But they can learn a lot about psychology by taking such a look, and by doing it over and over again. At the same time, they can bring a great deal to the field of psychobiography. (p. 5)

The present study offers an example from a non-Western culture, which I believe helps to highlight certain common human experiences and psychological processes. The case study approach as delineated by Runyan (1982) and practiced by Elms (1994) focuses on some specific issues during a relatively short and self-contained segment of the individual's life while containing some life-history information as context. As data, it draws upon the best available evidence surrounding the period. In this case, Ding Ling's creative writing helps to reveal the issues involved and the psychological processes of working through these issues.

Identity Formation in
Adolescence and Young Adulthood

Erikson (1963) characterized adolescence as having to resolve the crisis of identity versus role diffusion. Marcia (1966) operationalized the meaning of identity by developing an interview procedure to assess an individual's commitment to a vocation, to an ideological stance, and to a sexual orientation, which has stimulated a great deal of research in the West. The four identity status groups that Marcia (1980) has identified, Foreclosures, Identity Achievements, Moratoriums, and Identity Diffusions, are well-established categories. In a recent study of women's identity formation from college to midlife, Josselson (1996) offers an alternative set of labels, as follows: Guardians, Pathmakers, Searchers, and Drifters. Ding Ling, growing up in a turbulent period of Chinese history, resembles the American college women who grew up in the turbulent late 1960s to early '70s. Much like the Searchers in the United States, Ding Ling was self-reflective, self-conscious, and self-doubting in an intensely emotional manner. She was also idealistic, open to experience, opposed to external authority, and full of conflicts and inner contradictions. The above-mentioned three areas of choice and commitment were precisely what Ding Ling had to deal with during her transition into adulthood. China was undergoing wrenching soul-searching and rapid modernization. More options were opening up for women as gender roles were being redefined, but the concomitant risks were also enormous.

China in Transition

From its disastrous defeat in the Opium Wars of 1839-1842 and 1856-1860 to the fall of the last dynasty in 1911, China was reduced to a semicolonial state. Yet, the new Republic of 1912 was neither able to overcome foreign dominance nor capable of unifying the country divided up by regional warlords. The accumulated humiliation and frustration stimulated a series of reform movements. The May Fourth or New Culture Movement (roughly 1915 to 1922) among Chinese intellectuals was especially important to Ding Ling's development. But the liberation of women started long before then.

At the turn of the century, a reform movement had been under way to promote the idea that to strengthen the nation, China's economic and educational systems must be transformed. As women constituted half of the population, the reformers argued, they must be included in this effort. At the time, foot-binding, which had been practiced among the majority Han Chinese (94% of the population) for centuries, and illiteracy were seen as two ailments that needed to be cured. It was argued that foot-binding weakened women's bodies, thereby hampering their ability to bear physically strong children. Furthermore, lack of knowledge and skills prevented them from earning their own living, and they became an economic burden on society. Finally, because of their ignorance, they did not have the know-how to raise a high-quality next generation. Foot-binding and illiteracy were therefore among the root causes of the nation's poverty and weakness that needed to be eradicated (see Liao, 1989, p. 203). As public schools began to be established for girls, limited higher education was offered to women, primarily for training future teachers in girls' schools.

Ding Ling's mother, who had bound feet, lost her husband at the age of 30 when Ding Ling was 3 years old, but she was able to take advantage of the emerging opportunities to enter a newly opened normal girls' school in 1910. She managed to unbind her feet and became a crusader for women's education as well as for the eradication of foot-binding. She had an enormous influence on Ding Ling's upbringing. About that time, Ibsen's *A Doll's House* was introduced in China, and it encouraged increasing numbers of "emancipated Noras" to leave their traditional families, escaping arranged marriages and parental authority. However, in 1923, a well-known writer, Lu Xun, pointed out that after leaving home, a Chinese Nora would have only three choices: to starve, to "go to bad" (becoming a prostitute), or to return home. He argued that women's economic independence was the only way out of this bleak prospect, but he also knew that women would encounter immense obstacles in this struggle. Ding Ling was one of the "Noras" whom he was addressing.

Ding Ling's Childhood:
A Sketch

Ding Ling was born in 1904, a second daughter to her parents in a wealthy but declining gentry family. Her elder sister died within a year of her birth. When Ding Ling was 3 years old, her father died and her mother was pregnant with another child. Distraught at not having produced a male child to continue her husband's line of descent, Ding Ling's mother contemplated suicide. She was prepared to die in the event that the unborn child turned out to be another girl. She therefore arranged for Ding Ling to be betrothed to her younger brother's son, not an uncommon practice at the time, hoping that her beloved relatives would be kind to her. The newborn would be adopted by another relative who was still childless. Fortunately, the child was a boy.

Ding Ling was keenly aware of the fact that boys were valued much more highly than girls. In fact, her parents treated her much like a boy when she was the only child; she was often clothed in male attire. She tried to please her parents and to prove her worth by being better than boys. When her widowed mother was pursuing her own education to gain economic independence, Ding Ling was left with her younger brother for long stretches of time. She was affectionate to him and protective of him, as he was prone to sickness. She may have suppressed her own feelings of loneliness and resentment, however. Her mother observed that when she was reunited with her children after a separation, her son would joyfully throw himself into her arms whereas Ding Ling watched from a distance with tears in her eyes. Her mother elsewhere commented that Ding Ling was able to hold back her strong feelings, which she saw as her daughter's inner strength.

When Ding Ling was 13, her younger brother died of acute pneumonia. She took up the role of substitute son to comfort her devastated mother. From then on, mother and daughter leaned on each other for emotional support as well as economic survival, and their relationship grew close.

At the age of 15, Ding Ling was swept into the tide of the New Culture Movement, participating in student demonstrations and discussion meetings. In the summer of 1921, she and six older girls enrolled themselves in a previously all-male middle school that had just been made coeducational. The following year, she became a close friend of a girl 2 years her senior. This was Wang Jianghong, a younger sister of a former student of her mother's. Wang was excited about the prospect of going to the cosmopolitan city of Shanghai, a 3-day journey away from home by boat, to attend a progressive girls' school newly started by leftist intellectuals who were members of the newly formed Communist Party. When Ding Ling expressed her wish to go with Wang, her uncle, who was also the father of her fiance, objected. She openly quarreled with him, and with the support of her mother, she annulled her engagement and immediately set out for the big city with Wang.

Disappointed by the quality of the poorly financed fledgling school, 17-year-old Ding and 19-year-old Wang went to another big city, Nanjing (southern capital), to explore other possibilities. Unable to attend school or to obtain gainful employment, the two free spirits managed to survive on their meager pocket money. They audited classes at the university and bought books whenever they could. They were criticized for their demeanor, as they wore trousers most of the time and acted like men, talking and laughing loudly. Before long, they met a young dashing Marxist intellectual named Qu Qiubai who taught at Shanghai University. He persuaded them to return to Shanghai to attend his university. Wang and Qu soon fell passionately in love and got married. Sadly, Wang died of tuberculosis unexpectedly a year later during the time when Ding had returned to her mother's side for the summer vacation.

Distraught by the loss of her dear friend, Ding Ling set out alone for Beijing (northern capital), the cultural and artistic center of the entire nation, to further her education. Arriving too late to gain entrance into the university, she audited classes and took drawing lessons. She found the city bustling with new ideas. Names such as Goethe, Heine, Byron, Keats, Maupassant, Chekhov, Ibsen, Gorky, Tolstoy, and Shakespeare seemed to be on everyone's lips. Among the Chinese writers and thinkers, she especially admired Lu Xun for his humanism, his passionate patriotism, and his captivating lectures and literary works. Lu Xun abandoned his career goal of becoming a medical doctor in order to cure the Chinese of their spiritual ailments through teaching and writing, and his *Diary of a Madman,* published in 1917, served as a model for modern writers in the colloquial language that Ding was to emulate (see Lyell, 1990).

Transition to Adulthood

In traditional China, marriage marked the transition from childhood to adulthood for women (see Levy, 1949). However, in the 1920s, romantic love was a key concern among the avant-garde intellectuals with whom Ding Ling was associating. Women were seeking employment to gain economic independence, and the communist ideology was gaining ground. Ding Ling, therefore, had to deal with the aforementioned three areas of choice and commitment that Marcia and others have studied in the Western context. Her commitment followed the sequence of love and marriage, finding a vocation, and changing from anarchism to communism. We will examine how her writing of *Miss Sophie's Diary* may have helped her work through these issues.

Love and Marriage

A year after Wang's death, Ding was drawn into marrying a man a year younger than she, perhaps out of a sisterly affection for him. Ding met Hu Yepin in 1924, shortly after she reached Beijing. Hu fell in love with her right away. Ding related to him the circumstances of her younger brother's death and the devastation she felt for this loss. The following morning, Hu sent her a box of yellow roses with a note saying, "Respectfully proffered by your new younger brother" (Shen, 1992, pp. 42-44). Ding, however, did not respond to this overture and did not recall this incident in her writings about this period of her life.

Shortly after that, when Ding had gone back to Hunan to visit her mother, who was residing in an old temple residence, Hu suddenly appeared at the door one day, wearing a long plain white robe, his only luggage being a pair of trousers for change. She had only seen this man in Beijing two or three times, Ding thought. Why would such a casual acquaintance travel such a long distance, without a penny to his name, to visit her? The temple housed the school of which Ding's mother was the principal. It was empty of students and other personnel then, as it was during the summer vacation. Mother and daughter welcomed Hu to stay with them for a while, adding spice to their lonely existence.

Ding Ling was feeling depressed about her own lack of accomplishment and unobtrusively observed Hu. As she remembered it, he did not talk much. He often sat quietly, biting his fingernails, and after a while, he would write down some poetry full of sorrow and indignation. From his poetry, Ding surmised that he must have had a hard life and was in need of the warmth of family and hearth, as well as intimate friends with whom to share his pain. She was moved by his sadness but was also impressed by his courage, his passion, his persistence, and his optimism despite his dire poverty and uncertain future.

When Ding and Hu returned to Beijing, they established a common residence in the idyllic pastoral setting of the Western Hills and were seen as husband and wife (young intellectuals in those days rejected the ostentation of wedding ceremonies).

Shen Congwen, a close friend of the young couple at the time, in his *Reminiscences of Ding Ling* (published in 1934 when Ding was believed to have been killed; see Shen, 1992), observed that when he saw Ding for the first time after her marriage, her face exuded the glow of a newlywed. The young couple seemed to be living a rather carefree and romantic life in spite of dire poverty. They often took walks in the fields and would sit quietly somewhere to listen to the sounds of running creeks after the rain, to watch the beautiful sunset, or to gaze into the evening sky full of twinkling stars. Once they lost their way and got stuck in the mud for a while. They simply stood there and took in the poetic charm of the moment—the starry sky, the sounds of dogs barking in the distance, and the cool touch of the settling dew. The young couple did have occasional quarrels, but nothing out of the ordinary, in Shen's view. However, he was puzzled by the fact that Ding would occasionally go to a deserted place to shed tears alone (see Shen, 1992). She seems to have had bouts of mild depression while residing in Beijing before her "marriage" as well, for she would seek solitude in a graveyard in the evenings, and she talked about that period of her life as being lonely and of herself as being depressed because she was unable to find answers. Ding did not reveal her feelings toward Hu in terms of love and desire in any of her writings. Hu evidently continued to pretend to be her younger brother. For example, he wrote on his calling card "Ding Ling's younger brother" when he went to see the renowned author Lu Xun (Song, 1989, p. 39).

Sixty years later, Ding Ling was to reveal to a Japanese friend in a letter that she was not at all prepared for romantic love at the time and did not wish to be constrained by love or marriage; she desired freedom. "But because of circumstances," she had to accompany Hu to Beijing. She had intended to part with him on arrival, but "due to friends' (or a friend's) misunderstanding and objections," in a fit of anger, she said, "All right, we will cohabit!" She stated that they understood each other well and were considerate of each other, but "in reality did not have a husband-wife relationship." This was a Chinese way of saying that they did not have a sexual relationship. The fact that she did not become pregnant until after she had decided to "marry" him also supports this interpretation. In this letter, Ding continued to say that they were completely free and not at all duty-bound toward each other. However, "the situation gradually led into feeling as though it would be necessary to assume some human obligation [meaning sexual urges, I believe]." Realizing what she had envisioned was a mere illusion, in 1928, she decided to make her lifelong commitment with Hu and give up her fantasy (Zong, 1988, p. 45).

It was during the period when they were merely cohabiting in the Western Hills that Ding was reading a great deal of Western literature in Chinese translation, among which were *La Dame aux Camelias,* a Western counterpart of *The Dream of the Red Chamber,* a book that moved her to tears when she was just coming of age, and *Madame Bovary.* Hu did not tell Ding his heart-wrenching life story until 1927, 2 years after they had begun living together, and their feelings for each other deepened as a consequence. It was during this year that Ding started to write *Miss Sophie's Diary.* In the diary, the young protagonist is deeply concerned about the meaning of love and the consequences of sexual involvement. For example, Sophie's friends, a young couple who are very much in love, decide not to live together for fear of having a child. Sophie ponders, because they are kissing and hugging each other, why can't they hold each other's naked body under one quilt, if they are so much in love with each other?

The 20-year-old tubercular Sophie is temperamental, irritable, and full of complaints. She needs her friends and feels lonesome when they do not visit her, but when they come to see her, she often gives them a hard time, by her own admission. She cherishes her good friends, who care for her, yet she manipulates them. She lies to her friends so as to move near the object of her infatuation and away from her faithful boyfriend, causing him considerable grief and consternation. Sophie shifts between contradictory thoughts and emotions, "the see-saw battle of contradictory impulses" as Feuerwerker (1982, p. 29) puts it. The diary ended on a highly ambiguous note. Jenner's translation of Ding (1985) follows:

> Goodness only knows what impact my words had on him. He kissed me again but I evaded him, and his lips landed on my hand.

My mind was made up. My mind was clear enough for
me to insist that he went (sic). He looked rather disgruntled
and wouldn't leave me alone. "Why are you being so stub-
born?" I wondered. He didn't go till 12:30 a.m.

When he'd left I thought about what had just happened.
I wanted to hit my heart hard, with all my strength. Why did
I let a man I despise so much kiss me? I don't love him and I
was jeering at him, but why did I let him embrace me? Really it
was just because he looks like a knight that I feel so low.

In short, I've ruined myself. How in heaven's name am I
going to avenge and make up for all my losses when I'm my
own enemy?

Fortunately my life is mine alone in all the universe to
play with. I've already wasted enough of it. It doesn't seem
to be a matter of any importance that this experience has
thrown me into the very depths of grief.

But I refuse to stay in Beijing, let alone go to the Western
Hills. I've decided to take the train south to waste what's left
of my life where nobody knows me, and as a result my
wounded heart has perked up. I'm laughing wildly with self-
pity.

"Quietly go on living, and quietly die. I'm sorry for you,
Sophie." (p. 64)

Feuerwerker (1982) believes that Sophie is driven to "near suicidal
despair" (p. 43). I disagree with this interpretation. Ding was among
the newly emancipated young women adrift in the intellectual capital
of Beijing in search of a better life, free from the constraints of
arranged marriages. Although life was difficult and expression of
sexuality still highly problematic, these young people had hope and
optimism. Zeng Ke (1994) believes that Sophie is in pursuit of spiritual
purity as well as a beautiful and happy life. She sees elements of
forward-looking optimism, even though there is a great deal of
pessimism in her outlook. Li Daxuan (1991), likewise, perceives
Sophie as actively searching for something better and as having a
resilient and unyielding nature. He sees this as a reflection of Ding
Ling's character, which resembled that of her own resilient and
high-striving mother.

After loathing herself for all those sexual longings leading up to actually kissing his tender lips and yielding to his amorous embraces, Sophie is resolved to end all that silly agony and live out her life elsewhere, with all it might cost her. She takes charge of her own destiny, as she says: "Fortunately my life is mine alone in all the universe to play with." There is hope and renewal. This conclusion was written soon after Ding Ling received high praise for her first published work of fiction, followed by her decision to consummate her marriage. However, she was to continue to work through the question of self and other vis-à-vis her marital relationship.

The *Diary* can also be seen as a vehicle for self-reflection and healing. As mentioned earlier, Ding Ling was given to periodic brooding and weeping when she was residing in Beijing alone and continued to do so after her cohabitation with Hu. This conduct may have stemmed from prolonged grief over her past losses and her own uncertain future. Such ruminations, often accompanied by weeping and other symptoms of depression, are quite common among young females in their early twenties across many cultures (see Nolen-Hoeksema, 1990). Her mother did suffer from debilitating bipolar depression. Speaking through the character Sophie could very well have helped Ding Ling work through her feelings. Pennebaker (1989) has found that "writing about traumatic and/or significant experiences can be considered a form of psychic preservative maintenance" (p. 238).

Li Daxuan (1991) sees the Sophie-type characters in Ding Ling's early works as contemptuous of men in general and of weak ones in particular. He explains this in terms of the anti-male sentiment of the liberation movement, as well as the oppressive male-dominated family Ding and her mother experienced. The weak male character, Wei, depicted in the *Diary,* however, suggests a more personal linkage to her early childhood experiences. Wei's weeping, which so irritates Sophie, may have been rooted in her experience with her younger brother. As we have seen, Ding might have resented her younger brother for robbing her of her mother's exclusive love and attention. Moreover, when her mother was pursuing her own education, Ding was left with this physically fragile boy to care for, when she herself was lonely and in need of her mother's love. She could well have lost her patience when he whined and cried. It is interesting to note that

Wei is 4 years older than Sophie but is referred to as Wei di (younger brother).

Hu told Shen that Ding went crazy with grief when she told him about her deceased younger brother. Ding's cohabiting with Hu, a younger brother figure, was probably a way to redress the guilt she still felt for harboring those hostile feelings toward her younger brother and perhaps in some way causing his death as well, for she said that her brother caught the cold that developed into fatal pneumonia from her. If this was the case, the nature of their love would have to be clarified before Ding could actually marry him, for she would have been tempted to run away from that substitute brother as husband, given our aversion to marrying our own sibling (Wolf, 1995). The man as a steady companion and the one who is an object of her sexual desire would need to be fused. Even though Sophie has resolved to reject her object of sexual desire, her relationship with Wei is left hanging. In the light of Ding's subsequent marriages, I believe she continued to work through this issue. Her love for Hu grew, especially after he had changed into a self-confident and dedicated Communist, energetic and forward-looking. Sadly, he was executed in February 1931, shortly after the birth of their child.

That April, Ding left her baby with her mother in Hunan and returned to Shanghai to eke out a living on her own. She then started to write *Sophie's Diary II* (*Shafei riji dierbu*). This unfinished manuscript contains only two entries, dated May 4th and May 5th, which I believe were the actual dates. This project could well have served as a mechanism for working through the grieving process as well. What is remarkable to me is that even though Ding was speaking through the voice of Sophie, she was obviously describing her own experiences. She seemed to have abandoned the project, however, and wrote her heart-wrenching piece, *From Night till Daybreak* (*Cong yewan dao tianliang*), instead, for it was published on May 15. It appears that the rupture in her life had been so great that it was too difficult for her to continue with the persona of Sophie for self-expression. Instead, she referred to herself as simply "she."

Her second husband, Feng Da, was 3 years younger than she. He quietly entered her life when she was extremely lonesome in Shanghai. According to Ding's own account, he simply followed her around, much like a younger brother. He would help her cook and do household chores, and when it was time to eat, he would simply sit down to eat with her. It was a comfortable companionship. They went to bed together just as naturally but without passion on Ding's part. Their relationship was made all the more ambiguous because they were soon arrested and together put under house arrest by Chiang Kaishek's henchmen for 3 years in a sort of forced cohabitation. They stayed together under duress until she escaped to Yan'an, the Communist capital (see Ding, 1989). Like Hu, Feng seemed to be a weak character with an ambiguous status in society. His health was fragile, too, as he had tuberculosis. Again, she acted very much like an elder sister to him.

The third husband, Chen Ming, claims that Ding fell in love with him at first sight when he appeared on stage as Pavel in Gorky's play, *Mother*. It is significant to note that this character is a 24-year-old young man, a cripple, dominated by his mother and despised by his wife. He is someone to be pitied. Chen Ming himself was then a good-looking 22-year-old man, slender and delicate in appearance. He evidently elicited Ding's sisterly affection, for he talks about her overprotectiveness. Ding, by then a mature and seasoned woman of 34, was enjoying good health, power, and prestige in the general atmosphere of youthful exuberance in the Communist capital so glowingly described by Edgar Snow (1968) in his celebrated *Red Star Over China*. Having been pampered by two older sisters before he left home at the tender age of 10, Chen probably welcomed Ding's sisterly attention, even though, being an underling, he was flattered by her solicitude and felt somewhat ill at ease. Nonetheless, this relationship blossomed into a marriage full of passion and mutual devotion, spanning 44 years, until the end of her life in 1986. Her last words whispered to him were, "Kiss me!"

Finding a Vocation

At the time of writing the *Diary*, the 23-year-old Ding Ling had already gained a large measure of independence in breaking away from the control of her extended family, including the annulment of the engagement made in her infancy and getting married by first cohabiting with a man of her choice and informing her mother only after the fact. However, economically, she was still dependent on her mother's allowance, as her partner did not have a stable occupation. What her mother could give her was not adequate for maintaining a joint household, and so Ding set out to search for possible employment. She tried to be a governess, a private secretary, and an actress, all traditional women's occupations, without satisfaction. Only after she was disgusted by the treatment of women in the acting world did she again fall back on her gender-neutral although predominantly male writing skills. However, these experiences enabled her to write her first successful work of fiction, *Mengke,* published in December 1927. The subsequent success of *Miss Sophie's Diary* set her securely onto the path of becoming an accomplished writer with a good income.

From Anarchism to Communism

In *Ding Ling yanjiu wushinian* (Fifty Years of Ding Ling Research) published in 1990, Yuan Liangjun is puzzled by the fact that Ding Ling was in close contact with key Communist intellectuals very early on, but it took her 10 years to become an adherent of communism, which he thinks is very unusual.

Ding was a product of the New Culture Movement. She was a self-conscious rebel against the old society, in particular, the beliefs and practices that limited the lives of women. Being a naive anarchist, she resisted joining the Communist Party. When her husband was becoming an enthusiastic believer in the communist ideology, it was already very dangerous to be a member of the Communist Party, which had been driven underground by the ruling Nationalist Party after 1927. Besides, she had been successful in writing the sort of fiction that deals primarily with personal issues of romantic love, sexuality, marriage, and work, rather than societal issues of poverty, exploitation, class struggle, and so on. She joined the Communist Party after her husband was executed, along with 22 other Communists, in February 1931, shortly after the birth of their child. However, her true commitment to the communist ideology as practiced by the Chinese

Communist Party was to take a much longer time to develop, which is the focus of my analysis in a book-length manuscript.

Summary and Conclusion

While constructing Sophie out of models from fiction and real life, a unique and complex character, with whom millions of her contemporaries could identify, Ding Ling was fashioning her own self-identity, making commitments in at least two of the three major areas commonly found during the transition from childhood into adulthood. We see how she moved from cohabiting with a man she was not passionately in love with and evidently did not have sexual relations with into a marital relationship, after exploring the meaning of love and sexuality through reading and writing. This exercise also helped her shape her vocational direction. The success of *Miss Sophie's Diary* launched her into a brilliant writing career. The power of writing as a mechanism for the resolution of an identity crisis cannot be underestimated. Erikson applied his theory across two very different cultures in his seminal works, *Gandhi's Truth* (1969) and *Young Man Luther* (1958). Although Erikson's original formulation was based solely on the life course of men, Josselson (1996) has demonstrated well the applicability of his notion of identity to women by recognizing the fundamentally relational nature of their identity as well as their more subtle interior restructuring. The present case study bears a remarkable resemblance to the "Searchers" in her sample and serves to further illustrate the cross-cultural applicability of such psychological constructs, where the sociocultural context is well understood and can be specified.

References

Cowley, M. (1959). Introduction. In G. Flaubert, *Madame Bovary* (L. Bair, Trans.). New York: Bantam Books.

Ding, L. (1985). *Miss Sophie's diary and other stories* (W. J. F. Jenner, Trans.). Beijing: Panda Books.

Ding, L. (1988). *Wo zai aiqingzhong shengzhang.* Guilin: Lijiang chubanshe.

Elms, A. C. (1994). *Uncovering lives: The uneasy alliance of biography and psychology.* New York: Oxford University Press.

Erikson, E. H. (1958). *Young man Luther.* New York: Norton.

Erikson, E. H. (1963). *Childhood and society.* New York: Norton.

Erikson, E. H. (1969). *Gandhi's truth.* New York: Norton.

Feuerwerker, Y. M. (1982). *Ding Ling's fiction: Ideology and narrative in modern Chinese literature.* Cambridge, MA: Harvard University Press.

Feuerwerker, Y. M. (1986). Book review: *Miss Sophie's diary and other stories. CLEAR, 8*(1 & 2), 115-116.

Flaubert, G. (1959). *Madame Bovary* (L. Bair, Trans.). New York: Bantam. (Original work published 1857)

Heath S. (1992). *Gustave Flaubert: "Madame Bovary."* Cambridge, UK: Cambridge University Press.

Josselson, R. (1996). *Revising herself: The story of women's identity from college to midlife.* New York: Oxford University Press.

LaCapra D. (1982). *Madame Bovary on trial.* Ithaca, NY: Cornell University Press.

Levy, M. J., Jr. (1949). *The family revolution in modern China.* Cambridge, MA: Harvard University Press.

Li, D. (1991). *Ding Ling yu Shafei xilie xingxiang.* Changsha: Hunan wenyi chubanshe.

Liao, X. (1989). Qingmo nüxue zai xuezhisheng di yanjin ji nüzi xiaoxue jiaoyu di fazhan: 1897-1911. In Y. Li & Y. Zhang (Eds.), *Zhongguo funu" shilun wenji* (Vol. 2, pp. 203- 255). Taipei, Taiwan, ROC: Shangwu yinshuguan.

Lyell, W. A. (Trans.). (1990). *Lu Xun: Diary of a madman and other stories.* Honolulu: University of Hawaii Press.

Marcia, J. E. (1966). Development and validation of ego-identity status. *Journal of Personality and Social Psychology, 3,* 551-558.

Marcia J. E. (1980). Identity in adolescence. In J. Adelson (Ed.), *Handbook of adolescent psychology.* New York: John Wiley.

Nolen-Hoeksema, S. (1990). *Sex differences in depression.* Stanford, CA: Stanford University Press.

Pennebaker, J. W. (1989). Confession, inhibition, and desire. *Advances in Experimental Social Psychology, 22,* 211-244.

Runyan, W. M. (1982). *Life histories and psychobiography: Explorations in theory and method.* New York: Oxford University Press.

Shen, C. (1992). Ji Ding Ling: Reminiscences of Ding Ling, 1934. In Y. Liu et al. (Eds.), *Shen Congwen bieji.* Changsha: Yuelu Shushe.

Snow, E. (1968). *Red star over China.* New York: Grove.

Song, J. (1989). *Ding Ling pingzhuan.* Xian: Shaanxi renmin chubanshe.

Wolf, A. P. (1995). *Sexual attraction and childhood association: A Chinese brief for Edward Westermarck.* Stanford, CA: Stanford University Press.

Yuan, L. (1990). *Ding Ling yanjiu wushinian.* Tianjin: Jiaoyu chubanshe.

Zeng, K. (1994). Tan Ding Ling xiaoshuo nuxing renwu suozao. In *Zhongguo xiandang-dai wenxue yike yaoyan di juxing* (Proceedings of the International Symposium on the Literary Works of Ding Ling, pp. 130-137). Changsha: Hunan wenyi chubanshe.

Zong, C. (1988). *Fengyu renshen: Ding Ling zhuan.* Beijing: Zhongguo wenlian chuban gongsi.

❦   10   ❦

Love Stories in
Sexual Autobiographies

Elina Haavio-Mannila
J. P. Roos

*T*he experience of love is one of the most universal aspects of human life. With rare exceptions, some form of love is familiar to everybody. On the other hand, we assume that love experiences vary by gender, age, and generation. In this chapter, we shall discuss love experiences, that is, feelings of love and attraction using sexual life histories written by Finnish men and women (and also survey data). In the autobiographies, episodes of love are described almost as vividly when they happened 60 years earlier as when they took place yesterday. Even though the memories are influenced by the course of time, the material provides an excellent background for studying differences between sexual generations. Our main goal, however, is to develop a typology of love stories.

Finns, particularly men, rarely use the world *love*. In Finnish sexual autobiographies, there are few references to love. In some stories, love is mentioned infrequently or not at all. Only in exceptional cases is love a recurrent theme. Nevertheless, sexual autobiographies reveal subtle aspects of love that are difficult to capture by survey methods. When autobiographies and survey material are used together, as is done here, love discourses and processes of different genders and generations can be described and understood.

In the first part of this chapter, we describe love as a wonderful emotion giving meaning and enjoyment to life. Love in sexual relationships is analyzed on the basis of the rich material of the sexual life histories. Then, love as a process, a developmental cycle is analyzed. In the first section, life stories have been divided into fragments according to themes. In the second section, several types of life stories are distinguished, and passages of whole narratives are presented.

Concepts of Love

The sociology of emotion is a growing field in our discipline. Love and hate are probably the strongest human feelings. Love has been classified and defined in many ways. A distinction has often been made between *passionate* and *companionate* love. Elaine Hatfield and Richard L. Rapson (1993) define passionate love as a state of intense longing for union with another. It is

> a complex functional whole including appraisals or appreciations, subjective feelings, expressions, patterned physiological processes, action tendencies, and instrumental behaviours. Reciprocated love (union with the other) is associated with fulfilment and ecstasy. Unrequited love (separation) is associated with emptiness, anxiety, or despair. (1993, p. 67; 1996, p. 3)

Sex researchers tend to use the terms passionate love and *sexual desire* almost interchangeably, but it is more accurate to define sexual desire as "a longing for *sexual* union" (Hatfield & Rapson, 1996, p. 3). Passionate love has also been called *falling in love* (Alberoni, 1983), *romantic love* (Jallinoja, 1984), and *limerence* (Tennov, 1989).

Companionate love, which is sometimes also called true or marital love, is a warm, less intensive emotion than passionate love. It combines feelings of deep attachment, commitment, and intimacy. It is the affection and tenderness people feel for those with whom their lives are deeply entwined. In the same way as passionate love, companionate love includes appreciations, feelings, expressions, physiological processes, action tendencies, and instrumental behaviours (Hatfield & Rapson, 1996).

In Western societies today, life is flexible and adaptable; one can choose to live with someone else in a wide variety of ways. The romantic love complex has helped to carve a way to the formation of *pure relationships* in the domain of sexuality. Pure relationships, that is, intimate and demanding relationships between lovers or between very close friends, are characterized by Anthony Giddens (1991) as follows:

> In contrast to close personal ties in traditional contexts, the pure relationship is not anchored in external conditions of social or economic life—it is, as it were, free floating. . . . (Earlier) marriage was a contract, often initiated by parents or relatives rather than by the marital partners themselves. The contract was usually strongly influenced by economic considerations, and formed part of wider economic networks and transactions. . . . The tendency is towards the eradication of these pre-existing external involvements—a phenomena originally accompanied by the rise of romantic love as a basic motive for marriage. Marriage becomes more and more a relationship initiated for, and kept going for as long as it delivers emotional satisfaction to be derived from close contact with another. Other traits—even such seemingly fundamental ones as having children—tend to become sources of "inertial drag" on possible separation, rather than anchoring features of the relationship. (p. 89)

According to Giddens (1992, p. 27) the creation of *plastic sexuality*, severed from its age-old integration with reproduction, kinship, and the generations, was the precondition of the sexual revolution of the past several decades. Effective contraception signaled a deep transition in personal life. Sexuality became malleable, open to being shaped in diverse ways, and a potential "property" of the individual.

Separation of sexuality from reproduction and marriage has also meant separation of sexuality and love. According to a survey conducted in 1971 in Finland (Sievers, Koskelainen, & Leppo, 1974), three fourths of people ages 18 to 54 years agreed with the statement "sexual intercourse without love is wrong" whereas 20 years later, in 1992, only every other person thought so (Kontula, Haavio-Mannila, & Suoknuuti, 1994, pp. 86-87). In the Finnish sexual autobiographies (Kontula & Haavio-Mannila, 1995a, 1997), there is a lot of discussion about the relationship between love and sexual intercourse. The narrators are mostly of the opinion that a combination of emotional and physical love is an ideal state of affairs. Nevertheless, most of them admit that it is not always possible to achieve this.

Autobiographies and Survey Data

Autobiographies are cultural artifacts *par excellence*. They are influenced by the social and cultural norms and sanctions prevailing at the time of their writing. Also, the lives described in them are a result of various social and cultural factors and historical events. The present consensus seems to be that there is no life "as such," or life separate from its representations. We can thus speak of "overdetermination," so that it is not possible to say what really determines the presence of a given event in the life story. On the other hand, we may be sure that culturally significant valuations, relationships, and life events are present and highly visible in the texts and will not be lost in an anonymous mass of data.

Life stories are most fruitful when studying mentalities, basic views about life, social relationships, and expressions of emotions. They reveal how different historical events have affected people's lives and what kinds of social and cultural developments there have been. The more genuine or culturally unprocessed the qualitative data is, the better. A combination of detailed knowledge of the life of a relatively small number of individuals and quantifiable data on many people provides ideal possibilities for understanding and explaining the social world.

The purpose of this article is to study love in sexual autobiographies and survey data. What does love mean to people? What are their love experiences? How and in what connections do people use the word *love* in their sexual life histories? What are the typical love stories, and how does love develop as a process? Do love stories differ according to gender, age, and sexual generation?

The data for this article were gathered as part of the Finsex project, which consisted of three parts: (a) a national interview study representing the population ages 18 to 74, conducted in 1992 (Kontula & Haavio-Mannila, 1995b); (b) a content analysis of sex articles and pictures in the popular press in 1961, 1971, 1981, and 1991 (Kontula & Kosonen, 1994); and (c) a collection of sexual autobiographies in 1992 (Kontula & Haavio-Mannila, 1995a).

Finland is the only country in the world where the sexual life of representative samples of the adult population has consistently been followed over time. Because one of the most important objectives of the Finsex survey in 1992 was to make comparisons with the similar 1971 survey (Sievers et al., 1974), the method chosen was as close as possible to the one used in 1971, that is, a two-stage, face-to-face interview/self-administered questionnaire survey, to be implemented primarily in the home of the respondent.

One of the two questionnaires used in the survey was filled out by the interviewers, and the other by the respondents. The interviewer did not see the answers. The questionnaires were enclosed in envelopes for mailing to the research team. One third of the questions were exactly the same as those asked in the 1971 study. There were 207 questions and 404 variables. The sample for the study was drawn at random from the central population register. It was nationally representative of the population in the age bracket 18 to 74, excluding people permanently living in institutions.

The collecting of the data was conducted by 164 interviewers of Statistics Finland. In 1971, the interviews had been done by the public health nurses and midwives. The time spent on the interview and on filling out the questionnaire was 78 minutes, slightly less than in 1971.

In 1992, there were 2,250 responses to the survey, and the response rate was 75.9%, 77.7% for women and 74.2% for men. The most responsive age group were those under 25 (83.3%) and the least responsive (71.8%) those ages 35 to 44. In 1971, 2,188 people ages 18 to 54 responded to the survey, and the response rate was as high as 92.9%. The response rate in 1992 did not deviate from surveys made that year by Statistics Finland concerning the spending of leisure time and elections.

The decline of the response rate did not cause any systematic self-selection of the respondents. The responses concerning first sexual experiences were very much in agreement in the different age cohorts in 1992 and in 1971. For example, the 50-year-old people recalled and reported their first sexual experiences in 1992 in the same way as the 30-year-old people in 1971.

The autobiographical data were gathered through a competition published in newspapers and popular magazines. Of the 175 sexual life stories submitted, 166 could be used in the analysis.

In the guidelines of the competition, respondents were asked to write about the small things as well as the major changes in their sexual lives. They were encouraged to describe events, situations, feelings, and hopes they had experienced in a personal and realistic way. Certain phases in sexual life were listed in the leaflet: playing doctor and patient in childhood, growing up with problems in adolescence, dating and having sexual experiences for the first time, establishing a long-term relationship or contracting a marriage, having sexual adventures, establishing new relationships, paying or getting paid for love, having difficulties in achieving sexual gratification, facing the effects of aging, and so on. They were also encouraged to assess their lives: What are the central questions and the most important experiences relating to sexuality? What is it that sexuality has given you at its best?

The Finnish sexual life stories refer to emotions and events that have taken place at different stages of the life course: in youth, adulthood, and old age, and they have been written by people of different ages. This creates some methodological problems. Are the experiences of first love reported by young and old people comparable? Are people's memories of their emotions of love in youth different from their stories of feelings of love today? Descriptions of recent love experiences are probably more "accurate" than reminiscences from past decades. Only very strong upsurges of past emotion stay clearly in mind. Experiences of particularly passionate love are often very strong. Thus, we suppose that they have not been forgotten or become falsified with the course of time. Yet, it has also been observed that negative events and feelings are remembered better than positive ones (Roos, 1994).

Experiences of love were studied in three age groups/generations that were differentiated on the basis of sexual norms and practices prevailing at the time of their sexual initiation, that is, between 10 and 30 years of age:

1. *The generation of sexual repression* (or inhibition) born 1917 to 1936. In the youth of this generation, sexual matters were taboo and not to be discussed openly in front of others, especially children. As safe contraception techniques had not yet been developed, fear of pregnancy limited sexual intercourse. Double moral standards gave more sexual freedom to men than to most women; thus, there was a wide gender gap in sexual behavior.

2. *The generation of the sexual revolution* born 1937 to 1956. New contraceptive methods made it possible to engage in sexual relations without fear of pregnancy. Some feminists were critical of the pressure for casual sex and felt themselves exploited against their will. In general, however, sexual liberation was part of the gender equality and other radical social movements in the 1960s and 1970s.

3. *The generation of sexual ambivalence* (or gender equality) born 1957 to 1973. Our findings (Haavio-Mannila et al., 1996; Kontula & Haavio-Mannila, 1995a, 1995b) and American and Russian studies (Golod, personal communication, October, 20, 1994; Laumann, Gagnon, Michael, & Michaels, 1994) as well as University of Helsinki student surveys (Järvinen & Rikama-Alhainen, 1994) indicate that sexual attitudes and behavior of young people are not very coherent. The AIDS epidemic and efficient sex education in schools have made young people aware of the risks of casual and unprotected sexual activity. Other aspects to be taken into consideration in studying the youngest generation are individualization and gender equalization processes. They imply that one cannot coerce one's partner into coitus; both parties are supposed to have a genuine desire for it, as well as a right to initiate and refuse sexual contact.

In the following, the autobiographical love stories are analyzed on the basis of gender and age of the author. Mary Gergen (1992) notes that our identities are first defined by gender. We are recognized as "boy" or "girl" in our first moment of life. As personal identities are

TABLE 10.1 Absolute Numbers of Survey Respondents and Authors of Sexual
              Autobiographies in Finland in 1992

Sexual Generation	Survey Data		Sexual Life Stories	
	Men	Women	Men	Women
Ambivalence	409 (213)[a]	397 (241)	11	45
Revolution	469 (387)	441 (341)	24	47
Repression	226 (174)	306 (173)	18	20
Total	1,104 (774)	1,144 (755)	53	112

a. The numbers of married or cohabiting respondents to the survey are shown in parentheses.

always gendered, then so must life stories be. Gergen's concern is with the gendered nature of life stories. "What are manstories and woman-stories? How do they differ? And what difference do these differences make?" (p. 129.) To answer these questions, sexual autobiographies written by men and women will be compared.

The survey respondents and the people who wrote their sexual autobiographies are distributed by gender and generation as shown in Table 10.1. The autobiographers do not demographically deviate from the Finnish adult population as much as one would expect when using a self-selected sample. However, older men and educated, young, and non-cohabiting women are overrepresented. The frequency of sexual intercourse of the autobiographers is about the same as that of the survey respondents. The women had more sexual partners, the men had started their sexual life later, both genders had more homosexual experiences, and the men had more often had sex with prostitutes than was the case among the survey respondents.

The main purpose of this chapter is to illustrate different forms of love discourse in the three generations of men and women. A survey with structured questions and response alternatives gives information on the distribution of emotions and events in the population; the same emotions and events are spontaneously described and reflected on in the life stories. In this chapter, the use of the survey data is secondary to the analysis of the life stories. Survey results are presented to avoid criticism about a lack of statistical representativeness, as was the case of the Kinsey and Hite reports on sexual behavior (Hite, 1979, 1981;

Kinsey, Pomeroy, & Martin, 1948; Kinsey, Pomeroy, Martin, & Gebhard, 1953) in which self-selected samples also were used.

The first part of our analysis is based on those excerpts of the sexual life stories in which the Finnish word for love, *rakkaus,* was used. The passages were coded by using the computer software program "Word Perfect Index" developed by Pekka Sulkunen, Jukka Törrönen, Jussi Silvonen, Seppo Roponen, and Olli Kekäläinen at the University of Helsinki. The autobiographers are identified in parentheses by giving their running number in our files, gender (M = men, W = women), and age in the year 1992. For example, (45M61) means that the writer is number 45 in our files, a man, and 61 years old. All personal names mentioned in the fragments are pseudonyms.

Passionate Love

Falling in love is an almost universal life experience in Finland. Only 1% of Finns ages 18 to 74 have never fallen in love. The myth of only one great love during a lifetime applies to a minority of people: According to the survey data, 20% of men and 30% of women have fallen in love with only one person during their lifetime. The lifelong love pattern is more common in the generation of sexual repression (men 29% and women 35%) than in the younger generations. About half of the respondents have had two or three objects of love. About 28% of the men and 13% of the women have fallen in love with at least four people in their lives. The survey sample reported having fallen in love, on the average, with three people during their lifetime, the autobiographers with only two. In both the survey interviews and the sexual autobiographies, women reported fewer infatuations (in the interviews, on the average 2.7, and in the life stories, 2.0) than men did (3.9 and 2.2, respectively). The number of people one has fallen in love with during a lifetime is highest in the middle-aged group (Table 10.2).

One third of the autobiographers described feelings of love in their stories. Middle-aged women most often mentioned the word love in their stories when writing their sexual life histories.

TABLE 10.2 Proportion of Surveyed Men and Women Who Love and Are Loved by Somebody, and the Average Number of Lifetime Loves According to Sexual Generation in Finland in 1992

Sexual Generation	% Feels Love		% Receives Love		Average Number of People One Has Fallen in Love With	
	Men	Women	Men	Women	Men	Women
Ambivalence	72	82	69	81	3.2	2.3
Revolution	83	77	74	76	3.5	2.5
Repression	70	50	50	44	2.9	2.2
Total	76	72	67	69	3.9	2.7

We shall next discuss stories of passionate love by gender and generation starting from men of the oldest generation. Then, we turn to stories on companionate love.

Men's Stories of Passionate Love

The stories of passionate love written by male autobiographers belonging to the generation of sexual repression mostly refer to falling in love relatively late in life. Love at an early age seems to be less clearly recalled than more recent emotions. The feeling of passionate love at an advanced age may be extraordinarily intense because it often is a forbidden and hidden emotion that causes feelings of shame and guilt as it threatens important social bonds, particularly marital relations (cf. Scheff, 1990).

An example of falling in love is the story of an older married man who tells about his sudden infatuation at the age of 52 years. He is married to a chronically ill woman. The object of his love is the wife of an alcoholic.

> We just looked at each other. We immediately wanted to kiss each other. We accepted the face, the body and the smile of each other and already longed for the gleam of the eyes of the other. . . . We were happy when dancing in the crowded

> hall among other people. Oh, those tender glances and hugs.
> I, an old man, shivered, and her closeness made my legs
> weak. (123M64)

This love affair has continued for 12 years as a parallel (extramarital) semiplatonic relationship. The lovers meet secretly in connection with the man's jogging. The narrator lives happily enjoying the love of his two women. He waits for the few moments when his wife wants to make love with him. He has not yet had sexual intercourse with the other woman, even though he feels a strong sexual desire for her; the longing for sexual union is reciprocated by his beloved.

The love stories of older men also include feelings of guilt and shame, as well as health problems caused by conflicting pressures from their wives and other women. Heartache and suffering are reported by several men, particularly when the passionate attraction to a mistress has not led to a stable relationship with her. The deprivation felt by men who stay in poor matrimonial unions makes affairs very attractive. Obstacles against parallel relations strengthen the passion. If the man does not leave his wife, he may regret that he did not get a divorce, even though he was deeply in love with another woman. One such man (68M50) recommends that one should get a divorce if "a moderate happiness is to be expected."

Falling in love with another woman while married has led many men of the generation of sexual revolution into physical infidelity. Sexual autobiographies written by middle-aged married men include numerous vivid descriptions of episodes of sexual intercourse with a new object of love. The testimony of the life stories is supported by survey results, which show that 58% of all Finnish middle-aged men, 48% of younger men, and 49% of older men have had extra sexual relationships during a steady relationship. The generation of sexual revolution has thus been particularly inclined to break the bonds of marital faithfulness. Infidelity is, in most cases, not followed by a divorce: only 18% of Finnish married and cohabiting men have been married or cohabiting more than once.

Older and middle-aged male autobiographers almost exclusively describe passionate love in extramarital relationships. They do not mention the word love in connection with their relationship with their wives. An example of the association between passionate love and parallel sexual relationships is the story of the above-cited middle-aged man (68M50). He openly defends his casual and paid sexual relationships: "I do not know how I could have endured my life without these." But when an object of his love made a marriage proposal, he turned back.

Falling in love with a married woman may be very painful, as the following story of a man of the *ambivalent sexual generation* shows. This man describes his feelings of love toward his coworker:

> I noticed that I tremendously enjoyed your company. It was so easy to talk to you even about difficult things. You listened. Obviously you felt the same kinds of emotions toward me. Our relationship was exceptionally equal. First after that deeper development of friendship my feelings started to include a strong interest toward your body, too. Our acquaintance developed into friendship, friendship into affection, and finally into love. . . . I do not accuse you for flirting. But what did you seek when you came too close? I was like in fire. I would have liked to touch and fondle you. I remember the situation when we sat opposite each other, talked nonsense, and looked seriously into each other's eyes, right to the bottom. . . . I cannot get you out of my mind. When I wake early in the morning in solitude and silence, your picture floats before my eyes. I wonder what you are doing at the moment. Do you sleep, make love with your husband, or lie awake? Do you perhaps think of me? (38M29)

In this asymmetrical love relationship, the man's passion was expressed in sexual fantasies and masturbation.

Women's Stories of Passionate Love

Like older and middle-aged men, women of the generation of sexual repression report that the *context* of passionate love is mostly outside the institution of marriage. Although some of their love affairs took place at an early stage in their lives, the strong emotion of those affairs has not faded with the passing of the time.

Unlike the men, the older women autobiographers are often not married, although the partner is. This is because of greater marital fidelity among women. During any present or previous steady relationship, only 20% of the oldest, 34% of the middle-aged, and 33% of the youngest women have had extra sexual relationships (cf. the much higher proportions for men mentioned above).

One older woman now in a stable relationship has had several consecutive good sexual relationships. At the age of 31, she became infatuated with a married man. The falling in love took place literally in no time at all.

> The man had just turned 50, I was 19 years younger. Our friends joked about the mid-life crisis but we did not let it disturb us. I was in the clouds. We met in all possible and impossible places, and we rushed to get to bed. . . . We had 15 happy years together. During that time I had no desire to even look at anybody else. (76W62)

Another older woman (25W57) fell in love with her sister's husband when she was 17 years old. The infatuation took place while the sister was in the hospital giving birth to a baby. The autobiographer was deeply in love with her brother-in-law until his death at the age of 50. She loved him so much that she did not dare to tell him that she never had an orgasm with him; she was afraid that he would stop loving her and having sex with her. It was enough to be together with him. She had orgasms in sleep when dreaming about him. The lovers exchanged secret letters and "in those letters tender words were not spared." The same woman later fell in love with another married man, who had five children. They worked together far from the locality where his family lived. The man visited his wife once every 2 weeks, but at the work site "he gave enough love and tenderness for every hour in my days." This relationship lasted for 10 years. The narrator could be near the man she loved, and she felt really good in spite of some gnawing guilt feelings.

One elderly woman tells about her long-lasting affair with a married man, whose 10-years-older religious wife does not use contraceptives. Thus, the man has to rely on coitus interruptus. He has potency problems with his wife. In the extramarital relationship, he has no such problems. "Our love life grew really good with the passing of the years" (140W55).

The stories of passionate love by older female autobiographers are vivid both whether or not the infatuation has led to a permanent relationship. Many older women have lived through several consecutive or parallel love relationships, which they remember with great joy and pleasure.

Women of the generation of sexual revolution strongly believe in love. "Love includes everything worth living for. Every human being needs love in order to live well" (134W49). The positive side effects of warm affection on physical appearance are reported by several women. "I still believe that love is beautiful irrespective of age. It makes a human being beautiful both from inside and outside. The eyes get a miraculous glow and sparkle, it tickles continuously inside" (37W40).

Some middle-aged women have found a new love later in life. A divorced woman enthusiastically describes her recent infatuation with a bachelor:

> I only would like to be with him and fondle him and fuck.
> His tender touches, our mutual need for closeness, passion-
> ate tongue kisses, loving glances. . . . I thought that I had
> lost the beautiful and pure love, but I have found it by
> chance, nearer my sphere of life than I would have believed.
> Now I am happy and, like a young fool, madly in love.
> (37W40)

Passionate love at the age of 40 almost "took the life of" a woman (49W48). "I loved him both mentally and physically so that my soul ached. Perhaps one should not give one's spiritual self to another person so totally." The affair was too wonderful to last for more than 5 years; her recovery from the experience of being abandoned was very painful.

A woman who has had very many lovers thinks that a woman should simultaneously have several men in her life,

> one as an object of love, one as a partner in philosophizing, and one for making love. A single man cannot do all of this. . . . If I find a man who has two of these characteristics, the relationship can become a long one. (20W47)

In a case in which both partners were married to someone else, infatuation took place "like a flash" (136W49). Feelings of passionate love at the beginning of an extramarital relationship are vividly described in this narrative by another woman:

> We went to the dance floor—I looked into his eyes and we both were "sold." A tall man—he laid his hand on my waist and trembled. What happened to us? . . . I do not even remember if we danced one, two or many dances. . . . I had not known this man for more than a couple of hours, and he had confused my feelings. Not in a bad way but by kindling a brand new marvelous feeling in me! . . . I know that I have now fallen in love—in a moment. Can it be? . . . I hope that every mortal being would feel this kind of emotion at least once in life. I do not intend to go to bed with him and spoil all this beautiful. . . . The thought of the next week frightens and charms me at the same time. Can we control the fire inside us, or does it rule over us? Since I returned from that trip, I have woken up early in the mornings and fled in my thoughts back to those events! It is so easy to work and the world is more beautiful than before. (170W51)

Some women tell about almost incredible extramarital romances. It does not matter if the romance will soon end:

> I would not have believed that this kind of love would hit me. . . . Even if this would end tomorrow, I have gotten a lot, and I hope that I have been able to give as much. He is constantly in my thoughts. (87W42)

Occasionally, women get a divorce because of a sudden infatuation with another man. Even though the object of their love would not divorce, they may be happy in their new relationship. The passionate love of a woman toward her coworker lasted for 10 years when she was his mistress: "These years were the best ones in my life" (136W49).

Love is not only pleasure, it is also a part of the biological reproduction process. Strong emotions of love made a woman (87W42) want to have a child with her beloved, even though he was married to another woman. The narrator has not given up hope that the man will marry her.

A parallel sexual relationship can be quite satisfactory when there is love (87W42, 114W39). The relationship may help one endure an unsatisfactory marital relationship (107W42). Unusual although not rare cases are those in which a woman falls in love with an unattainable man (cf. Norwood, 1986). Infatuation with a man with whom it is impossible to have a real permanent relationship may enhance the emotion of love (64W53, 161W50). Some women even look upon an unfulfilled love as best (20W47).

In contrast to the love stories of elderly and middle-aged women, young women of the generation of sexual ambivalence tell about passionate love in marriage.

> Pekka is so superior compared to other men. He is a think-ing, feeling, but nevertheless strong man, and I know that he loves me as me, not as a mental picture. He is the best I ever have met. He makes everyday life a feast, also in bed. (40W26)

But there are also many desperate love stories written by younger women. One woman (78W30) fell totally under the spell of her idol. She floated in a golden bubble of happiness. She shivered after a night together, but the man was completely indifferent to her. In this case, the object of love was totally unattainable.

Fantasies of romantic love are common among young women (for example, 98W31). One woman (115W29) had earlier dreamed about and been in love with a rock singer. In her love story, she compares imaginary and personal love. The difference is that a real man is flesh and blood, that is, alive. Before her marriage, she had longed for a person she could love and touch. "A close and working couple relationship is the best that sexuality has given me."

Marital love does not always exclude feelings of attraction toward other people. A woman (116W31) who loved her husband nevertheless enjoyed it when a coworker flirted with her. This man radiated sex, and at a certain level, she wanted him, but she did not engage in sexual intercourse with him. The erotically attractive coworker represented something she hungrily longed for: a beloved.

Companionate Love

Companionate, true, or marital love is affection and tenderness that people feel for those with whom their lives are deeply entwined (Hatfield & Rapson, 1996, p. 25). Most episodes of falling in love take place at a relatively early age, and the period of passionate love usually lasts for 1 or 2 years (Tennov, 1989). The warm feelings of companionate love last longer. Loving and receiving love nowadays is relatively common: 73% of the Finns surveyed say that right now, there is some man or woman that they really love, and 68% of them think that right now, there is some man or woman who really loves them. Feeling and receiving love is most common in middle age, but also young women love and are loved to a great extent (Table 10.2).

Men's Stories of Companionate Love

Marital love is not described as enthusiastically as passionate love. Men especially point out problems. When writing about love in marriage, men of the generation of sexual repression comment positively on the endurance of love in marriage (12M65), lack of quarrels (19M59), satisfaction when they have been able to mentally support their wives (123M64), and good sexual lives (153M70).

Male autobiographers of the generation of sexual revolution often complain about their marriages. One (58M44) is dissatisfied with his wife's unwillingness to make love as often as he would like, that is, three times a day. This extreme case is an example of gender discrepancy in the strength of sexual desire. About 51% of the Finnish men surveyed in 1992, and 61% of the women, were of the opinion that "an adult man has a stronger sexual need than an adult woman." About 40% of the men and 16% of the women would prefer to have sexual intercourse more frequently than they now have in their present steady relationship. The above-mentioned man's wish to have coitus three times a day is an exceptionally high frequency of desired intercourse. The survey data show that most men would like to have intercourse more often in their present couple relationship when they have had their latest sexual intercourse more than 3 days ago. Most women long for more frequent intercourse when more than a month has elapsed from the last intercourse.

One man (70M40) is frustrated because during 15 years of marriage, his wife has not accepted his tenderness and love. He wants to love her during good and bad days. The wife expresses only hate and bitterness. But he has a strong will, and the couple has continued to stay together. The autobiographer does not love any other woman in the same way as he loves his wife. During the whole marriage, he has not had any outside sexual relations, not even infatuations worth mentioning.

According to many autobiographers, a rewarding sexual relationship is essential for marital love. One man (173M46) writes that he thinks that it is good to have had sexual experiences with many women before marriage.

None of the male autobiographers of the generation of sexual ambivalence have written about marital love in their sexual life stories.

Women's Stories of Companionate Love

In the later stages of marriage, companionate love often takes the place of passionate love. True love may flourish even when one or both of the spouses falls ill and the sexual life suffers. This happens relatively often: One fourth of the women of the generation of sexual repression reported that their own or their spouse's illness caused problems in sexual life.

In a beautiful love story, a woman (165W69) tells how she daily visited her husband in the hospital and fondled him. She even took his "little fellow" into her hand and tenderly pressed it. There was no longer passion but only love, which she wished would stream from her into him. When he was dying in the hospital, the spouses were left by themselves. She kissed his lips, which never again would whisper, "My dear wife." She kissed his little fellow, who had given her so many moments of joy.

A frequent problem in marital life is the lack of loving words. The emotional bond is taken for granted; one feels that there is no need to repeat self-evident things. Many older women complain about the lack of tender words spoken by the husband:

> My husband rarely spoke about his feelings. If I sometimes
> asked, he only said: "You should know." As a woman I
> would sometimes have longed for some mumble of love but
> it did not belong to his nature. However, I received plenty of
> care and security during our long marriage. That must per-
> haps be interpreted as love—the love of a Finnish man!
> (105W63)

Even though most women enjoy physical sex less than men do (Haavio-Mannila & Kontula, 1997), an older female autobiographer (105W63) writes that the sexual relationship gives warmth and close-ness to marriage. It helps to get over conflicts; it is a resource. The Finnish surveys of 1971 and 1992 show that the gender gap in finding sexual intercourse pleasurable has diminished during the last 20 years. An example of this is that one woman of the generation of sexual revolution (179W51) fell in love with her own husband at a late phase in her life when she finally learned to enjoy sexual intercourse. She is happy for being able to love and to be loved. "And now there is no need to be afraid of getting pregnant."

In the generation of sexual revolution, in the same way as in the preceding generation, men and women seem to have different opinions about how to express their feelings of love. Men do not think that nice words are necessary, whereas women expect verbal expressions of love (104W38). Sometimes, lack of words or harsh words are forgiven because the woman knows that the husband loves her even though he handles her badly. Several women complain about the silence of their husbands. A women (103W38) knows that her husband loves her but considers it futile to repeat it after many years of living together. The husband says that his actions should speak for his emotions. The narrator longs for the joy of receiving a small smile, a caress, or a touch of the hand in daily chores without implications that one should go to bed.

The process from passionate to companionate love is described by a woman (6W50) who tells how her happy marriage "in the course of more than twenty years has changed from love to companionship." One sexually satisfied woman (97W52) who has been married for 25 years gets a lot of joy from mutual marital love. "Our busy life necessarily brings problems and tries our patience, but having joint goals in life helps us to get over the difficulties."

But there is also skepticism in regard to the possibilities of achieving happiness in companionate marital life. A woman (32W42) doubts if satisfactory sexual activity can be included in marital and family life. She thinks that marriage is a degrading institution that makes women slaves. She cannot imagine that it might include real love and solidarity.

The women of the generation of sexual ambivalence do not take marital love as seriously as older women do. They are even able to laugh at the infidelity of their husbands. In one case, a woman tells how her husband fell in love with her again after having been unfaithful (38W28). But there are more traditional descriptions of really good marital love, too.

> Our life is happy, our sorrows are small and mostly related to money. We talk things through. Pekka is a real home psychiatrist and he peacefully opens my bottled-up feelings. He is for sure the first and last person in the world, in addition to our children, of whom I honestly can say that I truly love him. He is a skillful lover. (40W26)

In this case, the passionate love felt by the autobiographer (see the citation above) has not faded away in marriage.

Women more often than men emphasize the positive sides of companionate love. The older and middle-aged women write with some astonishment about love in their long-lasting marriages. Some younger women describe marital love almost as enthusiastically as passionate love. The deep feelings of infatuation have not yet withered away.

"Love Stories"—Love as a Process

Love is not just an emotional state, but rather a long process with different stages. The developmental processes are more or less regular. A feeling of passionate love changes into a calmer companionate love, or into indifference, bitterness, anger, or hate. But there are also different variants that are dependent on the context, that is, on the full life story. In the following, we shall present some typical love histories in Finnish sexual autobiographies.

The autobiographies reflect the idealized and highly idiosyncratic images of proper love life, which might be called *lovemaps*. A lovemap is not present at birth; it is a social construction, like a native language.

> It is a developmental representation or template in your mind/brain, and is dependent on input through the special senses. It depicts your idealized lover and what, as a pair, you do together in the idealized, romantic, erotic, and sexualized relationship. A lovemap exists in mental imaginary first, in dreams and fantasies, and then may be translated into action with a partner or partners. (Money, 1993, p. xvi)

A lovemap is an individual *social script,* a process whereby people are subconsciously and consciously conditioned and gradually programmed to follow those rules, values, and behavioral patterns by a society, subculture, ethnic, or socioeconomic group (Francoeur, 1990, p. 692). We shall not describe the development of people's lovemaps throughout their lives. Instead, we try to derive from our individual love stories some general types of love or prevailing love scripts that are shared by a certain number of Finns in the 20th century.

Many people experience various love episodes in the following order: arousal of interest in the other sex, falling in love, intercourse, cohabitation, pregnancy, marriage, end of love, finding new objects of love, divorce, or death of the partner. There are many exceptions to this pattern. Everybody does not go through all the different stages in the love process. And many people nowadays take their second, third, fourth, and so on chances in love.

We shall present only some variants of love stories and simplify them radically. We try to classify people according to their major love story/stories during their lifetimes. The method of selecting fragments on the basis of the word *rakkaus* may lead to a narrow view of love stories, as there are several other Finnish words that refer to the emotion of love without actually using the word. Thus, in the following classification, stories that did not include the Finnish word for love are also included.

We classified the 165 stories by giving three codes to each person, indicating the main love story type during his or her youth (18-34 years), middle age (35-54 years), and older age (55+ years). Then a general or main code was given to each person, trying to capture the essential type of story of love in his or her life. Only 11 of the 39 older people could be classified as the same love story type through the three stages of the life cycle. Of the 70 middle-aged people, 39 were categorized as the same story type in youth and middle age. This means that people's love life is not constant throughout life. The following versions of love stories—which are not unique or improbable—could be found in the texts:

1. *One great love* that is cherished and continues today. This may be connected with some searching first. Of all sexual narratives, 17% belong to this pattern (Table 10.3). This model is the classical ideal based on the Christian marriage contract, but perhaps it is not now considered to be an ideal life pattern. As examples of one and only love throughout life, the following two cases representing the generation of sexual repression are given: A woman (117W72) became

TABLE 10.3 Main Types of Love Stories by Gender and Sexual Generation in the Sexual Autobiographies in Finland in 1992 (in percentages)

| | Sexual Generation | | | | | | | |
| | Men | | | | Women | | | |
Type of Love Story	Ambivalence	Revolution	Repression	Total	Ambivalence	Revolution	Repression	Total
One great love		25	22	19	20	10	20	16
Consecutive loves	18	17	6	13	23	33	45	31
Searching	37	16	11	19	31	15	10	20
Devitalized union	18		22	11	4	19	5	11
Parallel relations	9	42	39	34	18	21	20	19
Other	18			4	4	2		3
Total	100	100	100	100	100	100	100	100
N	11	24	18	53	45	48	20	113

attracted to a married man during her wartime service, but this love did not lead to sexual intercourse. She got married at the age of 19 to her first and only sexual partner. The marriage lasted for 53 years. "I have still today not found anybody else to go to bed with other than my own husband." The other example is a man (123M64) who became engaged in a semiplatonic relationship later in life but who continues to love his sick wife.

A woman belonging to the generation of sexual revolution (161W50) had fantasies about a Lutheran minister during her searching period and finally married him. The husband wants her to totally avoid kissing other men. "This shows that he cares for me. We respect fidelity and a sexual union exists exclusively between us." A man (10M, no information on age) who has been married for 10 years says that neither of the spouses has ever had sex with other people. The couple had sexual intercourse for the first time on their wedding night. The author thinks that good sex at home is the best vaccination against infidelity. The spouses dress up for making love.

One variant of the story of permanent love throughout the life is told by a woman (38W28) of the generation of sexual ambivalence. She describes a love affair that cools, dies, and then flames up again. This kind of nostalgia for an old love and an ability to reawaken it is not very common in the autobiographies.

2. *Several consecutive loves,* each more or less important. This version of love stories may include several marriages, but more typically cohabitations or, among younger people, just going steady. These stories also describe failures in love, being left by the other, leaving the partner, and experiencing other disappointments. A typical case is a woman (32W43) whose story includes some elements of the illusionary love story type (6). Her real loves are seen as illusions, but sexually attractive, whereas the more realistic relationships lack sexual interest.

In the oldest age group, there are many women who have found new loves after the death of their husbands (92W61, 126W73, 164W80, 165W69). One older woman (174W68) got pregnant and married at an early age. She then fell in love with a married man, whom she met daily while pushing the baby carriage outdoors. The lovers moved in together, but after 5 happy years, the man died. The woman then had several consecutive relationships with men who often were younger than herself; some of them she met on vacations abroad. Now she is alone for the first time in her life. The physical signs of getting old make her insecure in relation to younger men.

Of the life stories, 26% were classified as consecutive loves. They are much more typical of women (31%) than of men (13%). Of the male narratives, one can mention the story of a man (22M69) who loved his wife who did not love him: "The only thing my wife was satisfied with were our bed affairs." The husband was faithful to his wife, but after 42 years of marriage, the spouses divorced. The man had several consecutive relationships with women he got acquainted with through advertisements in newspapers. One of these women wants to dominate and marry him, but he hesitates.

3. *Searching:* Several loves are failures until finally the writer finds the real one and the story continues as type 1 or ends at this stage. This is nowadays a sort of cultural ideal: Most people consciously seek partners and are either never satisfied or then finally find the right one (see, e.g., Jong, 1995). About 19% of the narratives can be characterized as continued searching, which is most common in the youngest age group. An example is a young woman (128W25) who dated for a year, gaining sexual self-esteem. Then, she fell in love with another man and felt she was in heaven. The couple stayed together for 7 years until the man made another woman pregnant. Since then, all her sexual relationships have been short-term, lasting for 2 months or so. She longs for a man to be at her side. "Is it my fate to be the other woman?" she asks.

4. *Devitalized union:* Love leads to marriage and dies but the marriage does not. About 11% of the sexual life stories represent this pattern. These versions of love stories are most common among older men and middle-aged women.

There is an interesting variant (12M65) where the elderly man loves his wife (his first and great love), who is not too interested in sex. He has other sexual relationships because the wife is not interested in having sexual intercourse. The whole story ends on a tragic note when the man learns to make love with his wife, but their sexual life ends at the same time due to her illness. So, throughout the story, the man loves his wife (but probably not vice versa).

Another, rather specific variant (17W49) is reported by a woman whose husband lives far away and has another woman there. The writer still loves her husband and does everything to keep him. She has no other relationships, even though the spouses do not often meet. This might also be classified as a love at a distance story (8).

The quality of the past or present couple relationship is important for the choices one makes when there are alternatives to traditional life patterns. In many relationships, the sexual appetites of the partners vary considerably. People clearly do not choose each other primarily because of their sexual compatibility. This is often described from both sides: The wives describe the disgusting insatiability of their husbands (51W46), and the husbands describe the disappointing disinterest of their wives (68M50). But men also can be completely disinterested, which sometimes causes great traumas for the wives.

5. *Complementary or parallel affairs:* Being in love with two or more people at the same time. These people are sexually active, often unmarried, divorced, or separated, and they enjoy sex and love. They are not necessarily only young but people who feel themselves to be young (20W47). In these cases, the enjoyment of life, openness to different relationships, and sexual ability are very impressive. The sexual lifestyle of these people recalls that of Don Juan, but many of them are able to enjoy their sexuality even after the phase of conquering a new partner.

Another variant of parallel relationships are devitalized marriages with one or more affairs, passions, and real loves. Here the writer falls in love, gets married, and notices his or her mistake but does not divorce. Instead, several new relationships come and go (or maybe one real love outside the marriage), and they are sometimes, but not often, described as having a positive effect on the marriage. If the relationship is revealed, the consequences vary from divorce to quiet acceptance.

These affairs do not normally begin immediately after the wedding or moving in together but after a period of faithfulness. Also, at a certain age (around 50 for men, somewhat earlier for women), they may become more intense. Many women describe extremely satisfying new love affairs at 40 and 50. Thus, the stereotype that men can begin a new life at 50 but women cannot does not seem to be valid.

Demographically, the chances for middle-aged women to find new partners are poorer than those of men. But when they have found a partner, even if this is a man married to somebody else, they seem to be very happy.

One fourth of the sexual life stories have as the main theme parallel sexual relationships. Parallel relations are much more common among older and middle-aged men than in the other groups.

The following types are more or less short episodes that usually do not take up the whole love story:

6. *Love for an illusory man or woman:* That is, a completely mistaken image of the "real" man/woman with whom one is in love. This is then revealed afterward and may result in divorce (168W24 and 146W33) or an unhappy marriage (51W46), which may last long.

7. *Love at a distance:* Love affairs where love is completely or almost one-sided, where the partner is elusive or disappearing, and where the loving partner never knows what the object of his or her love really felt. These stories vary from youthful loves for rock stars (115W29) to more mature cases where the lover does not show up too often or not at all or where the infatuation is the result of a few encounters. This is a modern variant of the classical romances, where the lovers either get each other in the end or don't, but the descriptions of love are always abstract, lacking any concrete forms, and mostly typical for women, but not always (168W24 and 17W49).

8. *Passion à la Annie Ernaux* (1993): The woman organizes her whole life just to be able to meet a man, who comes and goes as he pleases. Some such episodes are discussed by our authors, too (25W57).

9. *Loss of the loved one* and what happens next, or leaving the one who loves the autobiographer. In many of the above versions of love stories, the loss of the beloved plays an important part. But these losses may in some cases become full stories, where the loss structures the whole life of the author (141W, no information on age) or where the separation comes out of the blue: the husband just says one morning that he has found someone else and is leaving. In several other stories, the beloved dies or leaves the writer. But there is also the other side: The authors leave people who would not like to separate (41W21). Women may lengthen the affair out of pity. One woman describes how

she refused to accept the divorce until she was ready, and the partner agreed to wait. The couple separated, and now the old partner keeps in touch (20W47).

10. *Jealousy*: In many of the stories, jealousy is discussed, usually by the object of jealousy. Usually, it is the man who is extremely jealous, controls everything, and makes the writer's life unbearable. In a few cases, the authors themselves describe their feelings of jealousy, but only if they have been able to overcome them. It is thus conceivable that there are stories where the jealousy of the partner marks the life of the writer. She gives up affairs because she does not want to hurt the other, or she voluntarily restricts her life in other ways.

Because we did not specifically seek episodes about jealousy, we cannot yet describe in full all cases of jealousy in the autobiographies. For instance, case 146W33 is a description of the complete transformation of men from spiritual and sensual partners to egoistic, possessive, and, in the end, violent husbands. Jealousy in connection with male communication deficiency and alcoholism is a problem in Finland. These patterns of transformation and deception in love are well documented and analyzed by Finnish scholars (e.g., Heinämaa & Näre, 1994).

11. *No love*: Even though the proportion of people who have never fallen in love in their lifetime is only 1% of the population, there are some people who at present are outside the realm of human love. In some cases, they have earlier in their life been in love, and thus have a love story to tell.

When one looks at the frequency of people telling different types of love stories (the major type characterizing the life as a whole), there is a clear gender difference: Women more often report consecutive loves, whereas men more frequently tell about parallel, complementary love affairs (Table 10.3). The main generational difference is that young, sexually ambivalent people often are still searching for real love. Elderly and middle-aged people more often were classified as having partnerships or parallel loves.

We also classified the stories separately for each life stage, and we will now look at the type of love separately in youth, midlife, and old age for the three generations. Readers should keep in mind that the stories of youth and middle age of the older autobiographers and of youth of the middle-aged ones are retrospective, whereas the younger people describe more recent events and feelings.

The development of love life during the life course will be examined simultaneously from the point of view of age and generation (Table 10.4). Let us first look at how getting older influences love life in different generations, that is, the *effects of age* on type of love when generation is kept constant. Searching for love is clearly a phenomenon of youth in all three generations. Having only one great love is naturally equally frequent throughout the life cycle in both older generations in which one can follow the love process. Stories of consecutive loves increase when people get older. Parallel relations are very rare in youth, flourish in middle age, and decline after the age of 55. The effect of age on partnership is small.

We can also see the same results by looking at generational differences. Generation has no influence on the proportion of people searching for love, which is common to the youth of all three generations. The oldest generation cherishes one and only one great love throughout the life cycle. Consecutive and parallel loves are characteristic of the generation of sexual revolution, who appreciate "pure relationships" that are not determined by tradition. Partnership does not vary by generation.

There are some cases in which both age and generation have an independent influence on the type of life story. The generation of sexual revolution often (32%) takes a second chance in midlife when it enters into consecutive love affairs. The generation of sexual repression, which was very faithful in its youth (only 5% had parallel relations), became sexually liberated in its midlife by engaging in parallel sexual relationships (34%) but has decreased them in its older age (21%).

The age or life stage effects on central aspects of the love story can be summarized as follows: People search for love when young. They develop consecutive and parallel relations as they mature. Having only one great love in a lifetime and living in a partnership is not related to age when the influence of generation is controlled. The main generational difference in the life stories is that people of the generation of sexual repression tell about one great love more often than

TABLE 10.4 Types of Love Stories During Different Stages in the Life Course and Sexual Generation in the Sexual Autobiographies in Finland in 1992 (in percentages)

| | Sexual Generation | | | | | | | |
| | In Youth | | | | In Middle Age | | | In Older Age |
Type of Love Story	Ambivalence	Revolution	Repression	Total	Revolution	Repression	Total	Repression
One great love	16	14	29	18	17	26	20	26
Consecutive loves	22	20	18	20	32	21	27	27
Searching	32	28	40	32	11	3	8	5
Partnership	7	16	8	11	7	13	9	13
Parallel relations	16	21	5	16	30	34	31	21
Other	7	1		3	3	3	3	8
Total	100	100	100	100	100	100	100	100
N	56	71	38	165	71	38	109	38

those belonging to the generations of sexual revolution and ambivalence. It is also obvious that consecutive and parallel relations are most common in the generation of sexual revolution.

Even though the survey data could not be classified exactly in the same way as the autobiographies, both data sets indicate that about one fifth of Finns represent each of the five main types of love stories: one great love, consecutive loves, searching, devitalized union, and parallel loves (see Appendix). Also, the gender and generational variation of the story types follow the same pattern in both research materials. This gives us confidence in the reliability and validity of data on love and sexuality collected by using two different sociological methods.

Conclusion

In this study based on Finnish sexual autobiographies and survey data, the main question to be answered was: Are people's love discourses and maps universal, largely independent of gender, age, and generation, or can we discern patterns here?

The love stories by men and women have both different and similar elements. Men often report parallel relations alongside their marriage, whereas women tell about consecutive loves. Men do not talk about their feelings of love, and women complain about this lack of verbal expression of feeling. Particularly elderly men in devitalized marriages discuss the emptiness of the intellectual relationship with the wife, especially when they have found a new object of love. In the generation of sexual repression, men have had to find a reason for their unfaithfulness, whereas in the later generations, people can just change partners without explanation. Men often complain about the lack of interest in or even avoidance of sexual intercourse of their wives. Older and middle-aged women write bitter stories about the shock when a beloved man suddenly abandons them. Brave, independent young women finish their unsatisfactory romances easily themselves and feel great relief and joy after their decision.

The experience of feeling love seems to be the same for both men and women: Both are happy when they feel loved, and both tell in the same way of the ecstasy of passionate love and of the security of companionate love. In the quality and depth of the emotions of love, the manstories and womanstories resemble each other.

Most of the love stories in sexual autobiographies fell about equally into the following five types: (a) one great love, (b) consecutive loves, (c) searching, (d) devitalized union, and (e) parallel relationships. The consciously searching type of love story is most common among young people. The main love discourses of middle-aged and older people are more often concentrated on problems related to a devitalizing marriage, parallel relationships, and taking "other chances," establishing consecutive relationships that might be purer and more rewarding than their old relationships.

We also studied the central characteristics of love stories at different stages of the life course of the three generations. Searching for love is typical of the time of youth in all generations. In midlife, many people's love stories are characterized by consecutive and parallel relationships, irrespective of sexual generation. In older age, most people have stopped having parallel relations.

The effect of generation is most obvious when one looks at people having only one great love in their life. The proportion of these love stories is much higher in the generation of sexual repression than in the other generations. The influence of the sexual revolution can be seen in the high frequency of stories of consecutive and parallel love in both the youth and midlife of the presently middle-aged generation.

Finally, we shall present some general impressions of love stories in the postmodern world, where nothing can be taken for granted and many things that were earlier determined by tradition have to be negotiated and reinvented. In the light of the Finnish sexual life histories, faithful, monogamous love for a single person throughout the life course seems to be a rare thing. Most marriages are in the end quite disappointing. It needs a lot of active effort and interest to keep a marriage going. Instead of living in the same faithful relationship "until death do us part," most people are faithful in consecutive affairs, that is, in time-limited love relationships. And quite a few are regularly having several different relationships at the same time, often with work colleagues who also are married or cohabiting. In the

Finnish love stories, pregnancy is not an issue. The arguments for entering new relationships seem mostly to be sexual or emotional incompatibility with the earlier partner—not simply adventure. There are a few cases where marital happiness and extramarital affairs flourish simultaneously, but not too many. The happiest people seem to be those with an active and many-sided sexual life, with different experiences, and with well-functioning relationships at the present time.

Appendix
Comparing Types of Love Stories
in Autobiographies and Survey Data

The frequency of different types of love stories found in the sexual autobiographies can to some extent be compared with that in the total population. One great lifelong love is, according to both the autobiographical and the survey data, very rare. Only 21% of men who were married or cohabiting and loved somebody at the time of the interview ($N = 774$) and 27% of the respective women ($N = 757$) were *totally monogamous,* that is, had fallen in love only once in their lifetime, were in their first marriage, and had not had extra sexual relationships during any steady relationship. In the autobiographical data, one great love was reported by 19% of the men and 16% of the women. A logistic regression analysis of the survey data shows that total monogamy is characteristic of women, 18 to 24-year-old people (and least typical of people 35 to 44 years old), people with less education, and cohabiting versus married people.

Living through several consecutive marriages is much rarer than having had several sexual relationships consecutively (or simultaneously). Only 18% of the presently married or cohabiting Finns have been married more than once, whereas 87% of all Finnish men and 71% of all women have had more than one sexual partner during their life course. Of the sexual life histories, 27% were classified as consecutive love stories.

As an indicator of devitalized unions, one can use people in steady relationships who think that the relationship is unhappy or neither happy nor unhappy. Of both men ($N = 889$) and women ($N = 886$), 12% live in a devitalized marriage. If the percentages are calculated from the total sample, they are 10% for both genders. About 13% of the male autobiographers and 16% of the female ones tell stories of devitalized unions. People writing sexual autobiographies are a little less happy in their steady relationships than people in general, as was shown earlier (Kontula & Haavio-Mannila, 1995a).

Parallel sexual relations as the main love story type characterizes 35% of male and 20% of female autobiographies. This is less than the proportion of the surveyed people who have had sexual relationships during their steady relationships (52% of men and 29% of women). Most extra sexual relationships in Finland are casual and do not characterize people's whole lifestyles.

References

Alberoni, F. (1983). *Rakastuminen* [Falling in love]. Keuruu, Finland: Otava.

Ernaux, A. (1993). *Passion simple*. Paris: Gallimard.

Franceour, R. T. (1990). *Becoming a sexual person* (2nd ed.). New York: Macmillan.

Gergen, M. (1992). Life stories: Pieces of a dream. In G. Rosenwald & R. L. Ochberg (Eds.), *Storied lives: The cultural politics of self-understanding*. New Haven and London: Yale University Press.

Giddens, A. (1991). *Modernity and self-identity*. Stanford, CA: Stanford University Press.

Giddens, A. (1992). *The transformation of intimacy*. Stanford, CA: Stanford University Press.

Haavio-Mannila, E., & Kontula, O. (1997). Correlates of increased sexual satisfaction. *Archives of Sexual Behavior, 26*(4), 399-419.

Haavio-Mannila, E., Roos, J. P., & Kontula, O. (1996). Repression, revolution, and ambivalence: Sexual life of three generations. *Acta Sociologica, 4*, 409-430.

Hatfield, E., & Rapson, R. L. (1993). Historical and cross-cultural perspectives on passionate love and sexual desire. *Annual Review of Sex Research, 4*, 67-98.

Hatfield, E., & Rapson, R. L. (1996). *Love and sex: A cross-cultural perspective*. New York: Allyn & Bacon.

Heinämaa, S., & Näre, S. (Eds.). (1994). *Pahan tyttäret—Sukupuolitettu pelko, viha ja valta* [Daughters of evil—Gendered fear, hate, and power]. Tampere, Finland: Gaudeamus.

Hite, S. (1979). *The Hite report on female sexuality*. New York: Knopf.

Hite, S. (1981). *The Hite report on male sexuality*. New York: Knopf.

Jallinoja, R. (1984). Rakkauden kolmet kasvot [The three faces of love]. *Tiede ja Edistys, 3*, 105-115.

Järvinen, T., & Rikama-Alhainen, M. (1994). *Rakkaus ja seksi—Opiskelijoiden asenteiden muuttuminen suhtautumisessa rakkauden ja seksin yhdistämiseen 1980-luvulta 1990 luvulle* [Love and sex—Change in the attitudes of students toward combining love and sex from 1980s to 1990s]. Unpublished report, University of Helsinki, Department of Sociology, Helsinki, Finland.

Jong, E. (1995). *Fear of fifty* (2nd ed.). London: Vintage.

Kinsey, A. C., Pomeroy, W. B., & Martin, C. E. (1948). *Sexual behavior in the human male*. Philadelphia: Saunders.

Kinsey, A. C., Pomeroy, W. B., Martin, C. E., & Gebhard, P. H. (1953). *Sexual behavior in the human female*. Philadelphia: Saunders.

Kontula, O., & Haavio-Mannila, E. (1995a). *Matkalla intohimoon—Nuoruuden hurma ja kärsimys seksuaalielämäkertojen kuvaamana* [On the way to passion—The charm and suffering in youth as described by sexual autobiographies]. Helsinki, Finland: WSOY.

Kontula, O., & Haavio-Mannila, E. (1995b). *Sexual pleasures*. Dartmouth: Aldershot.

Kontula, O., & Haavio-Mannila, E. (1997). *Intohimon hetkiä—Seksuaalisen läheisyyden kaipuu ja täyttymys omaelämäkertojen kuvaamana* [Moments of passion—Longing for and reaching sexual closeness as described in sexual autobiographies]. Helsinki, Finland: WSOY.

Kontula, O., & Kosonen, K. (1994). *Seksiä lehtien sivuilla* [Sex on the pages of newspapers and magazines]. Helsinki, Finland: Painatuskeskus.

Kontula, O., Haavio-Mannila, E., & Suoknuuti, H. (1994). *Finnish sex: The tables of all the questions of the 1992 survey and the comparable questions of the 1971 survey* (Kansanterveystieteen julkaisuja M 113). Helsinki, Finland: Yliopistopaino.

Laumann, E. O., Gagnon, J. H., Michael, R. T., & Michaels, S. (1994). *The social organization of sexuality.* Chicago and London: University of Chicago Press.

Money, J. (1993). *Lovemaps.* Buffalo, NY: Prometheus.

Norwood, R. (1986). *Women who love too much.* London: Arrow.

Roos, J. P. (1994). The true life revisited: Autobiography and referentiality after the posts. *Auto/Biography, 3,* 1-16.

Scheff, T. J. (1990). *Microsociology—Discourse, emotion, and social structure.* Chicago: University of Chicago Press.

Sievers, K., Koskelainen, O., & Leppo, K. (1974). *Suomalaisten sukupuolielämä* [The sexual life of the Finns]. Helsinki, Finland: WSOY.

Tennov, D. (1989). *Love and limerence—On the experience of being in love.* Chelsea, MI: Scarborough House.

Index

About the Authors

Tineke A. Abma, PhD, is Associate Professor in the Department of Health Policy and Management at Erasmus University in Rotterdam, the Netherlands. She teaches in the areas of organizational studies, strategic management, and policy evaluation. Her research interests include policy evaluation, organizational transformation, and the history of ideas in the philosophy of social sciences (especially social constructivist theories). Recent evaluation projects involved a rehabilitation program within a mental hospital and a health promotion program in the Higher School for Theatre in Amsterdam. Her thesis was published in 1996, and she is the author of several international articles. Currently, she is editing a book on narrative and evaluation.

Mary E. Casey is a doctoral candidate at the Harvard Graduate School of Education and a member of the "Telling All One's Heart" research team.

Barbara Crowther is Senior Lecturer in Women's Studies at the University of Wolverhampton, UK, teaching media and cultural studies and women's writing. She took a literature degree at the University of York, England, and taught teenage children for some years before researching for an M. Phil degree at the University of Liverpool, and starting an academic career. She has been active in researching the representation of gender and sex in popular science, particularly in natural history television films.

Dora Shu-fang Dien, a native of Taiwan, holds a PhD in social psychology from Columbia University and is now Professor Emerita of Human Development at California State University, Hayward. She has published articles in both English and in Chinese.

Paul John Eakin teaches English at Indiana University. His principal publications in the field of autobiography include *Fictions in Autobiography: Studies in the Art of Self-Invention* (1985) and *Touching the World: Reference in Autobiography* (1992). He has also edited the essays of Philippe Lejeune, *On Autobiography* (1989) and a collection of essays by various hands, *American Autobiography: Retrospect and Prospect* (1991). His latest book, *Making Selves: Our Lives Become Stories,* is forthcoming.

Jennifer Ekert is a doctoral candidate at the Harvard Graduate School of Education and a member of the "Telling All One's Heart" research team.

Elina Haavio-Mannila is Professor of Sociology at the University of Helsinki, Finland. She has conducted research on village fights, history of Finnish sociology, health care professionals, immigrants, and comparative gender roles in family, work, and politics in northern Europe and the United States. Together with Osmo Kontula, she has conducted a national sex survey and collected sexual autobiographies in Finland. At present, she is engaged in a comparative study of sexual life in Russia, Estonia, and Finland based on survey data, autobiographies, and thematic interviews.

James Holland is a doctoral candidate at the Harvard Graduate School of Education and a member of the "Telling All One's Heart" research team.

Wendy Hollway is a reader in gender relations in the Department of Psychology, University of Leeds. In addition to her ESRC-funded project on "Gender Difference, Anxiety, and the Fear of Crime" (with Professor Jefferson), she has researched and published on questions to do with subjectivity, gender, sexuality, parenting, the history of work psychology, and gender relations in organizations. Her published works include *Changing the Subject* (1998, with Henriques, Urwin, Venn, and Walkerdine), *Mothering and Ambivalence* (1997, with Featherstone), *Work Psychology and Organizational Behaviour* (1991), and *Subjectivity and Method in Psychology* (1989).

Tony Jefferson is Professor of Criminology in the Department of Criminology, University of Keele. He has researched and published widely on questions to do with youth subcultures, the media, policing, race and crime, masculinity, and gender difference, anxiety, and the fear of crime, his ESRC-funded project (with Dr. Hollway). His published works include *Masculinities, Social Relations and Crime* (1996, with Pat Carlen), *The Case Against Paramilitary Policing* (1991), *Policing the Crisis* (1978, with Stuart Hall et al.) and *Resistance Through Rituals* (1976, with Pat Carlen).

Ruthellen Josselson is Professor of Psychology at Towson University and on the faculty of The Fielding Institute. Recipient of the APA Henry A. Murray Award (1994) and a Fulbright Research Fellowship (1989-1990), she has also recently been Visiting Professor at the Harvard Graduate School of Education and Forchheimer Professor of Psychology at the Hebrew University of Jerusalem. She is author of *Revising Herself: The Story of Women's Identity From College to Midlife, The Space Between Us: Exploring the Dimensions of Human Relationships,* and, most recently, with Terri Apter, *Best Friends: The Pleasures and Perils of Girls' and Women's Friendships.*

Amia Lieblich is Professor of Psychology at the Hebrew University of Jerusalem, where she served as chairperson from 1982 to 1985. She has just completed, with her two graduate students Rivka Tuval-Mashiach and Tamar Zilber, a book on qualitative methodology, titled *Narrative Research: Reading, Analysis, and Interpretation,* published by Sage.

Beverly Mizrachi is Lecturer in Sociology at Ashkelon Regional College and at the Hebrew University of Jerusalem. She studied at Temple University and the Hebrew University of Jerusalem. She received her PhD in sociology for her research on "The Recruitment of Women into Strategic National Elite Positions in Israel." She has received the Rivkah Mellis Prize for her research on women in management and the Tovah Zucker Award for her research on women in the workforce. She has been appointed to public committees on urban renewal projects, to a committee to study the integration and advancement of women in the public sector, and to a committee to study access to higher education in Israel. Her publications reflect her research in her areas of interest, which include stratification, gender, and the narrative life history methodology.

Victoria Nakkula is a doctoral candidate at the Harvard Graduate School of Education and a member of the "Telling All One's Heart" research team.

Harriet Bjerrum Nielsen is Professor of Women's Studies and Head of Research at the Centre for Feminist Research at the University of Oslo. She holds a master's degree in Danish language and literature from the University of Copenhagen. She has published books and articles in the fields of gender socialization, gender identity formation, and gender constructions among children and adolescents. She is the author (with Monica Rudberg) of *Psychological Gender and Modernity* (1994).

June Price is Assistant Professor at Fairleigh Dickinson University in Teaneck, New Jersey, and a clinical nursing specialist in child psychiatry. She received her doctorate from New York University in 1997. Her PhD dissertation concerned the history of relationships in mothers reported for child abuse.

Annie G. Rogers is Associate Professor of Human Development and Psychology at the Harvard Graduate School of Education, where she teaches courses on the psychology of girls and women, qualitative research methods, and psychological trauma. She is also a poet and principal investigator of "Telling All One's Heart": A Developmental Study of Children's Relationships, from which the examples here are excerpted. Her publications include *Marguerite Sechehaye and Renee: A Feminist Reading of Two Accounts of a Treatment; Voice, Play, and a Practice of Ordinary Courage in Women's and Girls' Lives;* and *A Shining Affliction: A Story of Harm and Healing in Psychotherapy.*

J. P. Roos is Professor of Social Policy at the University of Helsinki. He took his doctoral degree at his home university, but he also holds a master's degree from the University of Chicago. His research interests include welfare theory and social policy, ways of life, and lifestyles. Following the example of Pierre Bourdieau—whose books he has translated into Finnish—he has studied the field of intellectuals in Finland and is interested in the sociology of sport. He is a pioneer in using autobiographies in sociological research and has inspired the work of many others in this area.

Nurit Sheinberg is a doctoral candidate at the Harvard Graduate School of Education and a member of the "Telling All One's Heart" research team.

Printed in the United States
89815LV00006B/143/A